D1572712

Debugging Your Information Technology™ Career

Elegant Fix Press, LLC

Debugging Your Information Technology™ Career

A COMPASS TO NEW AND REWARDING
FIELDS THAT VALUE COMPUTER KNOWLEDGE

Janice Weinberg

Elegant
Fix
Press, LLC

Westport, Connecticut

ISBN 978-0-9793337-0-5
Library of Congress Control Number: 2007901155

First Edition
Printed in Canada

Published by Elegant Fix Press, LLC
Westport, Connecticut

To purchase this book, visit www.elegantfixpress.com.

CONTENTS

Part 3: Charting Your Course of Action 271

NOTES TO THE READER

The author has exerted considerable effort in ensuring the accuracy of the information contained herein, but she cannot guarantee that all information is accurate, complete, or current.

The suggestions and ideas presented in this book are based on the author's experience and reflect her best judgment, but she specifically disclaims liability for any adverse consequences experienced by the reader from acting on the advice contained herein.

The names of persons, publications, and organizations used in the Typical Workday segment of each career option are fictitious creations of the author. Any resemblance to actual persons, publications, or organizations is unintended and coincidental.

ACKNOWLEDGMENTS

I am deeply grateful to the following individuals who gave of their time to provide me with important information and insights into their professions. I know their contributions will be very valuable to readers of the book:

Art Brunton, Global Supply Chain Consultant, Southern Connecticut

Robert A. Garvey Jr., CPA, CFE, Cr.FA, Director-Forensic Accounting Practice, McLean, Koehler, Sparks & Hammond, Hunt Valley, Maryland

Cheyene Haase, President, BC Management, Inc., Irvine, California

Dr. David F. Hayes, Chairman (Retired), Computer Science Department, San Jose State University, San Jose, California

Thor Lundberg, Consultant, Digital Security and Forensic Investigations, Colorado

Lynda Nemeth, RN, MS, JD, In-house Counsel, Chief Compliance Officer, and Director of Risk Management, Norwalk Hospital, Norwalk, Connecticut

John Patzakis, Esq., Vice Chairman and Chief Legal Officer, Guidance Software, Pasadena, California

Steven Robinson, President, ISG International/CCBsure, Cambridge, Maryland

Scott Schleicher, Senior Vice President, ISG International/CCBsure, Cambridge, Maryland

A number of people provided me with advice and/or useful information. Larry Brauner and Henry Shove helped me set my goals for the book; Dick Mann advised me on choosing a printer; and Marta Campbell and Nancy Kuhn-Clark, two librarians at the Westport Library, took the time to step outside their professional roles to provide me with helpful information.

I would like to acknowledge some people I met while conducting research who went out of their way to assist me: Helen Degli-Angeli of the Manufacturers' Agents National Association; Terry Weller of McLean, Koehler, Sparks & Hammond; and Brad Gow. Lastly, I wish to acknowledge the Egyptian Cultural and Educational Bureau in Washington, DC for providing me with research assistance.

Part 1

The Changing Landscape of the Information Technology Profession

WEATHERING THE OUTSOURCING STORM

What began as a hurricane of media coverage of the offshoring of IT jobs has ebbed to a light rain, but only because the trend is no longer newsworthy — it is now a fact of life. Letters to the editor that follow articles on the subject typically include some from computer professionals expressing distress at their predicament, especially in light of their investment of time and money in acquiring undergraduate and graduate degrees. Computer professionals are not alone — architects, engineers, financial analysts, accountants, and a growing cadre of professionals who similarly completed rigorous educational curricula have felt offshoring's impact.

Not long after I began writing this book, the employment picture for U.S. computer professionals improved. Some companies were disappointed with the quality of offshore services or with deadlines missed on time-critical projects, motivating them to discontinue the practice. Others concluded that they needed both onshore and offshore teams. Still, in 2007, despite somewhat improved hiring rates of U.S. computer professionals, offshoring has become even more widespread, leaving no doubt that the IT profession's employment landscape has been dramatically — and permanently — altered.

While not diminishing the impact offshoring has had on the profession, it's important to keep the record straight. For although a significant loss of IT jobs could be ascribed to offshoring, the industry has also contracted due to productivity gains registered by U.S. companies. The irony in this is that the people whose intellectual capital and efforts yielded these efficiencies — including the dramatic reduction in telecommunication costs that rendered irrelevant the location of the providers of services in many occupations — found their employment jeopardized as a consequence of the advances made possible by their contributions.

Some government and industry leaders have suggested that education and training initiatives will lead to brighter employment prospects for those affected by offshoring. But computer professionals are among the most educated in society, with many having MS and MBA degrees, even PhDs. Very few professionals in other fields are expected to match the relentless demands for formal training and self-study required by the IT industry — demands driven by technological innovations. Coupled with the fact that educational institutions in countries with lower labor costs will continually upgrade their curricula to enable their students to compete for ever more complex jobs across all professions, why would U.S. IT professionals believe that further education and training will lead to a career that will insulate them from offshore competition?

Understandably then, thousands of computer professionals who have lost their jobs have switched to new careers, such as teaching, nursing, and the culinary arts. Concomitantly, enrollment has declined significantly in computer science educational programs as students seek careers that promise greater long-term job security. Moreover, those still employed in the industry have a markedly different perspective from that in the 1990s, when high salaries, sign-on bonuses, and a dizzying array of job offers were the norms. Today, their attitude is best described as cautious optimism. But that is how it should be. Computer professionals should regard the globalization of the labor market as reason to keep their resumes from ever needing to be "dusted off." They must be both proactive and creative in managing their careers. While having a complacent attitude about one's career in the 1990s wouldn't have penalized them — since employment opportunities abounded during that period — it would be imprudent to adopt that stance today.

Shifting the Paradigm

But something more than greater activism is needed. Traditionally, progress in the computer profession could be regarded as climbing a ladder, with each rung representing the principal route to advancement, for example: programmer, lead programmer, team lead, manager, and, on the top of the ladder, CIO or CTO. When offshoring began to make headlines, I wondered why there were no articles discussing the many fields that would be attractive alternatives for computer professionals because — although not on the traditional IT career ladder — employers in those fields would consider their technical knowledge a valuable asset.

As I thought more about this, the list kept growing. At the same time, however, I recognized that to take advantage of these alternatives, the ladder model of career progression would need to be replaced by a visual symbol more illustrative of the diversity of these options: a tree. As a living organism, a tree can sprout any number of branches in various directions, depending on the amount and direction of sunlight, as well as other nutrients it receives. A tree is also more reflective of the dynamic nature of the global information technology marketplace, since no one can predict with certainty what shape it will take. It symbolizes the need for computer professionals to continually adjust their career plans and strategies to capitalize on new trends, and to be prepared to seize opportunities that are, truly, "off the beaten path," rather than adopt a career planning approach dictated by prescribed steps.

Further, I realized, the tree analogy is appropriate because the computer knowledge base would constitute the trunk, or foundation, that would make the pursuit of a branch option possible. This new career paradigm could be adopted by any computer professional. Although many would still choose career paths that conformed to the ladder model, others would find these alternative options more appealing. New graduates could begin their careers in a traditional IT role, but they would also be qualified to immediately enter many of these other fields. Those who began their careers in traditional IT positions could make a transition to a branch option after 5, 10, 15, or more years in the profession — not only without being penalized financially, but with a higher value ascribed to their services. This, in contrast to the unwritten rules in many professions that define threshold levels of experience beyond which it is difficult — if not impossible — to make a successful transition. Moreover, depending on which alternative field the computer professional chose, it might be feasible to make the transition without switching employers.

This concept forms the cornerstone of this book — specifically, the careers I will describe in these pages. Most can be entered without further education beyond the undergraduate degree you probably already possess; some will require completion of one, or possibly two, certificate programs for entry. Only two, or possibly three, of the options require a commitment to a substantial educational program, but if you are willing to make that investment, you will be poised to reap the dividends of very favorable compensation and long-term job security.

At the same time, it's important to point out that offshore outsourcing is already underway in a number of the fields covered in the book. Although employers initially used offshore resources for entry-level tasks, to the extent that they have been satisfied, they have gained the confidence to outsource increasingly higher-level responsibilities. However, it's just as important to note that there are limitations to how high up the complexity scale offshoring remains feasible for these employers. The most significant limitation is the need to exercise judgment and manage relationships, rather than gain mastery of a set of procedures — a recipe for the commoditization that fueled the offshoring of software development. Further, laws and licensing requirements that mandate U.S. residency for practitioners are barriers to offshoring in some fields. Therefore, when I describe a career where offshoring has already occurred, or is likely to, I suggest strategies to protect you from the practice.

> **NOTE:** I have geared this book toward current and aspiring computer professionals (located anywhere in the world), but others — primarily engineers, architects, financial analysts, and accountants — who are similarly concerned about dimmer employment prospects, or who seek greater occupational fulfillment, can readily adapt the information and ideas presented here to their situations.

Cause for Optimism

There are a number of reasons why you should be optimistic about your career prospects, regardless of whether you wish to continue along the traditional IT career path or explore the options described in these pages.

Technology Is the Engine of Economic Growth and Productivity in Any Organization

In the early twentieth century, blacksmiths rightly concluded that their trade was in inexorable decline due to the advent of the automobile; and though it may be tempting to draw an analogy between that industrial upheaval and the issues affecting the computer profession, there is one salient difference: technology will only become more pervasive in commerce and society in the twenty-first century. All businesses need the latest technology to remain competitive, increase sales, and maximize profits. And, if nonprofit and government agencies are to remain viable over the long term, they, too, must control costs, creating similar pressure on them to continually adopt new technologies. With organizations of every stripe dependent on computer technology for their performance — indeed for their very survival — there should never be a dearth of opportunities for IT professionals. While you, a computer professional, may have to seek them out, rather than having them "knock on your door" as was typical in the 1990s, your efforts should be amply rewarded because, in contrast to the blacksmiths' situation, your services will continue to be in demand over the long term — as will become increasingly evident as you turn the pages of this book.

Computer Technology Is an Arcane Discipline

Relatively few people outside the profession understand computer technology. If you were to ask the parent of a software developer (perhaps yours?) how his child spends her workday, even highly educated parents — unless they are computer professionals, too — would probably say something like, "I can't tell you exactly what she does for a living. All I know is that she works with computers and writes software, whatever that is, and that it's very technical." Even in the business community — where computer technology drives every function — a mystique surrounds the work of computer professionals. The same cannot be said about marketing, sales, human resources, or public relations. In this regard, it's worth noting that the position of business analyst evolved in response to the communication gap between IT staff and the client community, as reflected in the delivery of applications that often lacked the functionality users expected. Business analysts are essentially interpreters who straddle the information technology and business functions, speaking to each in their own language.

Computer Professionals Require Special Capabilities

In the early 1990s, I read an article about the abysmally low percentage of U.S. college students majoring in computer science, as compared to that in other developed countries. The consensus of the experts cited was that, since the demand for computer science graduates was growing, it behooved U.S. universities to make students more aware of the many rewarding career opportunities in the computer industry. I disagreed, for two reasons. First, by the early 1990s, introductory computer science courses had long been part of the required curricula at most colleges and universities — even for liberal arts majors. Second, and more important, studies in vocational sociology have pointed to two primary determinants of occupational choice: one's ability, and the effort one is willing to apply.

Thus, the primary reason for the low rate of computer science majors was not students' *lack* of awareness of computer career opportunities; on the contrary, it was the *awareness* of the demands of computer science curricula that deterred many from the profession. And, although the percentage of computer science majors rose substantially in the late 1990s in response to aggressive efforts by industry and academia, the field has never attracted the same number of students who major in sociology, English, and business administration. Strong complex reasoning ability is needed to write a computer program that meets the stated requirements. Furthermore, a side-by-side comparison of the code in several software developers' programs that provide the identical functionality will reveal that — among the people who possess the reasoning ability to write a computer program — not all of them will do so in the most efficient manner.

Computer Professionals Are Well-Rounded

There is a widespread perception by people outside the industry that computer professionals are hyperintellectual, lack social skills, and focus on technology to the exclusion of other interests. Computer professionals are routinely described as nerds and geeks — which probably reflects the self-perception of those ascribing those labels. During my corporate career, I worked with scores of people both within and outside the computer industry. And I found computer professionals as a group to have multifaceted interests encompassing the arts, sports, and other cultural endeavors, and to be adept in human relations. (Of course, the fact that I was a computer professional has in no way affected my objectivity on this topic.)

Computer Professionals Are Passionate about Their Work

Many people choose a career by whittling down a list of possibilities to arrive at the one that is the most feasible and least unappealing. In contrast, most computer professionals are strongly attracted to the field, resulting in a greater percentage of them deriving career satisfaction than those whose selections were default options. I remember with pleasure from my programming days listening to colleagues describe their solutions to complex bugs: their excitement and delight was contagious; more, it was notable for its distinction from my observation that professionals in other fields always seemed to be discontent with their work. For my colleagues, programming was not work; it was a game of intellectual skill. In fact, software development has much in common with chess — winning at both "games" depends on the ability to see as many "moves" ahead as possible.

That brings up an important issue: If you were attracted to computer science because of the challenge of the software development "game," you may be concerned about the prospects of finding an alternative career embodying the same element of fun. Of course, whether you would find the fields I recommend in this book to be fun will depend on your definition of "fun." If it means the opportunity to apply your deductive and inductive reasoning abilities, you will not be disappointed. Furthermore, any deficit in the fun factor should be more than offset by the opportunity for substantially higher compensation and long-term job security. And you will almost certainly never have to put in another all-nighter to meet a deadline that was known to be a fantasy from the outset, or quickly became evident to be a figment of some higher-up's imagination as the project progressed.

A Self-Fulfilling Prophecy?

College students naturally want to major in subjects that will pave the way to satisfactory employment and advancement opportunities over the long term. Thus, it is understandable that many computer science students became alarmed about the job cuts in the industry. But if thousands of students respond by dashing their plans to enter the profession, they will only contribute to a shortage in the supply of computer science graduates relative to the demand. Ironically, if this happens, companies that would have preferred to keep part or all of their IT organizations in the United States will be forced to turn to foreign labor markets. Then all those would-be computer science students who instead became chefs, teachers, and nurses will exclaim, "Thank goodness I didn't invest the time and money to prepare for entering a profession with such gloomy employment prospects!"

Many academic and industry leaders have voiced concern about the impact of media reports of offshoring on students' choice of a career in computer science. According to Dr. David Hayes, who was Chairman of the Computer Science Department of San Jose State University from 2001 through 2006, current and aspiring computer science majors who change their career direction in response to the outsourcing trend will undermine the technology leadership position long held by the United States — an opinion echoed by many technology industry executives.

In commenting on the impact of outsourcing on San Jose State University's Computer Science Department while he was chairman, Hayes said that the number of computer science majors declined significantly after the dot-com bubble burst in 2001, reflecting both that students switched to other majors and that fewer students chose to major in computer science. However, he added, "From my observations, most of the students who switched their majors were not attracted to the field because of a strong interest in computer science, but rather because they viewed it as a route to a position at an Internet company, where they hoped to capitalize on the dot-com boom. The students who remained in the computer science program were more typical of the traditional computer science student, who is drawn to the field because of its intellectual challenges."

To enhance the potential of students to compete in today's global computer industry job market, Hayes led the incorporation of higher-level application development and software engineering courses into the university's undergraduate curriculum. He also promoted the addition of information technology security courses at the graduate level, while encouraging faculty to give students more challenging assignments. A clear result of these initiatives was that many of the department's graduates received multiple job offers from leading employers, and at very competitive salaries — including from some well-known companies known to engage in offshore outsourcing. This did not come as a surprise to Hayes, who said, "Although Silicon Valley companies established IT organizations in India, the same companies continued to build technical teams in Sunnyvale, which I believe reflected their appreciation of the importance of face-to-face interaction among technical personnel to the success of a software development project."

Furthermore, Hayes noted, beginning in 2004, the entry-level positions offered to the university's computer science graduates entailed responsibilities that previously required three to five years' experience, such as application development — a trend consistent with companies' offshoring the traditional entry-level technical support and quality assurance positions. Thus, the silver lining in the offshore outsourcing cloud is that U.S. computer science graduates now have the opportunity for advancement at a somewhat faster pace. And, though many companies have been outsourcing increasingly higher-level IT activities, their desire to maintain control over their trade secrets and computer architecture should act as built-in deterrents to offshoring many types of projects. Indeed, media reports of the difficulties faced by U.S. employers in meeting their domestic IT recruiting goals began to appear in 2005 and seem to be on the increase.

The bottom line? If you are an aspiring computer scientist, you have every reason to believe you will achieve your goals in your chosen field. If you continually strive to the highest level of performance and maintain the most current technical knowledge, there will always be employers who will recognize the contribution you can make — and be willing to compensate you accordingly. Also, by bucking the trend to switch to an occupation that today may seem to lie in "greener pastures," you will have fewer competitors for the most rewarding jobs. Finally, as you will learn in these pages, your education and experience will be your passport to many other rewarding professions, professions that place a premium on computer knowledge. A bad time to be a computer professional? Not only is it not a bad time — it's a wonderful time!

Open the Door to Opportunity

As I said earlier, even in the midst of the media storm caused by the high number of IT-related job losses attributed to overseas outsourcing, I wondered why no one was talking about the numerous alternative fields that represented attractive opportunities for computer professionals. At the time, I had begun to make a mental list of all the alternatives I could think of. That casual endeavor soon became more tangible, until finally, for the purpose of this book, I engaged in a formal process to identify additional possibilities. It consisted of three steps:

1. Sketch an organizational chart of a typical business.
2. List common position titles in each functional box, noting those where computer knowledge would be an asset.
3. Develop a guide to the career options.

When it came to step 2, listing position titles, in some instances — for example, product manager — it was obvious that a computer background would be advantageous in the technology sector only. In other cases, such as in the technology risk manager role, IT experience would be useful to any kind of organization. The number of fields that will be feasible for you will, of course, depend on your specific skills, interests, compensation goal, and practical needs, and whether you can complete any required educational program.

Step 3 — the guide to the career options — is the primary focus of the rest of Part 1. By familiarizing yourself with the format of this guide, you will be well positioned to take best advantage of the individual career options that follow in Part 2.

The Guide to the Career Options

Each of the career option sections contains 12 segments, in the same order of appearance throughout. So that you may reap the greatest value from the career sections, I strongly recommend that you resist the temptation to start "shopping" for your new career before you take the time to understand the meaning and significance of these sections. They are:

> Sector of the Economy
> Industry
> End-User Organizational Department
> Overview of the Function
> Position Titles
> Job Description Highlights
> Typical Workday
> Job-Hunting Strategies
> Recession Resistance
> Offshore Outsourcing Situation and Outlook
> Information Sources
> Your Ratings and Next Steps

The information you'll find in each segment follows.

Sector of the Economy

For the purposes of your career search, you need to decide which sector(s) of the economy you intend to target. You can think of the economy as comprising three sectors:

- **Private.** Although "private" may imply only privately owned businesses, this sector includes all for-profit enterprises, including both private and public.
- **Public.** All federal, state, and municipal government agencies are included in this sector; but be aware that some entities are hybrid private/public enterprises — for example, the United States Postal Service.
- **Nonprofit.** Social service agencies, foundations, museums, charities, most colleges and universities, and most hospitals fall within this sector.

If a career can be pursued in more than one sector, you will need to take note of important differences among them, which may influence your choice. These differences are:

- Compensation levels are generally lowest in the nonprofit sector and highest in the private sector.
- Job security is highest in the public sector, although tax revenue shortfalls can lead to budget cutbacks and, consequently, layoffs.
- Job security in nonprofits is strongly tied to grants and the success of fundraising campaigns.
- Job security in the private sector is highly dependent on the employer's financial performance. It is also affected by mergers and acquisitions, since they are usually motivated by the desire to consolidate redundant functions so as to enable workforce reductions.

Industry

Next you'll need to consider the industry or industries where you'll best be able to market your IT skills. Some careers will be viable options for computer professionals in a subset of the industries where the position title exists. When this is the case, you'll see the word "Recommended" at the beginning of this section. Other fields can be pursued in any industry.

End-User Organizational Department

In this section, I use the most common names for the functions where a position is located but, as you know, department names vary widely, so be sure to always verify where it fits into a specific organization where you seek employment.

Another important aspect of this section has to do with full-time versus consultancy needs. That is, although a company may engage in the activities described for a given career option, it may exclusively use consultants. On the one hand, for example, a company with annual sales of $20 million may expand through acquisitions, but the size and frequency of its transactions usually would not justify hiring corporate development staff. On the other hand, the frequency and size of a $40 billion company's acquisition transactions would justify such an organization — although it, too, might use consultants under certain circumstances.

Overview of the Function

In this section, I describe the objectives and responsibilities of the function, highlighting why it is an attractive option for computer professionals. Don't look for any mention of compensation here, however, as this is an ever-changing factor. An online search should lead you to a number of websites providing current compensation data for each field. Also, the publications and professional associations listed under "Information Sources" at the end of each career section may have conducted compensation surveys of their readers/members.

Position Titles

In this section, for each career option, you will find one or more titles commonly associated with the position. But keep in mind that particular employers may designate a title not included here for the same set of responsibilities.

Job Description Highlights

Although the responsibilities I list in this section for each of the career options are those typically associated with the position, the identical title at two companies may entail differences. For example, one company may give the title "Marketing Manager" to someone who oversees advertising and sales promotion programs, while the same title at another company would also encompass responsibility for the product management function.

Typical Workday

Many of my clients have told me that soon after entering a career they believed was right for them, they wanted to leave — they realized to their dismay that they had made the wrong choice. That is why I always present my recommendations for new careers in the most straightforward manner possible — no romanticizing allowed. This is also my rationale for including the typical workday section with each of the career options. If your overall reaction to this hypothetical "day in the trenches" is positive, regard it as cause to conduct research to validate your decision — it is not a guarantee that you will love the work. On the other hand, if your overall reaction is neutral or negative, it's probably safe to say that you would not be happy in the position. Remember, though, every job has unpleasant aspects, so a negative response to one or two tasks should not be a reason to reject it.

After reading each workday task, I ask you to record your reaction to it, as this will help you compare your reactions to alternative fields in a structured, consistent manner.

NOTE: You will no doubt notice that I have omitted one activity from the workday: time spent deleting spam e-mail — so perhaps I should have called it the "Typical *Fantasy* Workday." You will also note a time gap in the middle of each workday. Although these workplaces are fictitious, I don't want to be accused of having a sweatshop mentality; thus, I have given my "employees" a lunch break.

Job-Hunting Strategies

In this section of each career option, I'll give you specific search approaches relevant to the position, but here I want to cover general strategies that you will want to consider for most, if not all, options.

Number one is to target companies that would consider your experience relevant to their businesses. As an example, a software developer or business analyst who worked on a supply chain application for a restaurant chain could leverage his or her:

- *Functional* background, by targeting companies marketing supply chain software to any industry;
- *Industry* experience, by approaching companies marketing any type of software to the hospitality industry;
- *Functional and industry* experience, by targeting employers marketing supply chain software to the hospitality industry.

The second general strategy I recommend is to approach employers that sell IT products or services you have developed, evaluated, or used. Your resume, cover letter, and discussions with executives should be used as opportunities to demonstrate your knowledge of their customers' buying motivations, competitors' strategies and strengths/weaknesses, and emerging technological and industry trends that constitute opportunities or threats to their businesses.

Finally, I suggest you implement a three-part strategy that supplements the previous two. It requires that you: (1) decide whether you intend to seek full-time, in-house employment or become a consultant; (2) factor in company size when seeking a job; (3) choose the optimal method of seeking a job or consulting engagements.

Decide Between Consultant and In-house Employment

To help you decide whether to seek a job or build a consulting practice, it is important to first understand the differences between being an employee and a consultant. Any service can be performed by an employee of an end-user organization or a consultant engaged by the end-user organization. For example, a software engineer at a financial services company can work on a data warehousing application for his or her employer's exclusive use; in this case, the company is the end user. Alternatively, the company could have engaged a consulting firm that assigned a software engineer on its payroll to the project. And a company can simultaneously be both an end user and a consultant. If that same consulting firm engaged an advertising agency to promote its services, it would be the end user, and the advertising agency the consultant or supplier.

You can provide consulting services in any of the following ways:

- As an employee of a consulting firm
- As a subcontractor to a consulting firm, whereby you would work on projects for the firm's clients
- As an independent consultant who provides services directly to end users

Keep these possibilities in mind as you read about the career options, many of which offer the opportunity for entry through the consulting pathway.

Factor in Company Size

If your goal is to obtain a job — as opposed to building a consulting practice — an important consideration will be the optimal size of the companies you intend to target. But size definitions vary from one person to another, so let me begin by defining mine to ensure our numbers "add up":

- Very small: Up to $20 million annual sales
- Small: $20–$75 million annual sales
- Midsize: $75–$300 million annual sales
- Large: $300+ million annual sales

Now, some size-related factors that may have implications for your job-hunting strategy:

- Competition for jobs in large companies is much greater than in smaller enterprises. Even though large companies have the greatest number of positions, they also have access to numerous qualified candidates, meaning that your chances of making a transition to most new fields at a large company are very low — unless you know someone who can introduce you to an executive. There are a few exceptions to this generalization, which are noted in the relevant career sections.

- If you are a highly valued employee at a large company, you may be able to make the transition within the organization. In general, though, switching from a traditional IT position to a new field will be most feasible by targeting small-to-medium enterprises (SMEs).

- Positions in large companies are more specialized. In a large company, five employees may perform responsibilities that would all fall under a single title at a small firm.

- Large companies generally provide better benefits, but many smaller companies offer more favorable compensation to attract qualified personnel who would otherwise not consider them. Also, a startup may ultimately undergo an initial public offering (IPO), such that any stock options you might receive as an early employee could be very valuable — or worthless.

Among the career options, you will find I make frequent reference to the ideal company size to target for particular types of positions; but these are just recommendations: your situation may justify departing from them.

Choose the Optimal Method — or Methods

When it comes to method, there are five to consider:

- **Ads.** Many of my clients have obtained excellent positions through ads, but their backgrounds were almost always excellent matches for the qualifications sought. Even if you obtain a required certification or degree, most of your time should be spent researching and initiating contact with employers. The ideal situation for any job hunter — but especially a career changer — is to be the *only* candidate, which is not possible with an ad.

- **Posting Your Resume Online.** Although some of my clients have obtained employment through this method, I am not a fan of it. It is a passive approach that limits the number and quality of opportunities presented to the job-hunter. People who use this method are inclined to accept a position presented to them merely because it exists. They may subconsciously downplay the drawbacks of a position they find — or, more accurately, that finds them — through this method because accepting it will end the discomfort and, possibly, anxiety of finding a new job. If those who gravitate toward this method instead applied a moderate level of effort toward proactively seeking opportunities, they would significantly increase the probability of obtaining more satisfactory employment.

- **Recruiters.** Employers engage recruiters to find candidates with demonstrable qualifications in a field — which, by definition, you would lack if you are seeking your first job in the occupation. Although I am confident that many employers will value your technical knowledge, I doubt whether they would pay a 25 to 30 percent commission to a recruiter for sponsoring you. Recruiters are reluctant to even recommend a candidate who lacks the experience sought by the employer for fear of jeopardizing the relationship with the client — which, don't forget, you are not: you are "inventory." Yes, this may seem like a crass analogy, but the more you understand the recruitment business, the more likely you will choose the job-hunting method that will generate the most favorable results in the shortest period of time. After you gain one to three years' experience in the new field, recruiters should be receptive to working with you — although there would still be compelling reasons to manage that job hunt on your own.

- **Networking.** Many people rely too heavily on networking, only to conclude that their investment was not justified by the dividends it paid. There is nothing wrong with networking — people do find employment that way — as long as you augment it with a proactive campaign that does not rely on intermediaries to obtain introductions to executives.

- **Research and Contact.** Through my consulting experience, I can unequivocally state that the vast majority of people — whether seeking a career change or advancement in an occupation — will generate the most interviews by researching and initiating contact with employers. Furthermore, my clients who initiate contact by telephone *before* sending a resume consistently obtain the most interviews. Using this method requires advance preparation of a well-crafted, written script that includes responses to all possible objections the executive might raise for declining your request for an interview.

With these points in mind, be prepared to see the career sections feature an overriding emphasis on self-directed job-hunting techniques. If you have never sought employment this way, you may view it with trepidation, but I assure you, the guidance I provide will alleviate your concern in no time.

And once you put these strategies into action and begin to see the results, I am just as sure that you will feel increasingly confident about using this approach.

Recession Resistance

Certain industries are vulnerable to a recession, others are resistant, and still others even benefit from an economic downturn. If a career that appeals to you is associated with a *function,* rather than an *industry,* it may be easy to switch to the same function in another industry if you are affected by a recession. But even if an occupation is vulnerable, that is not necessarily a reason to reject it; it is merely one factor to weigh, along with many others.

Case in point: If one of my clients seeks a career in sales because she wants to earn a high income, I would always recommend commercial real estate because top performers can earn $400,000 to $1 million-plus annually. At the same time, because real estate is a cyclical industry, I would advise her to be prepared to earn as little as $10,000 annually in a recession — even as a high performer — but to consider her earnings potential over a decade. Thus, if she earned $250,000 in each of seven years, but only $10,000 in each of the remaining three, her annual amortized income would be $178,000.

Two more points here: First, not all companies will perform well even if their industries are insulated from an economic downturn; second, many factors other than a poor economy can cause an industry to contract — as you well know.

Offshore Outsourcing Situation and Outlook

The global marketplace is in a constant state of flux, and at a rate that has dramatically accelerated in recent years. Changes in the marketplace will continue to affect employment opportunities in the United States in both positive and negative ways. It hardly need be said that a major component of these changes is the offshoring trend. As this strongly relates to your career search, a good rule of thumb is to regard any professional position that exclusively or primarily involves researching, classifying, and analyzing data according to predefined procedures as very susceptible to being staffed overseas. More resistant to offshoring, as I noted earlier, are those positions where the exercise of independent judgment and the management of customer relationships are primary responsibilities.

Furthermore, despite the potential for immediate, substantial cost savings, under certain circumstances, management of an organization may decide not to offshore an activity. Let's now examine in detail each of the factors that could constitute an argument against offshoring:

- Importance of the customer/client relationship
- Requirement for experience
- Degree of required or desired control
- Importance of accurate and comprehensive communication
- Political factors

Let's look into each of these.

Importance of the Customer/Client Relationship

This factor may be the most instrumental in the decision to offshore a task because the sales function is so vital to any business. Without revenues being generated, profits and growth cannot be achieved — indeed, a company's survival would be jeopardized. And the degree of importance of a customer relationship will be a function of the price and complexity of the product or service, which — as they increase — will lengthen the sales cycle and involve more, and higher-level, personnel in the decision-making process. While individual businesses may have differing opinions regarding the particular criteria that would contraindicate offshoring the sales function, at some point in the price-complexity continuum, all would agree that it should be kept completely under in-house management.

Requirement for Experience

Without question, there will always be some responsibilities that can be mastered by a very intelligent person who lacks experience. Think back to the late 1990s, when thousands of inexperienced but computer-savvy teenagers became proficient programmers (leading many to drop out of school to seize the opportunity to earn a lot of money). But when data resulting from a research activity has to be evaluated in a way that cannot be prescribed by a set of rules, experience becomes essential.

Let me guess what you're thinking here: It's all well and good to talk about the importance of experience, but in practice, companies are being penny-wise and pound-foolish. They're outsourcing projects that cannot be completed with the same high quality that would apply to the work product of U.S. software developers — ignoring the fact that U.S. developers would *not* be more expensive if they factored all direct and indirect costs into the calculation. In fact, despite the media hype to the contrary, executives at legions of U.S. companies do appreciate the price-value relationship inherent in using experienced onshore professionals. Even if many of them engage in offshoring, a sufficient number place a premium on experience — especially when a project embodies particular characteristics.

DOLLARS AND SENSE: It would be interesting to conduct a controlled experiment in which U.S. and offshore teams of developers with the same amount of experience would each work independently to complete the identical project. All direct and indirect costs associated with each team's efforts would be calculated. Indirect costs would include such items as the opportunity cost of U.S. personnel's time spent communicating with offshore developers, which would not be required if in-house personnel managed the project. This category would also take into account the time spent by purchasing specialists, contract administrators, attorneys, and risk managers in preparing RFPs and reviewing bids, as well as structuring, reviewing, and negotiating the outsourcing contract.

One clear-cut reason that an organization would assign only the most eminently qualified personnel, whether employees or vendor staff — regardless of the cost — is when the activity has significant potential for liability. Thus, many of the fields I describe in the book revolve around the management of risk, such as the potential for a disruption in business operations, the violation of a law, or vulnerability to criminal activity. A risk-averse perspective can act as a strong deterrent to offshoring since, on the whole, offshore vendors may be perceived as less qualified than long-established U.S. vendors who can point to numerous Fortune 1000 clients.

The "flag-raiser" positions are the corporate risk managers, insurance advisors, and attorneys. For example, where a marketing manager will see only potential sales and profits to be gained by launching an innovative medical diagnostic test, risk-oriented professionals will envision lawsuits stemming from false negative or false positive test results.

One word of caution is in order here, however: As offshore vendors build a portfolio of satisfied, prominent clients, the risk factor in outsourcing projects with high liability potential will diminish — as it already has to some extent.

Degree of Required or Desired Control

Companies that engage in offshoring are gravely concerned about the misappropriation of their proprietary data, as well as confidential customer information. To address their clients' concerns, many offshore vendors have created workplaces that lack removable media, printers, and writing instruments; and they conduct physical screening of employees as they enter and leave the workplace. Nevertheless, of those companies that have embraced offshoring, many draw the line at outsourcing projects that would give outsiders access to their trade secrets or technology architecture.

The requirement for legal control would most often apply to companies that operate in regulated industries. For example, certain financial services companies must comply with regulations governing the outsourcing of their business processes, regardless of where their vendors are located.

Importance of Accurate and Comprehensive Communication

A friend who returned from a trip to France told me that, while walking in Paris, she and her husband were approached by a reporter. Upon learning that they were from the United States, the reporter asked what they thought about green peas. My friend was confused: "I couldn't imagine why they were interested in my opinion of a vegetable." Only after further interaction did it become clear that they were not being asked about a vegetable, but rather about Greenpeace, the environmental organization.

The failure to communicate can be a deal-breaker. And, as we all know from personal experience, communication problems can — and do — occur even when interacting with people of the same cultural and language background.

When the success of a business activity is at stake, and is strongly dependent on unambiguous and comprehensive communication, companies will express a clear bias toward hiring people who have a common understanding of the language — including the vernacular and topic-specific terminology used in everyday conversations. (This is not to say that they would have to share the same national origin and native language.)

Political Factors

A few years ago, a public outcry followed news that the State of Indiana had entered into an offshore outsourcing contract, leading to its cancellation. Since then, North Dakota enacted legislation that favors contractors in that state; New Jersey passed a law prohibiting services provided under state contract to be performed outside the United States. And numerous bills have been proposed in many states — some of which have become law — that impose restrictions on the awarding of state contracts involving the use of offshore labor, or that require companies bidding on state contracts to disclose their intention to use offshore labor.

But these initiatives apply only to state governments' contracts — not to businesses. Although some bills have been proposed in Congress that would impose limitations on offshoring by the private sector, none has become law. True, some corporations have curtailed or reduced their use of offshore labor for call center operations in response to customers' complaints. But, since software development is a "behind the scenes" activity, as long as corporate use of offshore software developers does not become public knowledge, companies will continue to engage in the practice to the extent that they are satisfied with the results and costs.

As you read the Offshore Outsourcing Situation and Outlook segment in each career section, you will see references to both the existence and degree of influence these factors will have on a particular field. At the same time, keep in mind that any number of factors other than offshoring may affect the demand for the services of particular professionals, such as advanced artificial intelligence methods that enable the automation of sophisticated decision-making processes.

Information Sources

The existence of the Internet means that no one can blame an unsuccessful job-hunting campaign on a dearth of information. To ensure that you don't overlook what I consider to be highly useful resources, I list some in each career option section.

Your Ratings and Next Steps

In this, the last section of each career option, you will find a form designed to help you clarify and record your thoughts and research findings so that you can compare your reactions to various options in a consistent manner.

- First the form asks you to assign a rating, between 0 and 10, of how compatible your skills are with the field.
- Below that is space to list skills and/or knowledge you will need before making contact with potential employers.
- Next is where you record your workday task ratings, with space for research notes.

- Last is a Contact Log for jotting down suggestions and referrals provided by people you approach for information about the field.

Before You Begin Your Search

I gave considerable thought to the sequencing of these career sections. My goal was that they parallel the order in which the practitioners in each field get involved in the business of an organization. Therefore, to get the most from any career section, I recommend that you read the options preceding it.

Part 2

The Career Options

CAREER OPTION:
PRODUCT MANAGER

SECTOR OF THE ECONOMY
Private

INDUSTRIES (RECOMMENDED)
Information technology, telecommunications

END-USER ORGANIZATIONAL DEPARTMENTS
Marketing, Product Management, Product Marketing, Engineering, Product Development

OVERVIEW OF THE PRODUCT MANAGEMENT FUNCTION
In the packaged goods, consumer electronics, and health and beauty care industries, it's probably safe to say that marketing would be considered the most influential part of the business. In contrast, in the early days of IT development, many successful companies were built on the basis of a novel technology, which was followed by the ad hoc identification of commercial applications — there was no deliberate marketing plan. Typically, the engineers who designed the technology assumed ownership of all facets of the program. In fact, this business model was prevalent in the computer industry well beyond its early stage of development. Now, however, it is much more common for technology companies to adopt the marketing model traditionally used by nontechnology industries, a cornerstone of which is a product management process.

Product managers continually seek opportunities for new products and features to address unmet and underserved customer needs. First they identify a concept with promise, then attempt to convince upper management to fund the program. If they win support for their idea, and the decision is made to proceed, they formulate detailed specifications for the planned offering. In the technology sector, these will be presented in a market requirements document (MRD). The product manager then negotiates commitments from technical managers to assign personnel to the program. During the development process, the manager monitors and expedites activities to ensure that the scheduled launch date is met, and works with advertising and sales promotion personnel to establish budgets and devise strategies for reaching the targeted customer segment.

The launch of a new product marks the end of the development process, but the beginning of a greater challenge: delivery of the projected financial results that persuaded senior management to approve the program. As they monitor changing economic, competitive, and customer factors, as well as the particular life-cycle phase of the product in which they occur, product managers must continually devise and adjust pricing and promotional strategies.

In the traditional product management model, a product's life span is defined in terms of four distinct phases, commonly referred to as *introduction, growth, market saturation,* and *decline.* If a company establishes a new, successful product category, it will have greater pricing power than in the growth phase, when competitors will try to wrest market share from it. If the company has built a preeminent reputation for technical support, it may retain significant pricing latitude during this phase. But, in general, the growth phase is marked by fierce competition — with the customer the beneficiary. During the final phase of a product's life — decline — the company's goal may be to discontinue the product, ideally without inconveniencing customers, as opposed to maximizing sales and profits.

A company's size, the number and variety of products it sells, and the differences among its customer segments will determine how many product managers it has. For example, at a small security software company that markets authentication, firewall, antivirus, and e-mail filtering products, responsibility for all of them may be assigned to one or two product managers. At a midsize or large company, one person may manage all products in only one of those categories. And, if the company operates in both the business-to-business (B2B) and consumer segments, one product manager may be responsible for the firewall product line marketed to businesses, government agencies, and educational institutions, while another will oversee those offerings for the consumer market. Product managers routinely "inherit" responsibility for products in various life-cycle stages.

Although it is feasible for someone without formal business administration training to enter and succeed in the marketing profession, it would be important to obtain an MBA to advance to the highest level in marketing.

POSITION TITLES

Product manager, associate product manager, assistant product manager, product development manager, product planner

JOB DESCRIPTION HIGHLIGHTS

These responsibilities are applicable to a product manager or an assistant/associate product manager position:

- Develop concepts for new products and enhancements to existing ones.
- Oversee market research studies, customer satisfaction surveys, and competitive analyses aimed at assessing the potential for new products and features, and at providing guidance in pricing, positioning, and advertising strategies.
- Prepare appropriation requests — or, as they are often called in the technology sector, "business cases." These describe the strategic importance of the program to the company's goals, the market research findings that point to commercial success, pricing structure, competitive strengths and weaknesses (if the category already exists), staffing levels, production requirements (if the product is manufactured), and financial projections for two to three years.
- Prepare a market requirements document (MRD) detailing the specifications for each proposed new product and feature. This would include technical specifications (e.g., scalability, interoperability), functionality, pricing, and the targeted customer segment.
- Establish a product development schedule and negotiate the assignment of technical personnel with their managers.
- Specify tests to obtain evidence supporting product claims (e.g., failover of servers within n seconds) for inclusion in advertising campaigns, website copy, and collateral materials. (Note: These must undergo a legal review before they can be used.)
- Work with internal and agency advertising and sales promotion personnel to establish budgets for advertising campaigns, direct marketing programs, trade show exhibits, conference sponsorships, and other marketing vehicles.
- Review agency proposals for advertising campaigns and media plans.
- Monitor sales of new and established products, modifying advertising,

promotion, and pricing strategies to address changing economic, competitive, and customer factors.

- Make decisions to phase out products because of declining customer demand, stronger competitive products, or because they are no longer strategically important.

TYPICAL WORKDAY

This is a typical workday that either a product manager or associate/assistant product manager might experience. In this scenario, the person is employed at Asset Arm-RE, a fictitious company that markets property management software to the real estate industry.

As you read, enter your reaction to each activity in the adjacent cell in the Rating column: an "L" (for like), "D" (for dislike), or "N" (for neutral, or no reaction). If you must conduct research before deciding, leave that cell blank for now.

Time	Activity	Rating
8:30– 9:20	Review responses to the questionnaire sent to participants in RE SoftRx V3.2's beta test to identify any comments that could be useful in the advertising campaign promoting the new release.	
9:20– 9:45	Call Mary R., Director of Technology, to find out when the Capital Equipment Lease v. Buy Analysis Module of RE SoftRx V3.2 will be ready to demonstrate to customers who are not participating in the beta test. Call Luke S., Strategic Partner Manager, to discuss the possibility of establishing alliances with capital equipment leasing companies that want exposure to property managers.	
9:45– 10:30	Go to *Property Manager Monthly's* website and read the results of the survey of property managers, where the categories of expenditures that increased last year at a rate higher than inflation are listed. E-mail a hyperlink to the survey to Gina M., Advertising and Sales Promotion Manager. Advise her that the ad campaign for RE SoftRx V3.2 should emphasize the Preventive Maintenance Module's ability to calculate the optimal *(cont...)*	

Time	Activity	Rating
(cont...) 9:45– 10:30	length of a boiler service contract, as well as the Energy Management Module feature that allows users to compare their energy costs to industry benchmarks for facilities of comparable use and similar square footage.	
10:30– 11:10	Meet with Steve H., Sales Manager, to review the results of a survey in which 22 percent of customers using RE Edge, the company's entry-level package, indicated their intention to upgrade to RE SoftRx V3.2 within six months of its launch to be eligible for a 10 percent license discount. Address the projected margin reduction of 3 percentage points on license revenues if all those customers upgraded — specifically, the fact that it's a necessary action to remain competitive.	
11:10– 11:50	Review a proposal from Mike L. of Instructional Innotech for the design of an avatar user training program to replace the current practice of using a training instructor. E-mail Mike a request for a price quote to design Spanish and Portuguese versions to support a planned expansion into Latin America next year.	
11:50– 12:20	Review February's revenue reports for each of Asset Arm-RE's four software packages. E-mail Lisa C., Midwest Region Sales Manager, asking for an explanation for the loss of five Chicago customers whose licenses were up for renewal.	
1:00– 1:45	Meet with Amy R., Financial Analyst, to review a preliminary advertising budget for next year. Call Ron M., Marketing Administration Manager, to try to negotiate a 20 percent increase in RE SoftRx V3.2's advertising budget to better compete with RE Pro — which, according to media reports, will have a $3 million advertising campaign supporting its next release.	
1:45– 2:30	Update a competitive matrix comparing the features of RE SoftRx V3.2 with those in the latest versions of the company's three biggest competitors.	

Time	Activity	Rating
2:30–3:20	Initiate a conference call with Gina (the Advertising and Sales Promotion Manager), Brian G., Account Executive for Tuckman Fostel, the company's ad agency, and Anne P., Tuckman Fostel's Media Planning Director, to review the proposed media plan for RE SoftRx V3.2. Listen to the agency executives' rationale for apportioning funds to two real estate magazines, three trade show sponsorships, the websites of two professional associations, and a direct mail campaign targeting property management executives.	
3:20–4:00	Read the study of the institutional property management marketplace, which details the unique issues associated with the management of prisons, nursing homes, and hospitals to assess the opportunity for designing an application tailored to each segment's needs.	
4:00–4:45	Review the results of a market research study conducted by Farriman Lochner Research. Evaluate the recommendations for future software features resulting from two focus groups: one in which eight property management executives at large companies participated; the other consisting of eight property management executives from SMEs.	
4:45–5:30	Take conference call with Keith P., General Counsel, Luke (the Strategic Partner Manager), and Rich D., CEO of RExpertech, a research firm serving the real estate industry. Discuss an alliance whereby RE SoftRx users will be able to calculate a projected ROI associated with implementing any of 65 energy-saving measures, to reflect both the direct cost savings resulting from the capital expenditure plus any available federal energy tax credits, as well as those offered by the state where the property is located.	

JOB-HUNTING STRATEGIES

Concentrate your job-hunting efforts on companies that would view your background as relevant to their business. Relevance could be inherent in your having developed commercial software that directly or tangentially relates to their product portfolios. Or, it could be demonstrated by your experience as a user of a targeted company's products or those of its competitors. Refer to page 15 for further guidance in using this strategy to identify employers. Provide details of the relevant aspects of your background in your resume, cover letter, and other communications with executives, and explain how your knowledge and experience qualify you to define the requirements of the products they market. Acquire as much knowledge as possible about the industry segment in which the company operates, as well as the buying motivations of its customers. Lastly, be prepared to demonstrate knowledge of the differences between the company's offerings and those of its competitors.

Ideally, your first product management position will be under an experienced product manager or marketing executive so that you can both contribute and learn. But be aware that the marketing executive at some technology companies may oversee advertising and promotional programs only, while Engineering or Technology will define and market new products — which might imply that the company does not have a formal product management process in place.

To maximize the probability that companies you contact have product management functions, concentrate on those with annual sales in the $50–$150 million range since larger companies are more likely to have achieved a level of sophistication in their product management functions that will bias them toward candidates with MBAs. When targeting any company in the recommended size segment, initiate contact with the CEO since he or she should be fairly accessible. Be prepared to be referred to the executive responsible for the marketing function, but you should interpret that as a positive sign since it suggests that the CEO is not ruling you out as a product management candidate.

RECESSION RESISTANCE

Certainly, the continual development of new products and features is critical to a business, but during a recession, a company whose sales are in decline may shift product development funds to more pressing needs. However, declining demand makes it more difficult to maintain market share — a critical measurement of performance — which, once lost, is very difficult to regain. As such, it would be very important to have a product manager who can devise pricing strategies and promotional programs to achieve the optimal balance of profits and market share during a troubled economic period.

The vulnerability of a technology industry product management or associate/assistant product management position will largely depend on the extent to which one's employer markets to customers that operate in cyclical industries. For example, real estate companies are quite sensitive to recessions, whereas pharmaceutical manufacturers are not. By concentrating on companies whose customers primarily or exclusively operate in industries that either resist or benefit from an economic downturn, you should be able to eliminate or significantly reduce your exposure.

OFFSHORE OUTSOURCING SITUATION AND OUTLOOK

The product management function relies extensively on research and data analysis to support market studies, customer satisfaction surveys, and competitive analyses — the very activities that lend themselves to outsourcing, and that have been outsourced to U.S. vendors since well before offshoring began. That said, the rationale for outsourcing a business process is to enable companies to focus on their core activities, and none is more vital than product management. If a company offshored its product management function, the offshoring of the departments with which product managers interact — such as Sales, Engineering, and Finance — would surely follow. At that point, virtually the entire company would have been outsourced.

INFORMATION SOURCES

Sales & Marketing Executives International (www.smei.org). This nonprofit organization offers educational programs, sponsors events, and publishes the *Who's Who in Sales & Marketing Directory.*

The Valuation of Information Technology: A Guide for Strategy Development, Valuation, and Financial Planning, by Christopher Gardner. (John Wiley & Sons, Inc., 2000). Computer professionals attracted to the product management field will learn methods for identifying customer needs, assessing the potential market for a technology-based product, formulating product requirements, and other techniques for developing a persuasive business case, and equally important, how to know whether a product concept lacks commercial potential.

Harvard Business Online (www.harvardbusinessonline.org). Articles, case studies, and books available through this website of Harvard Business School Publishing describe the ways companies have used product management and other marketing techniques to build successful companies, as well as turn around underperforming businesses.

PRODUCT MANAGER
YOUR RATINGS AND NEXT STEPS

How compatible is this field with my skills?

Assign a score of 0–10 (10 is highest): _____

Skills/Knowledge I Need to Acquire Before Contacting Employers

1._____

2._____

3._____

4._____

Typical Workday Task Ratings

After conducting research to fill in any ratings you initially left blank, calculate the total for each type of reaction (like, dislike, neutral). A field may be a good choice if you have at least six Ls and three or fewer Ds.

Total **L**s:_____ Total **D**s:_____ Total **N**s:_____

Research Notes

_____

_____

_____

_____

_____

_____

_____

_____

_____

Contact Log

Date:_____Name/Title:_____

Phone/E-mail:_____

Comments:_____

_____

_____

_____

Date:_____Name/Title:_____

Phone/E-mail:_____

Comments:_____

_____

_____

_____

Date:_____Name/Title:_____

Phone/E-mail:_____

Comments:_____

_____

_____

_____

Date:_____Name/Title:_____

Phone/E-mail:_____

Comments:_____

_____

_____

_____

CAREER OPTION: ACCOUNT EXECUTIVE

SECTOR OF THE ECONOMY
Private

INDUSTRIES (RECOMMENDED)
Information technology, telecommunications

END-USER ORGANIZATIONAL DEPARTMENTS
Sales, Account Management, Business Development

OVERVIEW OF THE ACCOUNT EXECUTIVE FUNCTION
As a computer professional, you may never have considered a sales career. But if you enjoy talking about technical subjects and would like to significantly improve your income potential — and who wouldn't? — a sales position might be just the right fit for you.

Sales positions are typically described either as "outside" or "inside." Outside sales positions, the most common, require at least occasional visits to customers. Inside sales personnel manage customer relationships remotely, whether by contacting prospects who responded to direct-marketing or other promotional programs, or by proactively researching and contacting prospects. Sales professionals may also be categorized as "hunters," whose job is to bring in new customers, or "farmers," who are responsible only for growing existing accounts. The vast majority of outside sales positions entail both activities.

Companies of all sizes and in all industries have a vested interest in selling products that are appropriate for their customers, and doing so in ways amenable to their target audience(s). But technology companies have greater difficulty in following this basic selling tenet, for one simple reason: Many of their customers lack the computer expertise to fully understand the capabilities of the complex computer systems and services they need to run their enterprises efficiently and cost-effectively. And that's where you come in.

Nontechnically trained customers in the market for computer systems and services — as opposed to IT professionals — have to rely solely on their account executive's representation of these products and services, and so the A/E is expected to be able both to recommend the most suitable product and to guide customers in deriving the maximum benefit from their purchases. To succeed in this dual-purpose role, A/Es either must understand the technology themselves or have technical support staff able to impart that knowledge to them or directly to their customers. It is this requirement that has provided the impetus for many technology companies to establish their pre- and post-sales engineer positions. Their management reasons that relieving account executives of technically oriented responsibilities will allow those personnel more time to focus on generating revenues. But looked at another way, the reasoning is faulty, because: To the extent that account executives can both formulate and respond to technical questions vital to winning a contract, companies would save the time spent communicating with and coordinating the activities of technical personnel. Adding more people to the communication loop will only lengthen the time required to fulfill a customer's request for a proposal or information. And the more people participating in the coordination and transmission of information to the customer, the higher the cost of sales.

Cost of sales can be measured in two ways:

- The allocation of technical personnel to assist account executives (whether they are formally designated as support staff or are application development personnel who provide support on a de facto basis) constitutes an incremental labor cost.
- As more staff become involved in the customer communication process, inevitably, the quality of information passed on to customers will begin to suffer. Even when misinformation (or insufficient information) is identified and corrected before any problems can occur, damage control must be counted as a labor cost. When errors are not identified until after the delivery of the product or service — when the customer may have been penalized financially — much greater costs will be incurred, especially if the dispute leads to litigation. At the very least, a technology company whose quality of information comes into question will "take a hit" to its reputation — customer trust, once impaired or lost, is rarely fully regained.

As an IT professional, you are well positioned to address these issues. You have what it takes to handle the sales process more independently and, therefore, more cost-effectively than those who lack equivalent training and experience. Equally important, as a technically proficient account executive, you will automatically have greater credibility with the customer, which will engender a higher level of confidence in your recommendations for configuration and other technical specifications — a distinct competitive advantage.

The point is, as an IT professional, you should have no difficulty obtaining a sales position at a technology company. And the more complex the products or services it markets, the more likely the employer will have learned — often, by losing customers — that its selling process demands a level of computer proficiency that requires technically trained account executives.

Most sales positions will entail serving as an employee of the manufacturer of a product or developer of a service, though many companies engage manufacturer's representative firms (often called "independent representatives") to promote their products (not services) in exchange for a commission on the sales they generate. Some companies use independent representative firms exclusively; others use a combination of employees and representative firms.

The independent representative sales model has long been popular in nontechnology segments because it is cost-efficient to promote the offerings of multiple noncompeting companies to the same customer during the same sales call. Manufacturers of hardware, software, peripherals, and supplies are increasingly adopting this method as well (see the Manufacturers' Agents National Association under Information Sources).

You can be employed in the manufacturer's representative segment either as an account executive at a representative firm or on a self-employed basis; in the latter case, you would negotiate commission agreements with companies whose products you wish to represent. If you choose the self-employment route, you would receive the full commission for your efforts and have the potential to hire others as your business grows.

POSITION TITLES

Account executive, business development representative, sales representative, account manager, sales engineer, independent representative, manufacturer's representative

JOB DESCRIPTION HIGHLIGHTS

Depending on a company's sales model, in this position you might perform the first and/or second responsibilities in the following list, as well as all other tasks.

- Develop sales from existing accounts, which may be assigned according to geography, industry, and/or annual sales level.
- Conduct cold-calling campaigns targeting new customers.
- Ascertain whether current and prospective customers use competitive products/services.
- Contact prospects who respond to advertising and direct-marketing campaigns.
- Design and deliver sales presentations.
- Prepare, or coordinate the development of, price quotes and proposals.
- Prepare weekly reports on campaign results, including contacts with prospects, the potential dollar value of their purchases, their concerns regarding the price and/or quality of your company's product or service, and the probability and timing of closing the sale.
- Obtain, or coordinate the acquisition of, prospective customers' technical data; using that data, determine which would benefit from your company's product or service. Define any compatibility issues that would have to be resolved.
- Coordinate internal technical evaluations aimed at defining the optimal product, configuration, and other specifications for each customer.
- Arrange for system installation, user training, and, if the product is hardware, maintenance and repair.
- Monitor competitive developments and their potential impact on the ability to retain and attract customers.
- Monitor customer utilization of your company's products/services to identify the need for additional training and support, opportunities to promote upgrades, and inroads made by competitors.
- Participate in trade shows, technical conferences, and internal regional/national sales meetings.
- Collect outstanding balances from past-due accounts.

TYPICAL WORKDAY

In this typical workday, the account executive works for the fictitious HoteliTech Systems, which markets an integrated front-office and back-office software package to companies in the hospitality industry. As you read, enter your reaction to each activity in the adjacent cell in the Rating column: an "L" (for like), "D" (for dislike), or "N" (for neutral, or no reaction). If you must conduct research before deciding, leave that cell blank for now.

Time	Activity	Rating
8:30–8:50	Review e-mails from two prospects to determine next steps to take with each: ■ The first canceled next week's scheduled sales presentation until the new CIO has reviewed the budget and prioritized expenditures to reflect the needs of the business — all vendor contracts are on hold. ■ The second has a question about two features in the Back-Office Module of our Ent-Apprise Gold System.	
8:50–9:20	Reread the current issue of *HospitaliTrends* to get details on the appointment of Caleb W. as the new CIO of Weltrue Lodging, a customer; then call Mr. W. to offer congratulations and make an appointment for a courtesy visit. In the same issue, read about another customer, Remingwood Resorts, which just acquired a chain of 12 hotels. Call Cynthia C., its CIO, to invite her to expand her company's license to allow up to 24 additional users. Offer to waive the fee for training any of the acquisition's employees if she does so within 60 days.	
9:20–9:40	Review cost and time estimates developed by our Technology Director, Len M., for incorporating a new feature into the next version of HoteliTech Platinum, which analyzes the performance of a customer's VIP Guest Program, including promotional mailing costs and response rates, program profits, level of repeat patronage generated by VIP members, and percentage of VIP member patronage by guests traveling for leisure versus business purposes.	
9:40–10:10	Review Al W.'s report detailing last week's user trouble reports at assigned accounts. According to Al, our systems engineer, it seems most of the problems reflect a lack of system knowledge. Are these new users? Did they complete the training program? E-mail Len M. (Technology Director) regarding two users' YTD Liquor and Food Expenditures reports: Why are *(cont…)*	

Time	Activity	Rating
(cont...) 9:40– 10:10	there zeroes in the Food column of the Banquet page? And why does the Restaurant page display the total food expenditures of both the Restaurant and Banquet operations?	
10:10– 11:25	Prepare slides for tomorrow's presentation to MerLuxe Hotels & Resorts execs. Remember to include a feature/benefit/cost comparison of our Platinum versus Selkross Data's Millennium III.	
11:25– 12:10	E-mail Fran R., Director of Sales, to inform her of the outcome of the sales presentation for six executives of Glendovus Resorts and Spas. They specified three requirements that must be met before they will sign a contract: (1) a predefined time period for correcting nonbug technical support problems in three progressively critical categories, to be specified in the SLA; (2) free training for any employee who replaces an existing user; and (3) a dedicated technical support person provided at no charge for the term of the contract.	
1:00– 1:10	Follow up on the e-mail from Sally R., Accounts Receivable Manager, regarding a 60-day past-due invoice sent to MerriMeadow Inns. Call Georgia L., MerriMeadow's Accounts Payable Manager, to remind her of the overdue bill and the contract clause that allows HoteliTech to discontinue technical support on any account with a balance aged 75 days or longer.	
1:10– 1:25	Download the e-mail from Karen O., COO of Casablanca Cove Resorts — she thanked us for our proposal and sales presentation, but gave the contract to another company. Need to call her (and send a backup e-mail) to find out if Casablanca has signed the contract yet; if not, and price was the reason for her decision, maybe we still have a chance to close the deal.	
1:25– 1:55	Call Ray D., CIO of Zirxea Hotels. His contract expires in 60 days — is he planning to renew? He wants to know whether the next version of HoteliTech Platinum will include two features already available in Selkross Data's Millennium III. We can't give him the 20 percent discount he requested for upgrading to Platinum, but we can waive the training fee for five new users and offer a complimentary one-year upgrade to Premium Technical Support.	

Time	Activity	Rating
1:55– 3:10	Answer most of the questions on the vendor qualification form included with Strasser Hotels's RFP. Forward it to Helen T., our CFO, to answer the six questions about the company's financial situation.	
3:10– 4:20	Call prospect Lou K., CIO of Halmizon Hotels, to discuss his review of Platinum's capabilities; set a date for a conference call sales presentation to Mr. K. and his colleagues. Based on Mr. K.'s comments, review this month's internal Competitive Intelligence Report to verify that the two other packages Halmizon is considering lack several capabilities that Platinum has. Start work on modifying the boilerplate sales presentation to emphasize the features that seem to be Halmizon's "hot button" items.	
4:20– 5:30	Talk with Ray V. of Regal SystemX, a HoteliTech channel partner, to discuss a planned joint sales presentation to a Virginia operator of eight inns. Focus on convincing management there that they are not too small to have such a system. Search the customer database for hotels of the same or smaller size; e-mail three account execs request for permission to use their customers as references.	

JOB-HUNTING STRATEGIES

Large well-known companies are inundated with employment applications — typically, they don't even have to advertise. This means they can screen candidates more carefully than smaller companies, so competition for sales positions at such companies can be stiff. However, you have the advantage of being among very few of the applicants who are technically proficient, simply because computer professionals are usually not attracted to sales. So don't hesitate to approach even the largest companies, especially those that place a premium on technically proficient sales professionals. But don't exclude SMEs because they can offer excellent opportunities as well.

As you fine-tune your job-hunting focus, keep in mind the following differences in sales functions based on company size:

- Large companies generally provide formal sales training programs, often entailing full-time study for one to three months or longer. Think of this as a benefit — it will prepare you for success in sales.

- Small and midsize information technology companies typically provide some in-house training, ranging from accompanying a salesperson on a few customer calls to as much as a week of classroom instruction. If you are attracted to a smaller company, but worry about a lack of formal training there, remember, there are many sales training programs on the market today. You can learn a lot from a high-quality program — especially if it features role-playing exercises that simulate a variety of challenging customer situations.
- Sales positions at small companies often entail nonselling responsibilities, which you should view as a significant benefit. Fulfilling these other responsibilities will broaden your understanding of the interrelationships among the various organizational functions and, therefore, your future marketability.

Do not let your lack of sales experience make you tentative in your job hunt. As you will discover, to employers that recognize that your background is important to improving their business, your lack of sales experience will not be an issue. You should, of course, target such employers. For help with that, go to page 15, where you'll find guidance in identifying employers that may be especially receptive to your candidacy. And on potential employer websites, be sure to visit their Channel Partners pages, where you may find other companies that meet your relevance criteria.

When it is time to submit your resume and cover letter, highlight any experience you have had in sales-related activities — business development presentations, proposals, preparation of price quotations, contract negotiations, and participation in customer conferences. In your cover letter, and later during discussions with employers, promote your technical experience further: Point out that your need to rely on presales engineers, technical support staff, and application development personnel will be minimal.

If a company you are targeting has branch offices throughout the United States, contact a regional executive who oversees several branches. The highest-ranking sales executive at the corporate headquarters of all other companies is the person to approach.

RECESSION RESISTANCE
If the accounts you are assigned — or are expected to target — are in

diverse industries, any recession-related decline in your revenue base should be cushioned to the extent that some will operate in noncyclical industries. Even if most, or all, of your customers are affected, you may experience no impact on your sales results if your customers consider the product or service you sell a necessity. For example:

- **If it is required by a core business function.** Products marketed to line functions generally have greater immunity to economic cycles than those promoted to staff functions. Thus, a manufacturer will typically view the purchase of process-control software as more urgent than, say, an HRIS application.
- **If it is required to comply with a law or regulation.** A publicly held manufacturer would probably consider document-control software a vital expenditure for ensuring compliance with the Sarbanes-Oxley Act. Naturally, as companies bring their systems and controls into compliance with Sarbanes-Oxley, the demand will decline.

OFFSHORE OUTSOURCING SITUATION AND OUTLOOK

U.S. companies have long used telemarketing campaigns to sell thousands of products and services, and the cost advantages inherent in offshore labor have prompted many to hire offshore telemarketing firms or establish proprietary offshore sales operations. To the extent that a telemarketer can close a sale, companies will continue to use that method. But remember, my rationale for recommending a sales career is the advantage conferred by your knowledge of information technology.

You are ideally qualified for an account executive position that will *never* be offshored because of the expertise and relationship management skills needed to sell myriad technologically complex products and services to the B2B community. And you can further bolster your immunity to offshoring by targeting companies whose offerings cost $100,000 or more — the higher the price tag, the more decision makers (and at higher levels) will be involved.

INFORMATION SOURCES

Sales & Marketing Executives International (www.smei.org). This nonprofit organization offers educational programs, sponsors events, and publishes the *Who's Who in Sales & Marketing Directory.*

Harvard Business Online (www.harvardbusinessonline.org). Articles, case studies, and books available through this website of Harvard Business School Publishing describe actual corporate sales organization restructuring programs, as well as sales turnaround strategies and customer relationship management approaches.

Manufacturers' Agents National Association (www.manaonline.org). MANA is the leading business development and trade association for manufacturers' agents. Its members include independent agents who represent thousands of low- to high-tech products. Over 70 MANA companies are listed in the Computer Hardware and Peripherals, Computer Software, and Computer Supplies member categories.

ACCOUNT EXECUTIVE
YOUR RATINGS AND NEXT STEPS

How compatible is this field with my skills?

Assign a score of 0–10 (10 is highest): _____

Skills/Knowledge I Need to Acquire Before Contacting Employers

1._____

2._____

3._____

4._____

Typical Workday Task Ratings

After conducting research to fill in any ratings you initially left blank, calculate the total for each type of reaction (like, dislike, neutral). A field may be a good choice if you have at least six Ls and three or fewer Ds.

Total **L**s:_____ Total **D**s:_____ Total **N**s:_____

Research Notes

_____

_____

_____

_____

_____

_____

_____

_____

_____

Contact Log

Date:_____Name/Title:_____

Phone/E-mail:_____

Comments:_____

_____

_____

_____

Date:_____Name/Title:_____

Phone/E-mail:_____

Comments:_____

_____

_____

_____

Date:_____Name/Title:_____

Phone/E-mail:_____

Comments:_____

_____

_____

_____

Date:_____Name/Title:_____

Phone/E-mail:_____

Comments:_____

_____

_____

_____

CAREER OPTION:
SYSTEMS ENGINEER

SECTOR OF THE ECONOMY
Private

INDUSTRIES
Information technology, telecommunications

END-USER ORGANIZATIONAL DEPARTMENTS
Sales, Systems Engineering, Technical Support, Product Support

OVERVIEW OF THE SYSTEMS ENGINEERING FUNCTION
Many companies that market software, hardware, and turnkey systems employ systems engineers to coordinate and oversee system installations, and to participate in the presales process. These professionals gather data about the customer's technical environment to identify compatibility issues that must be resolved before the system can be installed. Once the contract is signed, the systems engineer often serves as the primary customer representative, providing feedback to application development staff on users' problems, wish lists for new features, and satisfaction levels. They also play a key role in beta tests.

NOTE: "Systems engineer" also refers to a person who manages a software development project, and to a professional engaged in designing hardware. These are different positions from the one described here.

As a systems engineer, you would draw upon your technical training while participating peripherally in the sales process, which will also give you the opportunity to watch sales professionals at work. Then, if you later decide to switch to sales, you will already understand how account executives negotiate with customers, address competitive threats, and deal with the inevitable loss of customers — thereby smoothing the transition from the technical side of the business. Of course, you just might find systems engineering to be a fulfilling occupation over the long term.

POSITION TITLES

Systems engineer, sales engineer, customer engineer, presales engineer, postsales engineer

---

Note: The latter two positions focus on only one phase of the traditional systems engineering role, but they would be equally appropriate for someone attracted to systems engineering.

JOB DESCRIPTION HIGHLIGHTS

As a systems engineer, you can expect to be responsible for the following tasks:

- Evaluate the customer's computer infrastructure to determine product compatibility — will the customer be able to benefit from using the product? Based on this evaluation, assist sales personnel in developing proposals, presentations, and price quotes.
- Plan and coordinate the installation of employer's software and/or hardware; interact with customers' computer staff.
- Integrate third-party products with installed systems.
- Design and conduct user training.
- Respond to customers' technical questions during and after the sales process.
- Interact with helpdesk and technical support staff to identify customer issues requiring action. Are there bugs to correct? Do user problems point to the need for more training?
- Communicate user complaints and requests for new features to product development staff.
- Write user manuals and technical bulletins.
- Work with sales personnel to devise strategies for increasing revenues at accounts; identify potential new users at existing accounts.
- Participate in planning and overseeing beta tests.
- Stay informed about competitive products — in particular, customers' interest in those offerings. Convey that information to product development and sales staff.

TYPICAL WORKDAY

CliniCrest (a fictitious company) markets an integrated clinical and business management system to medical practices. A typical workday for a systems engineer there might be as follows. As you read, enter your reaction to each activity in the adjacent cell in the Rating column: an "L" (for like), "D" (for dislike), or "N" (for neutral, or no reaction). If you must conduct research before deciding, leave that cell blank for now.

Time	Activity	Rating
8:30–9:20	Meet with Fran M., Director of Application Development, and Charlie A., Director of Marketing, to review customer evaluations of the beta test version of V5.1, scheduled for release in three months.	
9:20–10:40	Draft user instructions for three new features in V5.1 and e-mail them to beta test participants for their assessments. Are the instructions clear?	
10:40–11:00	Call Melanie R., Operations Manager at Gracewood Medical Group, to explain how V5.1's Medication Module will comply with HIPAA when transmitting digital prescriptions to a pharmacy.	
11:00–11:30	Review responses to the questionnaire completed by Clarkson Medical Associates executives about its current computer installation. Based on their answers, e-mail Sonia D., Account Executive, a description of interoperability and scalability issues.	
11:30–12:20	Design a demonstration program for displaying the features of V5.1 at the upcoming International Health Horizons trade show.	
1:00–1:40	Conference call with Joe A., Account Executive, and Dr. Carl B., CEO of Waverly Westwood Associates. Be prepared to answer questions about V5.1's security features raised at Joe's sales presentation last week.	
1:40–2:30	Download four reports from the User Problem intranet. Verify that three were due to user error; review the related user instructions and revise one of them for enhanced clarity. E-mail the proposed changes to Fran (Director of Application Development); point out that the fourth trouble report appears to be a bug related to requests for the records of *(cont...)*	

Time	Activity	Rating
(cont...) 1:40– 2:30	patients who were members of two HMOs, each of which previously had contracts with the practice, but recently underwent a merger.	
2:30– 3:00	Review the matrix prepared by Charlie (Director of Marketing). It details the features he plans to incorporate into V6.0 (scheduled for release next year), including one that correlates physicians' recommendations for lifestyle modifications with changes in patients' lipid profiles, as well as their blood pressure, weight, and blood sugar readings.	
3:00– 3:15	Telephone Fred M., Strategic Alliance Manager for EntriKey, an alliance partner, to discuss several customers' interest in participating in the test of EntriKey's authentication software: They must first discuss their involvement with their legal counsel and insurance advisors to rule out any liability exposure.	
3:15– 3:45	Meet with Craig T., Director of Sales, to address a prospect's complaint that one of our account execs told her that V5.1 would have two capabilities that it won't. Follow up with a memo to all account execs reminding them to refer to the FAQ section of the Product Development Intranet *before* making representations to customers; and, when in doubt, to ask a systems engineer.	
3:45– 4:40	Meet with Ellen R., Account Executive, to review her upcoming presentation to Conklin Medical Group. Correct the table that compares V5.1 with Van Slyke Health's latest release, which Conklin is also considering — Van Slyke *does* issue automatic e-mail reminders to patients to make appointments for periodic examinations and medical tests.	
4:40– 6:00	Review the 85 user trouble reports logged in the past week; classify them as either: user error, bug, unclear documentation, installation error, determination of cause pending further study. E-mail the findings report to all distribution list recipients.	

JOB-HUNTING STRATEGIES

Most of the job-hunting techniques described for the account executive option are equally applicable to a systems engineering position. However, whereas all information technology companies use sales representatives to promote their offerings, not all of them will employ systems engineers. Only companies that market to the B2B segment use systems engineers — and only a subset of those. For example, a system marketed to health-care clinicians would be more likely to require systems engineers than one targeted to engineers, since the latter are generally well versed in computer technology.

For guidance in identifying employers where you can best capitalize on your functional, industry, and product experience, refer to page 15. And when conducting your online search, use keywords such as "turnkey," "computer," and "system," along with others that specifically reflect your product knowledge and experience. This approach should produce the names of numerous potential employers. As you begin to review the most promising from among these companies' websites, pay particular attention to any discussion of the level and scope of technical support provided before, during, and after the sale, as this may provide clues to a company's use of systems engineers.

When you have decided which companies you intend to focus on for your job search, emphasize in your resume, cover letter, and telephone script any experience you have in designing and delivering presentations — whether for training or sales purposes. Describe any contributions you made to beta tests, user documentation, product demonstrations, and the design or upgrade of change/problem/request management processes.

A word to the wise: Though you will probably generate the highest level of interest from SMEs, don't forgo large companies — especially if your functional, industry, or product experience is relevant to these businesses. When approaching a company that operates branch offices nationwide, contact the senior sales executive in your preferred region; and at the corporate headquarters of all other companies, the top sales executive would be the optimal person. Though many of these companies will have a manager of systems engineering, the higher rank of the sales executive will be more influential in obtaining an interview. In general, the lower the level of a manager, the more averse he or she will be to hiring someone whose background is not an exact fit for the desired qualifications.

RECESSION RESISTANCE

Computer applications that require systems engineering support are used by businesses, government agencies, and nonprofit organizations, meaning that systems engineers can be found at companies marketing to every industry. But to achieve the greatest insularity from a recession, you'll want to target those that exclusively serve customers in noncyclical industries.

An important upside to the systems engineer career option is that even if you lose your job because of the economy, it shouldn't be difficult to find new employment. For example, let's say you are laid off from a company that markets project management software to the construction industry, which is highly cyclical; you should easily be able to switch to a software company selling to the healthcare industry, one of the most resistant.

OFFSHORE OUTSOURCING SITUATION AND OUTLOOK

All businesses strive to minimize costs, so you can take it as a positive sign when a company employs systems engineers: it's likely a reflection that management believes it cannot offer customers adequate support on a remote basis alone. Another, equally important reason companies use the services of systems engineers is that these professionals are often the sole representatives to customers after an installation. Thus, they can be instrumental in a customer's decision to renew a contract — particularly if a comparable competitive product has a lower price tag. In fact, the systems engineer is often the first employee to learn that a customer is considering switching.

For these reasons, companies whose offerings entail a high level of user support regard the systems engineer as vital to retaining customers — not to mention motivating them to regularly upgrade to new releases. These are powerful factors against offshoring systems engineering positions. There is, however, one trend unrelated to offshoring that may reduce the demand for systems engineers: the increasing use of avatar training. Customers given the option of virtual instruction may choose it over the more expensive human training model. As users become comfortable with this training approach, it is only a matter of time before they will be receptive to being "walked through" installation processes previously directed by systems engineers. Even so, installation by users will be feasible only up to a limited level of complexity, and companies that encourage users to self-install beyond that point will be risking erosion in customer satisfaction and, therefore, their brands.

INFORMATION SOURCES

Association of Support Professionals (www.ASPonline.org). Among the programs and services offered by this organization, which is geared toward technical support practitioners, may be some that will be useful to individuals interested in becoming systems engineers. The site includes links to local chapters and affiliated organizations, as well as displays recruitment advertisements.

Independent Computer Consultants Association (www.icca.org). A review of the categories of professionals who are ICCA members suggests that aspiring systems engineers who attend its conferences and local chapter meetings may find leads to employment opportunities.

SYSTEMS ENGINEER
YOUR RATINGS AND NEXT STEPS

How compatible is this field with my skills?

Assign a score of 0–10 (10 is highest): _____

Skills/Knowledge I Need to Acquire Before Contacting Employers

1._____

2._____

3._____

4._____

Typical Workday Task Ratings

After conducting research to fill in any ratings you initially left blank, calculate the total for each type of reaction (like, dislike, neutral). A field may be a good choice if you have at least six Ls and three or fewer Ds.

Total **Ls:**_____ Total **Ds:**_____ Total **Ns:**_____

Research Notes

_____

_____

_____

_____

_____

_____

_____

_____

_____

_____

Contact Log

Date:_____Name/Title:_____

Phone/E-mail:_____

Comments:_____

_____

_____

_____

Date:_____Name/Title:_____

Phone/E-mail:_____

Comments:_____

_____

_____

_____

Date:_____Name/Title:_____

Phone/E-mail:_____

Comments:_____

_____

_____

_____

Date:_____Name/Title:_____

Phone/E-mail:_____

Comments:_____

_____

_____

_____

CAREER OPTION:
CHANNEL SALES MANAGER

SECTOR OF THE ECONOMY
Private

INDUSTRIES (RECOMMENDED)
Information technology, telecommunications

END-USER ORGANIZATIONAL DEPARTMENTS
Channel Sales, Channel Marketing, Sales, Business Development, Marketing

OVERVIEW OF THE CHANNEL SALES MANAGEMENT FUNCTION
A "channel" — sometimes called a "distribution channel" — is an avenue through which a product or service is sold to a particular customer segment. A channel partner differs from an alliance partner in that it is usually licensed or otherwise authorized to sell the partner's products. "Value-added reseller," or "VAR," widely refers to such companies, which typically include dealers, systems integrators, distributors, and consultants.

> **NOTE:** "Channel marketing manager" also refers to someone who devises promotions and products for particular retail distribution channels, such as computer specialty stores, mass merchants, and direct marketers, but is an entirely different position. The position I am recommending is found in companies in the B2B segment — that is, companies that sell to businesses, government agencies, school systems, universities, and nonprofit organizations.

Channel sales managers identify and qualify partners, as well as negotiate commission agreements for sales attributable to their efforts. They oversee training for channel partner personnel in the company's offerings and coordinate joint business development campaigns. A channel sales manager is not unlike a traditional territory sales manager in that both must ensure that sales personnel are properly trained in product knowledge and selling techniques. However, a key difference between the two is that the success of the partner relationship hinges on obtaining both a commitment and the necessary support from the partner's sales executive and other senior management. Since partners often enter into multiple channel agreements, multiple companies must vie for attention for their products or services.

POSITION TITLES

Manager of channel development, channel partner manager, channel sales manager, channel marketing manager

> **NOTE:** "Associate" or "Assistant" will typically precede the title of someone reporting to the channel manager.

JOB DESCRIPTION HIGHLIGHTS

A channel sales manager, or someone in an associate/assistant role, can typically expect to fulfill these responsibilities:

- Identify new channels for promoting the company's products/services.
- Negotiate and administer agreements with distributors, resellers, systems integrators, and consultants that authorize them to represent the company.
- Design and conduct training for partners' employees to qualify them to sell the company's offerings.
- Develop and administer budgets supporting channel relationships.
- Design joint advertising and direct-marketing campaigns with channel partners.
- Organize and participate in joint sales presentations, seminars, and conferences.
- Establish processes for informing channel partners about new products/services, pricing changes, and competitive developments.
- Prepare channel partner monthly/quarterly/annual sales forecasts, as well as reports of actual versus projected results.

TYPICAL WORKDAY

Imagine yourself as the channel sales manager at SensiTrust Solutions, a fictitious marketer of authentication software: The typical workday depicted here will give you a good idea if the field might appeal to you. As you read, record your reaction to each activity in the adjacent cell in the Rating column: an "L" (for like), "D" (for dislike), or "N" (for neutral, or no reaction). If you must conduct research before deciding, leave that cell blank for now.

Time	Activity	Rating
8:30–9:40	In preparation for selecting a new channel partner, call contacts at three companies for input on the reputations of two MSSPs. Then call Ronni F., Vice President of Sales at UniquiTech, one of the MSSPs, to explore the possibility of a relationship. Follow up with an e-mail containing Sensi-Trust's standard channel agreement and a questionnaire to make a preliminary determination as to whether the relationship would be mutually beneficial.	
	E-mail Sid H., SensiTrust's General Counsel, a request to send a confidentiality agreement to Ronni, and inform him that he will be receiving one from UniquiTech.	
9:40–10:15	Read the e-mail responses to the SensiTrust questionnaire from Steve P., President of Keymont Team, a systems integrator. Compare his answers to those of Omar M., Director of Sales for Sancana Systems, to determine which company might be a better partner — each wants exclusive Northeast representation.	
10:15–10:35	Download the e-mail from Corinne E., Vice President of Sales for Cooperman Sentry, an investigative services firm and SensiTrust partner. She listed 16 clients who requested a sales presentation in response to a joint direct-marketing campaign. Forward the report to Brenda D., SensiTrust's National Marketing and Sales Director, and ask her to assign her two top account execs to this effort.	
	E-mail Corinne to ask her to schedule the presentations. Can she find out in advance the password protection mechanism each client currently uses, along with the number and nature of security breaches they have had in the past year?	

Time	Activity	Rating
10:35–11:00	Write copy for the Partners web page announcing a new avatar partner certification program. Include a hyperlink to a demo; add information about three new channel partners.	
11:00–11:15	Return phone call from Inez C., Director of Sales for Laxlor Associates, a partner, to discuss her concern that Rogal Enterprises, a SensiTrust competitor, is offering a 20 percent license reduction to SensiTrust's customers. E-mail the information to Ken V., SensiTrust CEO, and Brenda (their Marketing Director) — emphasize the need to respond to Rogal's pricing move *now* to prevent customer defections.	
11:15–11:30	Respond to the e-mail from Christine G., Director of Sales for Mavon Worldwide, a partner. She wants to know when SensiTrust will launch V3.5. Two prospects are evaluating it against a competitive product that already has the same new features planned for V3.5.	
11:30–12:00	Search online for developments in Randallwort Consulting's planned acquisition of Rugitex Group, the top-performing SensiTrust channel partner. Call Greg K., Rugitex Group's Director of Sales — can he confirm a news report that the acquisition is a done deal? If so, how, if at all, might it affect the relationship?	
12:50–1:45	Reread the e-mail from Ken (SensiTrust CEO), before addressing his concern about Croshuck International's sales in the past quarter — they've ranked well below the average of the company's 12 channel partners, with virtually no increase in the past six months. Prepare an action plan to increase Croshuck's sales by at least 20 percent in 90 days, or terminate the relationship. Explore the websites of two systems integrators in Atlanta that could be replacements for Croshuck.	
1:45–3:10	Prepare the presentation for tomorrow's conference call with executives of Yeager Globex Solutions, a systems integrator considering a channel relationship. Include a matrix displaying the features and pricing of SensiTrust's product versus three competitive offerings.	

Time	Activity	Rating
3:10–3:40	Download the e-mail from Helene M., Director of Sales for M.S. Wilzon, Inc., a partner. She wants to know if Sensi-Trust will contribute 50 percent toward the cost of a direct-marketing campaign targeting hospitals if SensiTrust is promoted in it. Call her to ask about the campaign's size, total cost, contents, and method of selecting recipients. Then review YTD actual versus budgeted expenditures toward co-op partner programs to see whether it's feasible.	
3:40–4:30	Go to a banking industry association's website to track news of computer security vulnerabilities that may yield sales leads for channel partners. E-mail a hyperlink to a news item to Howard F., Vice President of Sales at Emb-ington Financial Solutions, a systems integrator serving financial institutions — recommend he contact an executive quoted in it.	
4:30–5:20	Conference call with Karl M., Sales Manager of Panocea PC, Les A., Panocea's Product Development Manager, and Randi H., SensiTrust's Product Development Manager, to discuss the feasibility of bundling SensiTrust with Pano-cea's PC system for the high-end business sector.	

JOB-HUNTING STRATEGIES

At large companies, a channel sales executive will oversee regional personnel located throughout the United States. Because of the considerable revenue potential of channel relationships, typically, top performers in the general sales force are recruited for channel sales positions. Channel sales professionals employed at competitors would also be desirable candidates. With a plentiful pool of candidates available to large companies, an IT professional without sales experience will be unlikely to win a channel sales job. Thus, if your experience has been limited to the technical side of the IT industry, the most feasible entry point will be in a nonmanagement channel sales role at an SME.

Look for companies whose businesses mesh with your background (see page 15 for guidance in this endeavor). It may be possible to obtain a channel sales manager position at one of these companies, but only if your background is highly relevant to its business, and its annual sales are below

$20 million. In this size range, the CEOs or sales executives typically manage the channel sales function until it becomes too cumbersome.

Regardless of whether you seek a channel sales management position or a subordinate role, use your resume, cover letter, and discussions with employers to emphasize your experience in sales presentations and proposals, user training, and in managing relationships with your employers' joint venture or alliance partners. Also highlight any project management and supervisory experience.

Always contact the CEO of any company that interests you, regardless of whether it has a channel sales executive. But before doing so, compare its channel partners to those of its competitors to see if you can identify deficiencies in its partner portfolio. Mention your observations in your conversation with the CEO — without characterizing them as weaknesses but, rather, unexploited opportunities. If favorably impressed, the CEO will introduce you to the channel sales executive. Be aware that the sales executive may feel threatened by your comments; and even if not, he or she probably will be more reticent to hire someone who lacks sales experience — that hire's poor performance will, after all, reflect on him or her. All that said, if you have impressed the CEO, you still have an excellent chance of being hired.

If any CEO you approach declines to meet with you on the basis that the company is too small to justify a full-time channel sales manager, don't give up: Mention that you could also contribute to the company's technology partner management function (see page 67 for a discussion of that field). It is not unusual for companies in this size range to consolidate responsibility for both under one manager.

RECESSION RESISTANCE

A number of factors motivate companies to exert a sustained high level of effort toward cultivating and maintaining channel partner relationships, regardless of the economic environment. First, companies that establish channel partner relationships invest substantial time in selecting and negotiating agreements with partners, and in training employees at those firms. During an economic downturn, it would be vital to maintain these relationships to capitalize on the inevitable postrecession sales rebound. And because there is often a lengthy time lapse between the initial discussions and the consummation of an agreement, a potential partner identified during a recession may not be authorized to begin promoting the company's products or services until the recession has ended. Likewise, a partner's employees would not be trained until after the agreement was signed, and so there would be a delay before they could begin to represent the company's offerings.

With this in mind, it's unlikely that a company whose sales suffer in a recession will react by reducing its channel sales organization. However, to protect yourself from the possibility that it could occur, you could exclusively target employers whose customers are unlikely to feel the impact of an economic downturn, such as a company that markets software to the healthcare industry.

OFFSHORE OUTSOURCING SITUATION AND OUTLOOK

A channel sales manager role has a strong relationship management component. Communications and contract negotiations between the two parties must be handled at the middle-management level or higher. Channel sales managers and their staff frequently interact with internal and partner marketing, sales, and technical managers; and trade shows and conferences are important avenues for identifying and initiating discussions with partner candidates, in addition to solidifying relationships with partners and their customers. These factors underscore both the impracticability and undesirability of offshoring the channel sales management function.

INFORMATION SOURCES

Sales & Marketing Executives International (www.smei.org). This nonprofit organization sponsors educational programs and events, and publishes the *Who's Who in Sales & Marketing Directory*.

Computer Technology Industry Association (www.comptia.org). This organization sponsors educational programs and events, as well as other opportunities for members to meet and form partnerships.

Harvard Business Online (www.harvardbusinessonline.org). At this site, which is operated by Harvard Business School Publishing, you will find case studies, notes, and articles discussing channel management strategies. A book available through the website, *Transforming Your Go-to-Market Strategy: The Three Disciplines of Channel Management*, provides a good overview of the function.

CHANNEL SALES MANAGER
YOUR RATINGS AND NEXT STEPS

How compatible is this field with my skills?

Assign a score of 0–10 (10 is highest): _____

Skills/Knowledge I Need to Acquire Before Contacting Employers

1._____

2._____

3._____

4._____

Typical Workday Task Ratings

After conducting research to fill in any ratings you initially left blank, calculate the total for each type of reaction (like, dislike, neutral). A field may be a good choice if you have at least six Ls and three or fewer Ds.

Total **Ls:** _____ Total **Ds:** _____ Total **Ns:** _____

Research Notes

_____

_____

_____

_____

_____

_____

_____

_____

_____

Contact Log

Date:_____Name/Title:_____

Phone/E-mail:_____

Comments:_____

_____

_____

_____

Date:_____Name/Title:_____

Phone/E-mail:_____

Comments:_____

_____

_____

_____

Date:_____Name/Title:_____

Phone/E-mail:_____

Comments:_____

_____

_____

_____

Date:_____Name/Title:_____

Phone/E-mail:_____

Comments:_____

_____

_____

_____

CAREER OPTION: TECHNOLOGY PARTNER MANAGER

SECTOR OF THE ECONOMY
Private

INDUSTRIES (RECOMMENDED)
Information technology, telecommunications

END-USER ORGANIZATIONAL DEPARTMENTS
Technology Partners, Technology Alliances, Strategic Partners, Strategic Alliances, Business Development, Corporate Development, Marketing

OVERVIEW OF THE TECHNOLOGY PARTNER MANAGEMENT FUNCTION
It would be a rare technology company indeed whose website lacked a Partners page, as the interdependence among software developers, hardware and peripherals manufacturers, and solutions providers has made the technology industry the leader in negotiating partnerships. Some companies' products may not even be usable without such relationships.

A popular type of alliance is motivated by a desire by one business to leverage another company's access to a targeted customer segment. For example, a company that markets enterprise restaurant management software would benefit from alliances with both a manufacturer of cash registers and a marketer of syndicated point-of-sale (POS) data since they sell to the same customers. Some partnerships involve the sharing of revenues generated from joint marketing and sales initiatives aimed at the same customers; others entail agreements whereby the allied parties agree to refer customers to each other.

The role of a technology partner manager is to identify and initiate contact with executives of potential partners. Assuming mutual interest, the manager will structure and negotiate the agreement and manage the ongoing relationship. Alliances between technology companies routinely require:

- Resolution of interoperability issues
- Design of interfaces
- Establishment of processes for conveying technical updates and information about new releases

Implicit in these requirements is the opportunity for you, a computer professional, to promote your ability to manage them independently. The benefit to the employer is clear: Technical personnel who might otherwise have to support the alliance manager will be free to attend to other responsibilities; therefore, your skills and experience contribute to their productivity as well. Your industry experience can also be an asset in identifying and qualifying prospective partners — especially when the technologies of competing companies must be evaluated for the purpose of selecting the most suitable business for an exclusive alliance.

To be a successful alliance manager, however, you will need more than computer expertise. Specifically, you will have to be able to *sell* executives of potential partners on the benefits of the relationship. And when a desirable partner wants an exclusive relationship with only one company in an industry segment, an even higher level of sales ability will be necessary. Presentation and budgeting skills are two other key requirements.

POSITION TITLES

Technology partner manager, technology alliance manager, strategic partner manager, strategic alliance manager, business development manager

---

NOTE: "Associate" or "Assistant" will typically precede the title of someone reporting to another person in one of these positions.

JOB DESCRIPTION HIGHLIGHTS

Typically, a technology partner manager or someone in a supporting role is expected to:

- Research and negotiate agreements with companies that market products and services that facilitate or enhance the use of the company's offerings.
- Research and negotiate agreements with companies selling noncompeting products/services to the same customer segment for referrals and other forms of exposure.
- Define technical issues, such as interoperability and scalability, that must be resolved before an alliance can be established.

- Develop and administer budgets to support alliances.
- Coordinate internal technical resources needed to support the relationship.
- Design and conduct training in partners' products for internal technical support and sales personnel.
- Organize technical conferences for prospects/customers, sponsored jointly with partners.
- Identify and purchase advertising on the websites of companies that attract users with the same profile.
- Specify the metrics by which the relationship will be evaluated; for example: revenues from customers referred by partners; the number of website visitors who transfer to/from a partner's website; online/offline purchases attributed to each party's customer referrals.
- Monitor the results attributable to alliance agreements for a satisfactory return on the investment of resources.

TYPICAL WORKDAY

Fantsho, Inc. (a fictitious company) markets WizarDispatch, an application that optimizes the assignment of field service engineers based on these factors: the impact of the problem on the customer's business; the proximity of a field engineer to the customer's facility, determined through GPS technology; the type and level of expertise needed; the cost of assigning a particular engineer to reflect both his or her compensation and the probability of overtime being required; other criteria defined by the customer. Assume you are a technology partner manager at Fantsho, and as you read the typical workday here, enter your reaction to each activity in the adjacent cell in the Rating column: an "L" (for like), "D" (for dislike), or "N" (for neutral, or no reaction). If you must conduct research before deciding, leave that cell blank for now.

Time	Activity	Rating
8:30–9:30	Prepare a proposal for Dave S., Business Development Manager of Anderville Mason, a vendor of outsourced field engineering services. Document an oral agreement for joint business development efforts, including the assignment of three dedicated helpdesk personnel and predefined thresholds of alliance-related sales volumes that will trigger the allocation of additional helpdesk staff.	
9:30–10:20	Conference call with Joe K., WizarDispatch Product Manager, Roy C., HR DynamiCorps's Strategic Alliance Manager, and Lisa K., HR DynamiCorps's Associate General Counsel. Discuss integrating WizarDispatch's deployment algorithm with HR DynamiCorps's HRIS application to enable its customers with field engineering operations to optimize the allocation of their personnel. E-mail Amanda R., Fantsho's Director of Application Development. Ask her to contact Dino M., Application Development Manager for HR DynamiCorps; we need to establish a schedule for designing an interface between the two applications. E-mail Kate F., Fantsho's General Counsel, a request to send a nondisclosure agreement to Lisa; inform Kate that she will be receiving HR DynamiCorps's NDA.	
10:20–11:15	Visit the website of Gibrich Safety, a manufacturer of electronic components for life-safety systems, to confirm that Audrey P. is the Strategic Partner Manager. Call her to propose an alliance whereby Gibrich Safety will promote WizarDispatch to its distributors, who will receive a 15 percent discount on any license agreement of at least two years' duration.	
11:15–12:05	Review the Internet media kits of three capital equipment financing companies; compare their third-party-audited page views during the past six months, as well as the composition of site visitors by position title and functional responsibility: Which would be the most cost-effective vehicle for placing advertising aimed at field engineering executives? Contact that company's alliance manager to propose providing exposure for its financing programs to Fantsho's customers in exchange for free advertising.	

Time	Activity	Rating
12:45–1:15	Review the draft of an agreement prepared by Anne M., Strategic Alliance Manager of Ragusa Acumen, a marketer of enterprise financial software. Ragusa proposes to promote WizarDispatch to its customers with field service operations, in exchange for which Fantsho will design software to update Ragusa's inventory management and financial reporting modules with each service call's labor/material costs and billing data.	
1:15–2:30	Write copy for the Technology Partner intranet to update sales personnel on four new partnerships, as well as the procedures for promoting each company's offerings to Fantsho's customers. Design, then upload, an online form for use by sales staff to record each customer's interest in being contacted by a partner representative. This should relieve me from spending 2–3 hours per week responding to sales personnel's questions.	
2:30–3:15	Conference call with Amanda R., Fantsho's Director of Application Development, and Hal F., Director of Application Development for Vopitch Solutions, which markets an operating system to manufacturers of handheld PCs. Itemize the interoperability issues that must be resolved before WizarDispatch can be included as an OEM application; draw up a schedule for addressing them.	
3:15–3:25	Review the latest monthly report detailing sales attributable to partner relationships, ranked in descending order.	
3:25–3:55	Develop the outline for a sales presentation for Kampman Rex, a manufacturer of CTP equipment for large commercial printers, in conjunction with its interest in promoting WizarDispatch to its distributors.	
3:55–4:30	Conduct a search for companies that market dispatch software to home-care and visiting nurse services in conjunction with the corporate strategy of identifying new applications for WizarDispatch outside the field-service sphere. Explore the websites of two such companies whose deployment algorithms appear to be based solely on the availability of personnel and their proximity to the site where service is needed. *(cont...)*	

Time	Activity	Rating
(cont...) 3:55– 4:30	Visit the websites of home-care and visiting-nurse trade associations to learn the names of their chief executives. Draft a letter to send as follow-up to a telephone call to each, proposing that they offer WizarDispatch as a membership benefit — a 15 percent discount on any license agreement of at least two years.	
4:30– 5:00	Telephone call from Harry T., Strategic Alliance Manager for Charlap Partners. His company markets a data mining tool that predicts when manufactured parts are likely to fail, and minimizes the cost of equipment maintenance through statistical analyses that optimize the scope and scheduling of maintenance. Discuss his proposal for an alliance whereby Charlap's software would be integrated with WizarDispatch. Afterward, visit the Charlap website to watch a demo of the software.	
5:00– 5:50	Conference call with Joe (WizarDispatch Product Manager), and Phil M., Strategic Alliance Manager of Pulzen, a vendor of computer break-fix services. Discuss the programming resources and implementation schedule for adapting Fantsho for use by corporate helpdesk functions, which Pulzen will promote to its customers in exchange for a commission on license fees resulting from its efforts.	

JOB-HUNTING STRATEGIES

When you're ready to prepare your resume, cover letter, and telephone script, be sure to emphasize your experience in:

- Qualifying vendors
- Interacting with your employer's alliance and joint venture partner personnel
- Participating in developing sales proposals and presentations
- Conducting training programs for sales personnel and customers

Your potential for obtaining a position as a technology partner manager will be based on the extent to which your experience is relevant to the business of a company (see page 15 for guidance in identifying such companies). Another, equally important screening criterion is whether the company already has someone in that role. The annual sales level that will trigger the establishment of a technology partner management position will vary from one company to another, but a good guideline is to start by focusing on companies with $10 to $25 million in annual sales. The CEOs and sales/marketing executives of companies in this size range will usually negotiate and manage partner relationships until those activities encroach on their other responsibilities, causing them to consider hiring a dedicated alliance manager. Unless your background paints a picture of a strong candidate for a management role, concentrate on companies in the $25 to $100 million annual sales range since they are likely to have a manager in place, and you might be considered for a subordinate role.

After zeroing in on a desirable employer, you'll want to focus on identifying weaknesses in the number and prominence of their partners, as that might suggest that the company is attempting to upgrade its portfolio. Visit competitor websites to help you ferret out this information. Then, sift through the results of your research, and try to think of entire categories of partners that are not represented on either the company's or its competitors' sites. Mention your observations on these topics in discussions with executives — without implying any deficiency in the company's management of its alliance function, but rather as opportunities for them to further leverage their internal resources.

> **NOTE OF CAUTION:** An executive may eagerly listen to your ideas for upgrading the company's technology alliance function — only to use them without offering you a job. However, because you have no track record in the field, it's probably a risk worth taking.

Regardless of whether you seek a technology alliance manager position or a subordinate role, contact the CEO, as this executive should be directly accessible at companies in the size ranges I recommend. If the CEO is impressed by your observations about competitive weaknesses and suggestions for targeting untapped partner categories, you are virtually guaranteed an interview with the company's technology alliance manager, if one is on staff. And if the company has not yet established such a position, your insights may result in an offer to head the function.

One last point: If you approach the CEO of a company that does not have a technology alliance manager on staff, the only obstacle to hiring you may be that the company is too small to justify the cost of appointing a full-time employee to that activity. If so, you could propose that the company structure a position that would entail responsibility for managing both the technology partner and channel sales functions (see page 58 for a discussion of channel sales). In many companies, both are subsumed under the same management.

RECESSION RESISTANCE

Because a single alliance can provide exposure for a company's offerings to all of a partner's customers, its revenue potential is much greater than that feasible through the efforts of a single account executive. Not surprisingly, therefore, considerable time is invested in finalizing and administering alliance agreements. As such, any disappointing results attributed to the impact of a recession on a partner typically are not seen as reason to terminate such an agreement, since the assumption is there will be an improvement once the recovery begins.

Similarly, once negotiated, these relationships are not regarded as self-sustaining, meaning that the alliance manager is viewed as essential to their ongoing and long-term success. Moreover, because significant time may elapse between the initiation of discussions and the negotiation of an agreement, it's important for a company to exert a sustained effort during a recession so as to immediately capitalize on opportunities that arise after it ends. Thus, a strategic alliance position should be relatively insulated from the impact of an economic downturn.

OFFSHORE OUTSOURCING SITUATION AND OUTLOOK

Technology partnerships are negotiated and administered at mid to high management levels. During the course of these relationships, the manager or a subordinate will regularly interact with internal and partner sales, marketing, and technical managers. Issues with the potential to impair the relationship can arise at any time, requiring resolution at a high level. In addition, people in these positions regularly attend trade shows and conferences to identify new potential partners and solidify relationships with existing ones. These factors make it both impractical and unwise to outsource the alliance function, whether to an onshore or offshore vendor.

INFORMATION SOURCES

Association of Strategic Alliance Professionals (www.strategic-alliances .org). This nonprofit organization sponsors conferences and workshops, and provides publications and other resources useful to those seeking alliances. The agendas and schedules of programs sponsored by U.S. and foreign chapters are available on the website.

Harvard Business Online (www.harvardbusinessonline.org). Articles, case studies, and books on strategic alliances are available through this website of Harvard Business School Publishing. A collection of articles covering various aspects of alliances is contained in the book, *Harvard Business Review on Strategic Alliances*.

TECHNOLOGY PARTNER MANAGER
YOUR RATINGS AND NEXT STEPS

How compatible is this field with my skills?

Assign a score of 0–10 (10 is highest): _____

Skills/Knowledge I Need to Acquire Before Contacting Employers

1._____

2._____

3._____

4._____

Typical Workday Task Ratings

After conducting research to fill in any ratings you initially left blank, calculate the total for each type of reaction (like, dislike, neutral). A field may be a good choice if you have at least six Ls and three or fewer Ds.

Total **L**s:_____ Total **D**s:_____ Total **N**s:_____

Research Notes

_____

_____

_____

_____

_____

_____

_____

_____

_____

Contact Log

Date:_____ Name/Title:_____

Phone/E-mail:_____

Comments:_____

_____

_____

_____

Date:_____ Name/Title:_____

Phone/E-mail:_____

Comments:_____

_____

_____

_____

Date:_____ Name/Title:_____

Phone/E-mail:_____

Comments:_____

_____

_____

_____

Date:_____ Name/Title:_____

Phone/E-mail:_____

Comments:_____

_____

_____

_____

CAREER OPTION:
PROCUREMENT PROJECT MANAGER

SECTORS OF THE ECONOMY
Private, public, nonprofit

PRIVATE SECTOR INDUSTRIES
All

END-USER ORGANIZATIONAL DEPARTMENTS
Purchasing, Procurement

OVERVIEW OF THE PROCUREMENT PROJECT MANAGEMENT FUNCTION
The procurement function of an organization defines the policies by which goods and services are bought, including both direct and indirect purchases. "Direct" primarily refers to those purchases needed to manufacture a product, for example, materials, components, packaging, and fabrication services. "Indirect" refers to all other goods and services, such as vehicles, furniture, computers, security systems, placement services, and office supplies. Obviously, manufacturing companies are the principal buyers of direct goods and services. Companies in the services sector, such as banks, insurers, and brokerages, as well as such nonbusiness entities as universities and municipalities, mainly purchase indirect goods and services.

The procurement function defines the standards by which vendor offerings are evaluated, which generally fall into the categories of pricing, quality, innovation, and compliance. Naturally, standards will be tailored to each particular product or service category. For example, materials and components used to manufacture a product must often meet performance standards for strength, durability, and heat resistance, which will not apply to, say, desks and office supplies. However, many indirect items must also conform to standards. For example, carpeting may have to meet requirements for fire-resistance, regardless of whether they are mandated by the building codes of the jurisdictions in which the company operates.

In the past few years, large companies have begun implementing worldwide centralized procurement processes to replace their traditional practice of allowing business units to independently manage those functions. The forces driving these initiatives are:

- **Globalization of trade:** The same phenomenon that fueled the offshoring of information technology positions has motivated organizations to define standards to ensure consistency across all categories of the goods and services they purchase.
- **Economies of scale:** By consolidating all purchases of a good or service into a significantly reduced supply base, companies maximize their purchasing leverage, achieving substantial cost savings.
- **Use of the Internet as a primary purchasing platform:** A key advantage of the Internet is its capability to connect buyers and sellers quickly and efficiently, thus reducing or eliminating the need for intermediaries. One e-procurement method that is gaining broad popularity is the *reverse auction,* whereby companies convey their needs for products and services through a website, inviting sellers to bid on the opportunity to provide them.
- **Heightened emphasis on vendor due diligence:** The globalization of trade has created opportunities for companies throughout the world to serve customers located anywhere. At the same time, in a post-9/11 environment, businesses have a heightened awareness of the vulnerability of their supply chains to criminal acts. Finally, the Sarbanes-Oxley Act, passed in 2002, imposes rigorous controls and reporting requirements on U.S. public corporations, which has led many to escalate their due diligence of suppliers.

Implementing a centralized global procurement process can take one to two years, depending on the size of an organization and the number of business units it has. Procurement organizations can be found in any business, government agency, and nonprofit organization large enough to justify a structured function. However, when implementing a centralized procurement processes, organizations almost always engage a consulting firm, which will assign a program manager from its staff. Reporting to the program manager will be one or more project managers, with each overseeing activities pertaining to one or more categories of expenditures. When multiple project managers are involved, they usually comprise personnel representing both the client and the consulting firm. Depending on the scope and complexity of the initiative, each project manager may supervise one or more associates, who will compile, analyze, and interpret data to support process decisions made at higher levels.

As a consultant to major multinational companies, Art Brunton has served as the program manager on global procurement process implementations, including individual contracts entailing the coordination of project management consultants and employees in as many as 17 countries. When asked to describe the work of a project manager in a single word, Brunton chose "communication." "The day of a project manager," he said, "is filled with both formal and informal meetings with one or more people, numerous e-mail and voice messages, the transmittal of files, and the preparation of written and oral status reports. All of these activities are components of a formal project plan that encompasses measurable objectives and a strong governance structure."

Having supervised project managers with functional backgrounds in finance, purchasing, and IT, Brunton is a strong supporter of IT professionals in procurement project management roles because their work regularly entails the planning and implementation of complex processes. As he noted, "A global procurement initiative calls for the same strong reasoning abilities that computer professionals routinely apply to IT projects. In the procurement process environment, those abilities are required to ensure that all necessary resources are defined, potential obstacles are identified and addressed, and the steps entailed in the process are executed in the optimal sequence. Since interdepartmental coordination and communication have always been integral components of IT professionals' responsibilities in serving internal and external clients, they should also be quite adept at performing the cross-functional responsibilities of a procurement project manager. And I want to emphasize that I believe IT professionals can be highly effective procurement project managers for any category of expenditure — not just computer technology."

Brunton estimates that only about 20 percent of Fortune 1000 companies have implemented formal global strategic sourcing processes. "The remaining 80 percent," he said, "will probably undertake them in the next five to seven years. And, since SMEs typically emulate the Fortune 1000 in adopting new processes, the demand for procurement project managers should be robust over the long term."

POSITION TITLES
Global procurement project manager, procurement project manager

JOB DESCRIPTION HIGHLIGHTS
A procurement project manager can expect to:

- Research laws and regulations governing the sale of products and services in particular jurisdictions.
- Study the purchasing customs pertaining to specific categories of goods and services, drawing upon trade publications, industry associations, and other resources.
- Identify categories of expenditures that can be pooled by business units and subsidiaries to gain greater purchasing leverage when negotiating with suppliers.
- Define measurable quality standards for assigned categories of expenditures.
- Design questionnaires aimed at assessing vendors' quality, pricing, innovation, and compliance within assigned product/service categories.
- Develop the format for Requests for Information (RFIs) and Requests for Proposal/Quotation (RFP/Q) documents.
- Work with legal counsel and contract administrators to define general terms and conditions pertaining to all purchases, as well as those applicable to specific categories.
- Formulate policies to guide the establishment of relationships with alternate suppliers to protect against vulnerabilities inherent in single-source relationships.
- Establish policies pertaining to long-term purchasing contracts to lock in prices for items whose costs have the potential to rise dramatically.
- Participate in defining the analytical and reporting requirements for procurement process software applications.
- Establish policies regarding purchasing approval authority for specified levels of expenditures.
- Design and conduct training programs in sourcing strategies for purchasing department staff.

TYPICAL WORKDAY

A project manager on a global procurement program implementation at Melzor Worldwide, a (fictitious) confectionery manufacturer, is responsible for two categories of expenditures: information technology and marketing services. As you follow along through this manager's day, note your reaction to each activity in the adjacent cell in the Rating column: an "L" (for like), "D" (for dislike), or "N" (for neutral, or no reaction). If you must conduct research before deciding, leave that cell blank for now.

Time	Activity	Rating
8:30–9:40	Meet with Jack F., Melzor's Marketing Services Director, and Chuck A., Melzor's Director of Purchasing, to review a preliminary list of criteria for selecting advertising and sales promotion agencies, trade show exhibit design houses, graphic designers, and other marketing services suppliers. Discuss importance of adding two criteria: (1) that the client billing system of any advertising agency must be audited by a public accounting firm; (2) all contracts must contain a clause indemnifying Melzor from the vendor's use of design, copy, or other creative products that violate any person's proprietary or privacy rights. E-mail final criteria to Connie P., Associate Counsel; ask her to translate them into "legalese."	
9:40–10:20	Conference call with Mike W., Melzor's Manager of Application Development, and Sharon R., Global Procurement Program Manager — we need to pick three of the six consulting firms that submitted proposals for developing a reverse auction system to deliver presentations. E-mail the contact person at the three finalists to tell them they're on the short list and what they need to do next.	
10:20–10:45	Review a report showing the ratio of marketing services expenditures to the number of new product launches at each of Melzor's five divisions for the past two years. E-mail the report to Vince E., Melzor's Assistant Controller, and Jack (the Marketing Services Director). Suggest incorporating into the budgeting process a formula for allocating marketing services funding to reflect the number of new products planned by each division for the forthcoming 12 months — those expenditures are often incurred well in advance of a product's commercial introduction.	
10:45–11:15	Conference call with three members of the Helpdesk Task Force to discuss their preliminary selection criteria for helpdesk training vendors. Recommend adding a requirement that all vendors must offer avatar training as an option — it's much less expensive than human trainers.	

Time	Activity	Rating
11:15–11:40	Develop outline for tomorrow's presentation to Sharon, Global Procurement Program Manager; Rick C., Melzor's CIO; and Chuck, Melzor's Director of Purchasing. In preparation, compile information on the status and outcome of each assignment given to the IT Spend Task Force last month.	
11:40–11:55	Review the spreadsheet detailing Melzor's IT expenditures in six categories of purchases. E-mail Ashley C., Global Procurement Associate, a request to add a column comparing Melzor's expenditures in each category to the average for all manufacturers of comparable size in the same period — refer her to a consultant's study.	
11:55–12:30	Review the report prepared by Ashley that itemizes each division's IT consulting expenditures in the past three years, as well as current approval authority levels for development projects and proposed changes to those threshold figures. Finish drafting a revised IT Project Requisition form. We need to get it approved at the IT Spend Task Force's next meeting and implemented online.	
1:15–2:10	Meet with Mike (Melzor's Manager of Application Development) to define a process for deciding whether to develop an application internally or use a vendor's product. If internally developed, what criteria should be used to determine whether contract employees should be engaged to augment staff? E-mail Ashley to ask her to add to the IT Spend Task Force's meeting agenda the specification of procurement criteria for using IT personnel provided by manpower leasing firms. Remind her also to confirm with Max V. in Risk Management that Melzor's liability insurance policy covers leased employees at any company site worldwide.	
2:10–3:00	Review the draft of a new RFP form prepared by the Sales Promotion Task Force. E-mail Alex B., Melzor's Sales Promotion Manager and Task Force Lead, a request to insert "fiscal" before "year" in the clause requiring a 6 percent volume rebate on all purchases exceeding $5 million in any year. We need to avoid the interpretation that expenditures are to be calculated on a calendar year basis, since Melzor's fiscal year ends on September 30.	

Time	Activity	Rating
3:00–3:40	Review a report prepared by Vera L., Global Procurement Associate. Pay particular attention to the table listing the 24 printing vendors used by the divisions in the past two years — it shows how well each would have met the 12 selection criteria just defined by the Marketing Services Spend Task Force. E-mail Vera a hyperlink to an article in a trade publication, citing 10 mistakes to avoid when buying printing. Ask her how, if at all, these affect our new selection criteria.	
3:40–4:30	Prepare the outline for a strategic sourcing workshop for Melzor's procurement staff: Include procedures for researching, qualifying, and managing relationships with vendors of indirect products and services.	
4:30–5:30	E-mail Vera to request an addition to tomorrow's Ad Agency Task Force meeting agenda: We need to discuss requiring any agency to use a quantitative methodology for measuring the performance of creative campaigns. Ask her whether Monica S., Melzor's Manager of Advertising, can obtain data from a trade association on the number and names of agencies whose fee structures are based on measurable results. Conduct an online search for articles on the prevalence of performance-based fee structures in the industry; e-mail hyperlinks to two articles to Vera and Monica.	

JOB-HUNTING STRATEGIES

As Art Brunton pointed out, computer professionals are well positioned to present themselves as credible candidates for procurement project manager roles pertaining to *any* category of expenditure. To capitalize on your IT background, use your resume, cover letter, and discussions with employers to:

- Highlight any experience you have in developing software supporting the purchasing or procurement function.
- Describe any role you played in defining vendor qualification criteria,

preparing RFPs, reviewing bids, negotiating fees and terms, and managing vendor relationships.

- Since global procurement implementation projects are almost universally directed by consultants, detail your contributions to sales proposals and presentations.
- Specify any experience you have in managing client relationships, noting the names of any prominent companies and describing your interaction with executives at the C level or higher.

To find employers, search for midsize and large consulting firms with procurement practices, as well as small firms that exclusively provide procurement and supply chain services. Specify these keywords: procurement, strategic, sourcing, supply, chain, global. When targeting consulting firms with multiple practice areas, contact the head of the supply chain group. The CEO of a dedicated procurement or supply chain consulting firm would be the optimal person to approach. If the person you seek is not identified on the company's website, a search using the company name and the preceding keywords may yield articles, white papers, and panel discussions that reveal it. In fact, even if you already know the name of your targeted executive, you should still search for those materials, as their contents may be useful in preparing your initial approach.

Note that if you are employed in the IT department of a large company, you may have to look no further for an initial project management role. If the company is planning to implement a global procurement process, one or more IT staff may be chosen as project managers. Gaining such experience would enhance your candidacy for a project management position with a consulting firm — in particular, the one engaged by your employer.

RECESSION RESISTANCE

Global procurement processes can always be linked to substantial cost savings, and the prospect of that benefit would seem to motivate companies to undertake such programs even if a recession negatively affects their businesses. The reality is another story. According to Brunton, many companies will postpone implementing such projects — the cost of which can range from $1 to $5 million for a Fortune 1000 — if they experience weak financial performance. But do not let this deter you because, as mentioned, the vast majority of the Fortune 1000, as well as SMEs, have yet to implement centralized procurement processes. This, coupled with the fact that many industries are resistant to a recession, augurs well for sustained demand over the long term for procurement project managers, regardless of the economic environment.

OFFSHORE OUTSOURCING SITUATION AND OUTLOOK

There is a distinct advantage in having all members of a global process initiative within the same physical facility, believes Brunton. "Face-to-face contact," he said, "can be very helpful in negotiating the cooperation of stakeholders that is vital to a successful procurement initiative. However, my engagements increasingly involve telephone, video, and web conference communications among participants — including project managers deployed at sites spanning the East Coast to Hawaii. These programs have been just as successful as those where all parties were in the same physical facility. Even so, despite the widespread use of virtual communications in global procurement process implementations today, I have not heard of any company outsourcing such an initiative to an offshore vendor."

INFORMATION SOURCES

Institute for Supply Management (www.ism.ws). This association for supply management professionals offers certifications, sponsors conferences and programs, and provides other resources for members.

Procurement and Supply-Chain Benchmarking Association (www.pasba .com). This organization conducts benchmarking studies of procurement and supply chain processes, and sponsors roundtable discussions of its member organizations. There are also forums where people in particular industries, or with an interest in the same business processes, can share information.

PROCUREMENT PROJECT MANAGER
YOUR RATINGS AND NEXT STEPS

How compatible is this field with my skills?

Assign a score of 0–10 (10 is highest): _____

Skills/Knowledge I Need to Acquire Before Contacting Employers

1._____

2._____

3._____

4._____

Typical Workday Task Ratings

After conducting research to fill in any ratings you initially left blank, calculate the total for each type of reaction (like, dislike, neutral). A field may be a good choice if you have at least six Ls and three or fewer Ds.

Total **L**s:_____ Total **D**s:_____ Total **N**s:_____

Research Notes

_____

_____

_____

_____

_____

_____

_____

_____

_____

Contact Log

Date:_____Name/Title:_____

Phone/E-mail:_____

Comments:_____

_____

_____

_____

Date:_____Name/Title:_____

Phone/E-mail:_____

Comments:_____

_____

_____

_____

Date:_____Name/Title:_____

Phone/E-mail:_____

Comments:_____

_____

_____

_____

Date:_____Name/Title:_____

Phone/E-mail:_____

Comments:_____

_____

_____

_____

CAREER OPTION:
CORPORATE DEVELOPMENT ANALYST

SECTOR OF THE ECONOMY
Private

INDUSTRIES (RECOMMENDED)
Information technology, telecommunications

END-USER ORGANIZATIONAL DEPARTMENTS
Corporate Development, Strategy and Corporate Development, Strategic Development, Mergers and Acquisitions, Business Planning

OVERVIEW OF THE CORPORATE DEVELOPMENT FUNCTION
Businesses continually look for new ways to increase their sales, profits, and market share. In addition to introducing new products and services to achieve these goals, they engage in mergers, acquisitions, and joint ventures; invest in other companies; and purchase business units, product lines, technologies, and other assets. And, obviously, for any company that buys an asset, another is selling it because it needs cash, it no longer considers the asset important, the owners are retiring, or other reasons.

These purchase and sale decisions are always made at the senior executive level and, when the company has reached a certain size, by a function dedicated to that activity: the corporate development office (CDO). But it is not only CDOs that are negotiating acquisitions and investing in companies: Private equity and venture capital firms often compete against corporations in their quest to identify companies they deem worthy of purchase and investment.

Some CDOs are staffed by only one person, a corporate development officer; at other companies, one or more corporate development analysts will report to that executive. Corporate development officers and their staff work with internal senior executives, and occasionally management consultants and investment bankers, to define the criteria for selecting acquisition and merger candidates. An employee in the CDO will typically initiate contact with a counterpart at a potential targeted acquisition, joint venture, or merger partner to determine its receptivity to such an agreement.

Once a preliminary screening has qualified a potential transaction partner, a due diligence team will be established under the leadership of the CDO, typically comprised of personnel borrowed from the marketing, sales, operations, IT, risk management, and legal areas. Although many transactions never make it beyond this stage — mainly because of differences in the two parties' valuation of the deal — for those that do, and once an agreement has been finalized, the next step is for each party to establish an integration team. It is common practice for members of the due diligence team to also engineer the integration because of the time savings inherent in the knowledge already gained about the other party's processes.

Given the high level of merger and acquisition activity in the technology sector, computer professionals with an interest in corporate development should seize the opportunity to make a transition to this field. A computer industry background can be advantageous, for these reasons:

- To identify businesses and assets consistent with a technology company's strategic plan.
- To analyze product functionality and competitive strengths, product development and R&D processes, and management and staff competencies.
- If the other party sells to the computer industry, to bring a user's perspective to the evaluation of its technology.
- To conduct due diligence of a counterparty's computer infrastructure, and participate in post-transaction integration activities.

The feasibility of making a transition directly from IT to a corporate development position will depend on the extent to which an employer perceives your background as relevant to its business, whether stemming from your experience as a buyer or a user of the products marketed by the company or its competitors. If you have developed applications for non-IT functions, such as finance or human resources, or that are unique to particular industries, companies that either operate in or target customers in those segments might consider your experience valuable in supporting their corporate development initiatives.

POSITION TITLES
Corporate development analyst, strategy development analyst

JOB DESCRIPTION HIGHLIGHTS

As a corporate or strategy development analyst, you can expect your job requirements to include some or all of the following:

- Define standardized, quantitative criteria by which potential acquisitions will be evaluated (e.g., targeted industry segments, market share, annual sales range, profitability, proprietary technology).
- Engage and manage relationships with consultants and investment bankers who may assist in defining the selection criteria for transaction partners and investors, identifying companies meeting those requirements, devising approaches for financing transactions, and negotiating the terms of those agreements.
- Work with internal business unit executives to specify the attributes of acquisitions consistent with their expansion goals (e.g., product segment, geographic scope).
- Identify prospective transaction partners by studying information in the public domain or available for purchase. Subsequently, commission custom market studies, and interview vendors and customers of companies that rise to the top of the candidate slate.
- Contact executives of companies that meet initial screening criteria to gauge their interest in a transaction, and determine the feasibility of reaching an agreement.
- During on-site visits to acquisition and merger partner candidates that have passed a preliminary screening process, lead a due diligence team in interviewing their management and staff to obtain additional information to validate the desirability of the transaction.
- Prepare reports on due diligence findings.
- Participate in making decisions regarding selling the company, finding investors, and serving as a liaison to prospective buyers and investors.
- Manage projects unrelated to mergers and acquisitions. These might include: selecting assets for divestiture, identifying new channels of distribution for the company's products/services, negotiating licensing agreements, and identifying foreign markets where the company should establish a presence.

TYPICAL WORKDAY

Imagine yourself experiencing this typical workday of a corporate development analyst at Manyon LogiShip, a fictitious marketer of supply chain software. As you "shadow" this person during the workday, enter your reaction to each activity in the adjacent cell in the Rating column: an "L" (for like), "D" (for dislike), or "N" (for neutral, or no reaction). If you must conduct research before deciding, leave that cell blank for now.

> **NOTE:** Although corporate development analyst positions often entail technology due diligence and merger/acquisition integration responsibilities, I have omitted them from the workday here because the career option that follows, Technology Due Diligence Analyst, is dedicated to that role. Thus, keep in mind that some activities in that option's Typical Workday could also apply to this position.

Time	Activity	Rating
8:30–9:45	Prepare next week's presentation to the M&A Committee of the board on the status of acquisition discussions with two procurement process consulting firms. Highlight several issues that can potentially kill each deal.	
9:45–10:30	Meet with Cassie A., CEO, and Shawn K., Vice President of Marketing, to present and discuss a matrix comparing the capabilities of three companies marketing software and databases that ensure compliance with federal transportation regulations. Based on the wish list we drew up last week, one appears to be more desirable than the other two. However, the other two may be priced low enough to justify allocating Manyon staff to add the functionality they lack. Need to talk to IT about assigning an application developer to assist in evaluating that option.	
10:30–10:45	Call Bobbi D., a former colleague and currently Vice President of Sales at a systems integrator, to ask if she knows anything about the culture, sales turnover rates, and customer satisfaction levels at any of three systems integrators Manyon is considering buying.	

Time	Activity	Rating
10:45–11:20	Interview Sylvane C., CIO of Ardizzent Global Chartering, a former licensee of ContainMent-R, a developer of RFID technology for the shipping industry, which Manyon is considering acquiring. She says poor customer service, not license price, was the reason for not renewing the contract. Find out whether Ms. C.'s experience is an isolated situation — interview two other ContainMent-R licensees tomorrow.	
11:20–12:35	Download the website contents of three Australian procurement consulting firms as a first step toward choosing one to acquire to support our Pacific Rim expansion goals. E-mail a list of each company's alliance partners to Manyon's Sales, Marketing, and Finance VPs asking for any "insider info" about management and service quality at the firms.	
1:00–2:30	Meet with Terry E., Manyon's Vice President of Sales, to review confidential customer and sales data of Higbee Pathways, a logistics-management software developer. The board wants to see a concrete plan and timetable for maximizing the savings from consolidating the two companies' sales forces, beginning immediately after the deal is closed. We have the potential for a net annual savings of $3.8 million if we: (1) assign the majority of Higbee's accounts to Manyon's existing sales force, (2) consolidate and transfer responsibility for the 10 accounts that comprise 60 percent of Higbee's revenues under a new National Accounts team, and (3) add two systems engineers and four helpdesk personnel.	
2:30–3:00	Read a consultant's report on the cultural, competitive, and regulatory issues associated with entering the Latin American marketplace, including information on the largest Latin American developers of supply chain software. The acquisition route appears much more promising than opening a branch and, possibly, "spinning our wheels" on foreign terrain.	

Time	Activity	Rating
3:00–3:40	Conduct an online search for geopolitical risk consulting firms to help allay our clients' nervousness about global hot spots disrupting their supply chains. They want advance notice of potential problems so they can adjust their processes as quickly as possible. Review two of these websites, then look for any media coverage on their forecasting accuracy to see which might be the better potential acquisition candidate.	
3:40–4:30	Download the e-mail from Stan I., Manyon's Vice President of Human Resources, relating to two significant personnel issues that will have to be factored into the Higbee deal: (1) Higbee is obligated to pay two-years' severance to four executives; (2) the company recently failed to have a wrongful discharge lawsuit dismissed through a motion for summary judgment.	
4:30–4:50	Telephone call from Marlene P., Manyon's General Counsel, regarding the red flag raised by a review of Higbee's intellectual property: Two of the three people who developed its software were consultants, and Higbee had no work-for-hire agreement with them; nor did it get them to assign their rights in the software to the company. E-mail Ralph L., CFO: How much should we offer those consultants for all rights to the software — assuming we can find them?	
4:50–5:40	Download the e-mail from Judy U., Chief Operating Officer of Cabot Market Pulse, a company that sells syndicated supply-chain research. Cabot has just accepted an acquisition offer from a private equity firm and, therefore, will not be pursuing further discussions. Send her best wishes — but emphasize that we'd be glad to reopen discussions if the deal doesn't go through.	
5:40–6:10	Prepare a report for the board on the desirability of acquiring an operations research consulting firm. Stress the competitive edge we'd have by being able to offer our clients quantitative methods for selecting distribution center sites to minimize their shipping costs.	

JOB-HUNTING STRATEGIES

The profile of a company most likely to be receptive to your candidacy as a corporate development analyst is one whose business is relevant to your functional or industry background, or that markets a product in which you are proficient. (Refer to page 15 for specific guidance in capitalizing on the relevance factor method of targeting employers.) In your resume, cover letter, and other communications with executives, be sure to draw parallels between your background and their businesses. Also, because U.S. companies are buying and investing in foreign businesses at a very brisk pace, mention any foreign language skills you have. If you are a native of a country that is a focus of a high level of U.S. acquisition activity, or you learned about the culture through an overseas assignment, emphasize that as well.

It is common for companies to describe their corporate development activities on their websites, which are often characterized as "organically based" (through expansion of their existing businesses) and/or "inorganically driven" (the acquisition route). Thus, an online search using the terms "inorganic," "growth," and "acquisition," coupled with keywords reflecting your functional, industry, and product experience should yield many prospective employers. But then you must filter those results because not all of those companies will have an in-house corporate development staff, since during a company's initial period of growth, the CEO, CFO, and chair will manage the corporate development function. Only when such responsibilities begin to encroach on their time will they install a corporate development officer. However, typically, at this juncture they would almost certainly include only experienced corporate development professionals on their candidate slates.

As to company size to target, it might seem that the largest companies would be fertile sources of corporate development employment opportunities because of the frequency and size of their acquisitions, but the reality is another story. The CDOs of even the largest multinationals are usually staffed by only a handful of people, typically corporate development and finance professionals and, occasionally, an attorney. Because of the volume of their transactions, these companies regularly establish due diligence and integration teams, pulling people from their IT, finance, legal, and risk management departments to augment their CDO staff. Thus, they have an ample pool of internal, experienced personnel who would be given preference when a CDO position opens up. Many large companies have even implemented formal professional development processes to ensure that top-performing employees are rotated through these assignments, which, because of the exposure they provide to senior management and the opportunity to broaden one's skills portfolio, are highly coveted. None of these factors should dissuade you, however, from marketing your experience to well-researched large companies that could most benefit from it.

In general, though, entering the corporate development field will be most feasible by targeting businesses whose annual sales are in the $100 to $150 million range, where there is likely to be a corporate development officer in place, but with either no subordinates or only one analyst on staff. The advantage of targeting this size company is that you'll be less likely to find yourself competing against experienced corporate development analysts. Ideally, contact the CEO, as he or she probably will be directly accessible at companies in this size range. But if you are unable to connect with that executive after several attempts, present your qualifications to the corporate development officer.

Another potential entry point to the CDO field is at a private equity or venture capital firm, whose businesses revolve entirely around buying and investing in businesses. They employ analysts who perform responsibilities comparable to those of corporate development analysts in traditional corporate environments. Just be aware that like large companies, they, too, tend to favor candidates with demonstrable corporate development experience, or an investment banking or management consulting background. Still, you need only one job, so if you are attracted to the private equity and venture capital environments, test the waters, concentrating your efforts on those exclusively engaged in technology sector investments. Another aspect of your approach should be to target a managing director or corporate executive whose biography shows stints at technology companies — as opposed to a background exclusively in investment banking or management consulting.

If you consistently encounter roadblocks in the private equity and venture capital community, do not be discouraged. Shift your emphasis to CDOs, and after gaining two to three years' experience, knock on the doors of those same companies again. I predict you'll receive a much better reception.

RECESSION RESISTANCE

Historically, merger and acquisition activity declines in a recession, since the ability to finance an acquisition will be contingent on a company's cash position, stock price, and debt-financing ability. If a recession has hurt a company's financial performance, all three financing options may have been impaired. That said, to the extent that a company can finance an acquisition, it may view a recession as an opportunity to purchase businesses and assets at more attractive prices than during an economic boom. A McKinsey & Co. study validates this. It charted the M&A activity of 1,200 U.S. companies over a 20-year period and showed the prevalence of this opportunistic perspective during a troubled economic period; it also enumerated the benefits that can accrue to companies that adopt it. According to the study, "Leading companies that retained their leadership status conducted 33 percent more M&A activity during the recession and 75 percent less activity outside the recession than did their unsuccessful peers. The suggestion: successful top-quartile incumbents benefit from opportunistically picking up failing competitors at known-down prices or by making surgical acquisitions of specific desired assets".[1]

Another finding was that companies that were successful in challenging the leading firms in their segments did so through opportunistic acquisitions as well. But in contrast to the leaders — which also escalated their acquisition activity during a recession — challengers made more aggressive use of their excess cash during a recession, while also cutting their capital and noncapital expenditures at a significantly higher rate.

And even if a company curtails or reduces its M&A activity in response to a recession, that alone would not necessarily constitute a threat to a corporate development analyst's job security. Keep in mind, an analyst's role in a CDO could encompass various other responsibilities, such as identifying assets that should be sold for strategic or cost reasons, as well as managing those transactions; researching and evaluating opportunities for distributing the company's products or services through new channels; and participating in crafting an organizational restructuring. True, an analyst could be assigned to these kinds of projects during prosperous economic periods, but a company whose performance suffers during a recession might have no choice but to undertake them as a means for survival.

OFFSHORE OUTSOURCING SITUATION AND OUTLOOK

The CDO is a high-visibility organization, making it an unlikely candidate

---

1 "Moving Up in a Downturn," *McKinsey on Finance*, Winter 2002, p. 9. Reprinted by permission of McKinsey & Co., © 2002, McKinsey & Co. All rights reserved.

for outsourcing. Remember, the activities of a CDO are critical to a company's growth in its current market and its ability to establish a foothold in new, strategically important segments. And even, as discussed previously, should the chair, CEO, and CFO at young companies decide to delegate responsibility for the corporate development function, this in no way reflects a lessening of its importance, only that it has become too demanding for them to oversee personally. And, again, generally they prefer to delegate responsibility for the CDO to in-house personnel. Even though the ideal initial position for a computer professional is one reporting to a corporate development officer, it is quite common for junior staff members to participate in meetings with senior management and the board of directors.

Confidentiality is another vital component when it comes to the decision to keep the CDO position in-house. Obviously, confidentiality must be maintained throughout the course of discussions between the company and its transaction counterparties, for if a competitor of a pursuing company learns of transaction discussions in progress with an enterprise that it, too, considers desirable, it may present a more attractive offer. Of course, confidentiality can never be guaranteed, but when all persons participating in corporate development transactions have a vested interest in their success, company management generally feels more secure, potentially biasing them toward keeping the entire initiative "on the home front." Certainly, the company could establish an offshore CDO, but a deterrent to that practice is the critical importance of all involved parties sharing an understanding of the culture, the vernacular, and the terminology.

Another deterrent to outsourcing stems from the importance of who makes initial contact with a potential partner, as this interaction lays the groundwork for a successful transaction. The person on the receiving end of an acquisition or merger overture will always be a senior executive, which means the initiating executive should be at a comparable level so as to underscore the importance the company ascribes to the relationship. Executives at this level usually remain at company headquarters.

Considered individually and collectively, these factors make it both infeasible and undesirable to outsource the corporate development *function*. On the other hand, these factors are less likely to discourage private equity and venture capital firms from offshoring some of their corporate development *activities*, such as researching acquisition candidates and

managing the due diligence phase. The reason? These firms have a reputation of being earlier adopters of new approaches to business management.
In particular, since venture capital firms are requiring the companies they
fund to present them with business plans that incorporate offshoring initiatives from the outset, it should not be surprising that they would embrace
the same practice for their internal activities. Nevertheless, don't hesitate
to pursue an analyst position at those companies. They need people who
understand information technology to participate in evaluating potential
investment opportunities, regardless of whether they involve investments
in technology sector companies — and this need should grow exponentially, thus creating ample opportunities for any computer professionals
who are willing to acquire the experience and apply the effort needed to
obtain them.

INFORMATION SOURCES

**The Technology M&A Guidebook, by Ed Paulson. (John Wiley & Sons, Inc.,
2000).** This book describes each phase of the M&A process that takes
place in any industry. It also discusses the particular issues presented by
M&A transactions in each of five technology industry segments.

The Deal (www.thedeal.com). *The Deal*, a print publication available through
this website, reports mergers and acquisitions in all industries, and includes
articles that will provide the newcomer with an excellent overview of the
challenges and opportunities in such transactions. *Tech Confidential*, which
focuses on M&A activity in the technology sector, provides information
about companies and executives that could be useful leads to corporate
development positions and consulting engagements.

Association for Corporate Growth (www.acg.org). This organization sponsors conferences, training seminars, and networking opportunities for corporations, private equity firms, and individuals engaged in middle-market
corporate development activities. Computer professionals with an interest
in corporate development should contact the heads of chapters in their
localities to explore the possibility of attending events as either a member
or nonmember.

Galante's Venture Capital & Private Equity Directory. This Dow Jones publication lists more than 2,800 firms, and includes the names of executives, the size of their average yearly new investments, and the industries in
which they specialize. A local library with an extensive business reference
section may have it in its collection.

CORPORATE DEVELOPMENT ANALYST
YOUR RATINGS AND NEXT STEPS

How compatible is this field with my skills?

Assign a score of 0–10 (10 is highest): _____

Skills/Knowledge I Need to Acquire Before Contacting Employers

1._____

2._____

3._____

4._____

Typical Workday Task Ratings

After conducting research to fill in any ratings you initially left blank, calculate the total for each type of reaction (like, dislike, neutral). A field may be a good choice if you have at least six Ls and three or fewer Ds.

Total **L**s:_____ Total **D**s:_____ Total **N**s:_____

Research Notes

_____

_____

_____

_____

_____

_____

_____

_____

_____

Contact Log

Date:_____Name/Title:_____

Phone/E-mail:_____

Comments:_____

_____

_____

_____

Date:_____Name/Title:_____

Phone/E-mail:_____

Comments:_____

_____

_____

_____

Date:_____Name/Title:_____

Phone/E-mail:_____

Comments:_____

_____

_____

_____

Date:_____Name/Title:_____

Phone/E-mail:_____

Comments:_____

_____

_____

_____

CAREER OPTION:
TECHNOLOGY DUE DILIGENCE ANALYST

SECTOR OF THE ECONOMY
Private

INDUSTRIES
All

END-USER ORGANIZATIONAL DEPARTMENTS
Corporate Development, Strategy and Corporate Development, Strategic Development, Mergers and Acquisitions, Business Planning

OVERVIEW OF THE TECHNOLOGY DUE DILIGENCE FUNCTION
In the preceding career option (Corporate Development Analyst), I described the process by which companies acquire businesses, manufacturing plants, intellectual property, and other assets. I also alluded to the due diligence they conduct, both to justify the decision to consummate the transaction and to arrive at a price that reflects the value of the business or asset.

> **NOTE:** If you have not already done so, I strongly recommend that you read the Corporate Development Analyst career option section (beginning on page 89) before continuing here. That will ensure you derive the most value from this material.

Today, so much of the infrastructure of any business — not just technology companies — depends on computers; thus, a major focus of the due diligence process is an examination of the counterparty's computer network, systems, and applications from the standpoints of functionality, security, interoperability, and other characteristics, as all of these have implications for the desirability and feasibility of the transaction. For example, it may cost a lot to replace a targeted company's obsolete systems or to integrate the disparate systems of the acquisition and parent. Obviously, the expense of these initiatives must be factored into the purchase price.

Naturally, when the company undergoing due diligence is in the technology sector, the scope of that endeavor will be more extensive than, say, for a cosmetics or stationery products manufacturer. Its technical staff and management, software and hardware architecture, product development process, and quality of customer support must be evaluated along with its internal computer infrastructure. Even if the transaction is not a merger or acquisition, but the purchase of a product line only, conducting thorough technology due diligence will be no less important. It would also be critical to assess industry trends and economic factors with the potential to influence the performance of the company or technology under consideration for acquisition.

Though not all corporate development transactions are driven by the potential cost savings from combining the computer infrastructures of both parties, the vast majority are. Thus, the integration effort begins before the ink is dry on the final agreement in order to reap the financial benefits as quickly as possible. And to the extent that the personnel who participated in the technology due diligence also engineer the integration, its costs will be minimized by avoiding the learning curve that would have to be scaled if a new cadre were assigned to that task.

Both the technology due diligence and integration processes must be entrusted to people with the knowledge demanded by the nature and complexity of the particular business or asset. And herein lies yet another opportunity for computer professionals — in particular, those with architecting experience — to leverage that background as a springboard to a new field.

POSITION TITLES

Information technology due diligence analyst, information technology merger/integration analyst

JOB DESCRIPTION HIGHLIGHTS

Most of the responsibilities described here apply to the time frame when a company or business unit in any industry is being considered for acquisition or merger. It will be apparent to you, a computer professional, which will apply only to technology companies or product lines.

- Participate in devising the due diligence plan (to include the sequence of the steps and the content of each), questions to be asked during interviews with the counterparty's personnel, reporting requirements, and implementation timetable.

- Interview the transaction partner's IT personnel to identify issues that may affect the feasibility, desirability, or price of the transaction, or the integration plan. Also, identify employees who should be assigned to the integration effort and/or offered permanent employment.
- Identify opportunities to reduce the costs of the combined infrastructures, processes, and staffs of the two entities.
- Design and conduct tests of commercial and noncommercial software to verify that it performs as claimed by the counterparty.
- Analyze the architecture, development processes, scalability, and other technical aspects of the counterparty's commercial software.
- Interview current and former customers of the acquisition/merger candidate or asset being considered for purchase.
- Evaluate products and services that compete with those of the counterparty.
- Review the software and processes used by the counterparty to protect its intellectual property and detect infringement.
- Develop time and cost estimates associated with upgrading the other party's computer infrastructure and, if an IT company, its products and/or services.
- Prepare reports and deliver presentations on the findings of due diligence interviews, software tests, document reviews, and other investigative activities.
- Participate in planning and managing the integration of the computer infrastructure of an acquisition or merger partner.
- Evaluate the features, benefits, and costs of alternative software, hardware, and services, to facilitate decisions about entering into purchase, lease, license, joint venture, and alliance agreements.

TYPICAL WORKDAY

Imagine you are an associate at Michtelson Associates, a fictitious consulting firm that markets technology due diligence services to companies in all industries. As you "work" through this typical day there, enter your reaction to each activity in the adjacent cell in the Rating column: an "L" (for like), "D" (for dislike), or "N" (for neutral, or no reaction). If you must conduct research before deciding, leave that cell blank for now.

Time	Activity	Rating
8:30–9:10	With Valerie C., Michtelson's Account Manager, set up conference call with Don L., the CIO of Mannheimer Manufacturing, and Vic B., its Chief Risk Officer, to discuss their reactions to a report comparing the enterprise risk management applications of four vendors. Based on their comments, will draft an RFP to send to the two companies in that group that appear to satisfy all of Mannheimer's technical requirements.	
9:10–9:30	Prepare the outline for a presentation to Fiorentino Development on a plan for integrating its applications with those of Wiskern Properties. Goal: Leverage each company's unique SOA modules, and combine those with overlapping functionality. E-mail the outline to Charlie M., CEO of Michtelson Associates, for his review before developing the presentation content.	
9:30–10:30	Meet with members of the IT due diligence team for Frashi Associates now that its merger with Graland International has been approved by both companies' boards. Next step: Develop the plan and schedule for integrating their systems. Review the list of IT personnel selected for the project. E-mail Wu L., CFO of Frashi, telling him to plan on 4–6 months for the integration based on the experience levels implied by the titles of the personnel selected, coupled with the fact that most of his apps are client-server-based and most of Graland's are mainframe-based.	
10:30–11:05	Interview Sharon W., Engineering Manager of Masor Associates, a licensee of the CAD software package marketed by a company that a Michtelson client intends to buy. High turnover in the acquisition candidate's tech support group, she says, is making it difficult for her staff to get their problems resolved. Ask for a list of those problems, then arrange to test the software for bugs, documentation issues, and other causes.	

Time	Activity	Rating
11:05–12:35	Review responses to a questionnaire completed by Kai N., Operations Manager for Lorinsten Group, regarding the management of its 1,000-plus PCs. E-mail Gretchen M., Managing Director of Timparosso Partners, a private-equity firm considering an acquisition of the company. Point out the cost savings and other benefits if Lorinsten shifts from manual to automated patch management, reduces the number of unique PC configurations it allows, and centralizes the application-provisioning processes of its four divisions — including elimination of several IT positions, reduction in PC lease costs, and improvement in user productivity through less downtime.	
1:05–2:30	Write a results report on phase one of a project aimed at selecting a change/request/problem management software package for Kantor Bakery. Include a matrix comparing the capabilities, service quality, and license structures of four companies' packages, drawing upon information on their websites, interviews of their customers, and articles in the media. E-mail the matrix to Sy R., CIO of Kantor Bakery, recommending two of those companies to send RFPs for the project; copy Valerie (Michtelson's Account Manager).	
2:30–3:00	Review six months' of user problem reports for DockeTech, a document control software application that Callaman Systems wants to buy. Based on software tests that duplicated 20 randomly selected problems, four designated as "user error" by Siazo Digital (owner of DockeTech) need to be reclassified as "software defects." Examine DockeTech's beta test documentation to learn how many of these problems were reported prior to commercial launch — the client might have to expand the size of the problem report sample, as this could be just the "tip of the iceberg."	

Time	Activity	Rating
3:00–3:40	As background for possible acquisition of Wright Suburban Bank by Univista Bank, review the line items in Wright's annual helpdesk budget against benchmark helpdesk costs for banks with comparable assets, detailed in a vendor's research study. Alert Lisa M., Univista's CFO, that Wright's helpdesk staffing and break-fix costs exceed the typical range for banks of its size by 24 percent. Schedule on-site interviews for next week with Wright helpdesk personnel and several users. Goal: Identify possible cost reductions through improved staff training, user communications, and automated patch management, as well as other steps to bring Wright's costs in line with its peer bank group.	
3:40–4:30	Write a report for Amundsen Industries management summarizing last week's on-site interviews of six IT employees at Martinson Electronics, a potential acquisition. Point out that, according to a vendor's research study, Martinson's discretionary IT expenditures for the past two years were 15 percent to 23 percent higher than the average for distributors of comparable size. Possibly because Martinson has more advanced systems and applications than companies in its size category? Suggest Amundsen conduct further research to answer that question. (Perhaps an off-the-shelf research study of Martinson's industry segment has already been done.)	
4:30–4:50	Initial telephone discussion with Les I., Corporate Development Officer of Alnoor Technologies. Alnoor wants to buy Kenz Industrial Hygiene and integrate its software with Alnoor's HRIS package to expand its footprint in the manufacturing segment. Discuss the framework for a due diligence plan. In addition to testing the software, Les wants a telephone survey of Kenz's customers, to include an equal number of interviews with users with less than one year's experience and with more than three years' experience. For most accurate customer assessments, suggest he ask Kenz for a list of its top 10 customers in each of the two user experience categories, in order to deliberately exclude them from the survey.	

Time	Activity	Rating
4:50–5:40	E-mail Phyllis E., Corporate Development Officer of XPC Assets, to tell her that, based on my review of the interview responses and resumes of four project managers employed at Silveritask Solutions, a potential acquisition, all four appear equally qualified to oversee the integration plan from the acquisition side. Recommend she offer a retention agreement to the least expensive of the four.	
5:40–6:10	Prepare a Technology Due Diligence Status Report on the potential acquisition of Callaman Systems by Timparosso Partners. Address the delays attributed to the need to research some discrepancies between Callaman's description of its IT controls and audit trails on various applications and actual findings of the team. E-mail the report to Valerie (Michtelson's Account Manager), for her review prior to transmittal to Gretchen (the Timparosso Managing Director), who is overseeing the project.	

JOB-HUNTING STRATEGIES

Depending on the degree to which your particular computer competencies are the type needed for a technology due diligence endeavor, you may be able to enter the field in any of the three workplace environments discussed. Here are some strategies for maximizing the results of your efforts toward each one of those settings.

For a Position with an End User

The largest end-user companies regularly engage in acquisitions and other transactions requiring technology due diligence, whether or not they are in the technology sector. And, as discussed, the scope and depth of technology due diligence at an information technology company will be far more extensive than in a low-tech business. Despite this, the prospects for a computer professional without technology due diligence experience to obtain an initial position at a large company — even one in the technology sector — are not promising. Even at large technology companies, CDO staff do not usually include IT professionals because, typically, the preliminary due diligence is limited to a review of the financial picture of the potential transaction partner.

Once the transaction has passed a preliminary review, IT staff immediately become involved. However, because of the frequency and size of their acquisitions, large companies have implemented structured approaches for rotating their high-performing IT employees through these assignments. And although SMEs are less likely to have these formal processes in place, they, too, would probably assign their staff to these initiatives, albeit on a more ad hoc basis — that is, anyone not allocated to a 24/7 project. Keep in mind, too, that, in contrast to the continuous nature of a corporate development analyst position, the requirement for a full-blown technology due diligence arises only if a potential acquisition has passed an initial, less rigorous evaluation; many fall by the wayside, obviating the need for technology due diligence.

The most feasible point of entry into the end-user segment will be in a technology company in the SME segment — in particular, one engaged in an aggressive corporate development program predicated on inorganic growth. Such a company might find it difficult to adequately address its acquisition technology due diligence with internal resources, as diverting its staff from product development initiatives could undermine its ability to fund the acquisitions. Companies in this situation might be inclined to draw upon consultants; but when their needs reach a continuous, predictable level that demands a full-time employee, a cost-benefit analysis more likely will lead to the conclusion that it is time to hire a dedicated technology due diligence specialist. Yes, a company in the SME segment might also give preference for such a position to its IT staff, but you will have less competition here.

To identify prospective employers, take these steps:

1. Search for companies most likely to consider your background relevant to the nature of the technology due diligence they perform. For guidance in applying this strategy to your situation, refer to page 15.
2. Narrow the list of companies that surfaced through step 1 to focus only on those in the SME segment.
3. Visit the websites of the companies that pass the filtering process in step 2 to identify those that describe ambitious inorganically based corporate development programs.

The CEOs of companies in the SME segment are relatively accessible, so make those executives your primary targets, with the corporate development officer next on your list if several attempts to reach the CEO prove futile. Although both executives will probably be named on the company's website, it's still worthwhile to conduct an online search for discussions or articles containing comments attributed to them, as this information may be useful in developing your initial presentation.

For a Position with a Private Equity or Venture Capital Firm

As discussed in the Corporate Development Analyst career section, companies with CDOs regularly compete against private equity firms in making acquisitions. These companies, as well as venture capital firms, regularly perform due diligence on companies they purchase or in which they invest. Some will always engage consultants for these projects, but others are large enough — or so heavily concentrated (sometimes exclusively) in the technology sector — that they have a continuous need for technology due diligence expertise, justifying the hiring of dedicated due diligence staff.

When you visit the websites of venture capital and private equity firms — of course, focusing on those dedicated to the technology sector — look for a corporate officer or managing director whose biography describes experience in the computer industry, rather than an investment banking or management consulting background. In other words, you want to find someone astute enough to appreciate the contribution you could make to the firm's due diligence projects, and who would be more likely to empathize with your situation.

For Employment or Subcontracting Relationships with Consulting Firms

You'll find many consulting firms specializing in technology due diligence through an online search using these keywords: M&A, technology, diligence, risk, advisory, transaction.

Two other search guidelines to keep in mind: First, when targeting employers, don't exclude companies that are not in your locality — consultants routinely travel to assignments. Second, when approaching a large multidisciplinary consulting firm, introduce yourself to the head of the practice that provides technology due diligence services. An online search may yield the executive's name, if the website does not, because consulting firms actively seek media coverage. The CEO of a dedicated technology due diligence consulting firm would be the appropriate person to contact.

Regardless of the type of workplace you prefer, in your resume, cover letter, and telephone script, be sure to:

- Emphasize your experience evaluating computer products, services, and processes, whether relating to the selection of vendors or merger/acquisition due diligence.
- Describe any participation in quality programs, including internal company initiatives and those performed in connection with a third-party audit or certification process, such as ISO 17799.
- Highlight any IT auditing background you have because an acquisition or merger involving a public U.S. corporation will almost always necessitate a Sarbanes-Oxley Section 404 review.
- Point out any part you played in white box or black box tests of commercial software and in Y2K remediation activities.
- Specify any IT staff management experience, since a key technology due diligence activity is the selection of personnel to retain for the integration effort, or to offer permanent employment.
- Mention any foreign language ability you have. Though unrelated to your technology expertise, this could be instrumental in getting a prospective employer's attention. Mergers and acquisitions are occurring at a very high rate between U.S. and foreign companies, and between European companies. And the globalization of commerce will only add further fuel to these transactions. Your ability to speak both "computerese" and the language of a counterparty's country will greatly enhance your candidacy with some employers.

RECESSION RESISTANCE

Although M&A activity tends to decline during a recession, as discussed in the Recession Resistance portion of the Corporate Development Analyst section (page 96), a McKinsey & Co. study demonstrated that many companies view an economic downturn as an opportunity to make favorable acquisitions. Although the McKinsey study cited a decline in the average value of transactions that occur during a recession — which could certainly have implications for the demand for technology due diligence competency — other events that commonly occur during recessions should offset that decline.

Companies in financial distress may be forced to sell business units, manufacturing plants, product lines, and intellectual property. And the same precarious cash flow situation that drives these transactions might also undermine the debt-servicing ability of companies, motivating them to try to negotiate loan workout agreements. Lenders who are approached for these accommodations will conduct due diligence to help them determine the degree of restructuring flexibility that is consistent with the level of risk. All of these situations can necessitate technology due diligence expertise.

Remember, too, that many companies operate in industries that resist or benefit from a recession, meaning they will not be applying an economic brake on either their acquisition activities or technology purchases. Even among recession-vulnerable companies, some will have the cash or debt-financing ability to make an acquisition, and may be presented with well-priced acquisitions.

In sum, the drivers of the demand for technology due diligence may shift in a recession, but its level should not be materially affected. Furthermore, as pervasive as technology is today, it will only become more so in the future; thus, if anything, the need for people with the skills to critically evaluate computer networks, systems, applications, and processes in connection with corporate development transactions will only increase.

OFFSHORE OUTSOURCING SITUATION AND OUTLOOK

The due diligence processes of M&A transactions almost universally share two characteristics that tend to act as deterrents to offshoring:

Time-critical deadlines: Before either party invests the resources required for a final-stage due diligence, the assumption is that sufficient preliminary work has pointed to the feasibility and desirability of an agreement. A key component of that effort will be an estimate of the financial benefits to be reaped after the transaction has been completed. As you can imagine, there is a tremendous incentive to translate those potential benefits into tangible bottom-line results. Because time is of the essence, the many issues that inevitably arise during discussions between the due diligence teams of the two parties — intensive, almost 24/7 activities — demand real-time resolution.

Face-to-face meetings: The time-critical nature of the due diligence process always necessitates an on-site visit to an acquisition's facility, where both one-on-one interviews and group meetings take place. Greater emphasis is on the group format because it precludes the need for one team member to relay important new information to another — a time-waster. Members of the team continually exchange information gleaned from interviews with the other party's staff, which inevitably prompts new questions. For example, an IT team member may learn that a counterparty's commercial software application was developed by a consultant who did not assign the rights in the software to the company. Naturally, an attorney team member would have to get immediately involved.

While these two factors constitute compelling arguments against off-shoring technology due diligence, they could be addressed through rigorous advance planning, such that the entire due diligence process could be conducted remotely. A team of offshore personnel, all in the same room, could conduct video meetings with the counterparty's representatives, who would likewise all be gathered together at a remote locale. And provision could be made to establish a communication process between the onshore staff of the acquiring company and the offshore personnel, so that employees of both the buyer and vendor could be immediately accessible to one another.

Of course, revamping the logistical processes underlying the technology due diligence function presupposes that offshore personnel would be qualified to handle what can in no way be considered a cookie-cutter methodology. Although veteran "acquirers" have developed questionnaires and checklists for eliciting preliminary information about potential transaction partners, by the time the final due diligence phase is ready to begin, open-ended discussions will be the rule. To assign this task to anyone other than personnel with a preeminent level of knowledge of best practices, processes, and computer infrastructure would expose the potential buyer to unacceptable risk. Yet many offshore computer professionals have acquired the technology expertise to qualify them for participating in a challenging technology due diligence project. And more and more will do so in the future.

All that said, there is still one factor that could be a deterrent: the risk element. As I noted in Part 1, this is one of the contraindications to the offshoring of *any* process. As much as M&A transactions embody very high upside potential, they are fraught with an equal measure of downside risk. True, on-site due diligence visits could be replaced with virtual visits, but the importance of a shared understanding of the language and vernacular by participants in the ensuing conversations would still be vital. Experience has shown that even when no cultural differences existed between the two parties' representatives, companies have had to deal with unpleasant post-transaction surprises following what they viewed as a thorough due diligence process.

Notwithstanding the deterrent impact of the risk consideration, and even without revamping the traditional M&A process, some types of technology due diligence could be offshored without undermining the ability to either obtain all needed information or to complete the project under time-critical deadlines. For example, consider the need for evaluating a commercial software package and comparing it to competitive offerings, regardless of whether the transaction involves only the purchase of the software or the acquisition of the company that markets it. Personnel located anywhere in the world could test the functionality, scalability, and interoperability of those applications in accordance with criteria that either they or the potential buyer defined.

But here, too, a cogent counterargument could be made against offshoring this kind of project. Specifically, it would be important to obtain customer assessments of the quality of technical support and beta test management processes, whether or not the transaction also entails the acquisition of the vendor's staff. For these to be performed properly, the interviewers and customers should have a shared understanding of the terminology and vernacular used by the other party to the conversation. Interviewers must be capable of being clearly understood by customers, and vice versa. Naturally, this phase of the due diligence process could be undermined if cultural differences existed between the interviewer and customer.

What, you might ask, about having offshore personnel evaluate the software and competitive products, and onshore staff administer the customer satisfaction survey? On the surface, this approach would appear a feasible way to still benefit from lower-priced offshore labor. But consider this: The personnel assigned to the customer satisfaction survey would still have to learn the workings of both the seller's software and those of its competitors. Otherwise, how could they understand the significance of customer responses? And acquiring that knowledge would be necessary to formulate probing follow-up questions to obtain vital information that would: (1) help the buyer decide whether to proceed with the transaction, and (2) determine the costs of addressing any identified deficiencies. And let us not forget the learning curve for onshore personnel, which would have to be factored into the cost equation. Ultimately, the savings might just prove to be illusory even before adding in the indirect costs of contract preparation, risk management, and communications between onshore and offshore personnel.

Although this scenario could give IT management pause when deciding whether to offshore the technology due diligence of customer-facing applications, it would probably not discourage them from the evaluation of an acquisition or merger partner's internal applications, notwithstanding the existence of cultural differences. Of course, there would still be the potential for miscommunication between the IT staff of the two parties, which could range from minor to material. And the time spent on addressing these issues would certainly have a cost — which could be much higher if it were discovered after the transaction had been consummated.

Notwithstanding the deterrents I have cited, offshoring of technology due diligence is already taking place. The globalization of the marketplace has been reflected in a dramatic increase in cross-border mergers and acquisitions. Many are occurring between companies in the United States and those in non-English-speaking countries, and the number of these transactions between European countries with disparate cultures and languages has been rising dramatically. More companies that engage in international acquisitions and mergers are drawing upon offshore resources; and because IT professionals in offshore markets are quickly moving up the technology knowledge escalator, it is inevitable that they will increasingly become candidates for managing complex IT due diligence assignments. But as a qualified U.S. computer professional, it would be a mistake for you to be discouraged from pursuing an interest in technology due diligence. The dramatic growth rate in the adoption of computer tools by businesses means that the technology component of the M&A due diligence process will command an increasing proportion of the time required for such projects. In short, there should be ample opportunities for qualified computer professionals in any country.

INFORMATION SOURCES

Association for Corporate Growth (www.acg.org). This organization sponsors conferences, training seminars, and networking opportunities for corporations, private equity firms, and individuals engaged in middle-market corporate development activities. Contact the head of the chapter in your locality to explore the possibility of attending events as a nonmember, even if you would not qualify for membership, as these may offer exposure to people who can assist with your search.

The Technology M&A Guidebook, by Ed Paulson. (John Wiley & Sons, Inc., 2000). This book describes each phase of the M&A process that takes place in any industry, including due diligence. It also discusses the particular issues presented by such transactions in each of five technology industry segments.

The Deal (www.thedeal.com). The company that operates this website publishes *The Deal,* a weekly print magazine covering mergers and acquisitions in all industries. If you are a newcomer to this area, read *The Deal* to gain an excellent overview of the challenges and opportunities presented by such transactions. Also check out *Tech Confidential,* another publication available through this website, which exclusively covers M&A activity in the technology sector, and could be a fruitful source of leads to due diligence positions and consulting opportunities.

Galante's Venture Capital & Private Equity Directory. This Dow Jones publication lists more than 2,800 firms, and includes the names of executives, the size of their average yearly new investments, and the industries in which they specialize. The subscription price is rather high, so a trip to your local public or university library with an extensive business reference section may be in order.

TECHNOLOGY DUE DILIGENCE ANALYST
YOUR RATINGS AND NEXT STEPS

How compatible is this field with my skills?

Assign a score of 0–10 (10 is highest): _____

Skills/Knowledge I Need to Acquire Before Contacting Employers

1._____

2._____

3._____

4._____

Typical Workday Task Ratings

After conducting research to fill in any ratings you initially left blank, calculate the total for each type of reaction (like, dislike, neutral). A field may be a good choice if you have at least six Ls and three or fewer Ds.

Total **L**s:_____ Total **D**s:_____ Total **N**s:_____

Research Notes

_____

_____

_____

_____

_____

_____

_____

_____

_____

Contact Log

Date:_____Name/Title:_____

Phone/E-mail:_____

Comments:_____

_____

_____

_____

Date:_____Name/Title:_____

Phone/E-mail:_____

Comments:_____

_____

_____

_____

Date:_____Name/Title:_____

Phone/E-mail:_____

Comments:_____

_____

_____

_____

Date:_____Name/Title:_____

Phone/E-mail:_____

Comments:_____

_____

_____

_____

CAREER OPTION: INFORMATION TECHNOLOGY AUDITOR

SECTORS OF THE ECONOMY
Private, public, nonprofit

PRIVATE SECTOR INDUSTRIES
All

END-USER ORGANIZATIONAL DEPARTMENTS
Information Technology, Risk Management

OVERVIEW OF THE INFORMATION TECHNOLOGY AUDITING FUNCTION
Concomitant with the increasing reliance on computer systems and networks across all organizational boundaries is the growing appreciation for the consequences of inadequate controls. Along with this heightened sensitivity naturally follows more focused attention on the IT auditing function, for it is the IT auditors who identify weaknesses in computer system and application controls. It is they who sound the alarm about the potential for errors and vulnerability to criminal threats, whether stemming from internal or external sources. And it is they who, based on their ultimate findings, specify remedial actions to address exposures. For example, they may determine that employee access to company systems and servers is beyond the scope of what is needed to perform their responsibilities.

In 2002, the already-high IT auditing profile was elevated further that year with the passage of the Sarbanes-Oxley Act (SOX). Crafted in response to a rash of accounting scandals at public companies, SOX imposes rigid requirements for internal controls and obligates CEOs to sign off on — that is, attest to — the accuracy of their companies' financial statements. Although the driving force behind SOX was the need to provide investors with greater confidence in the financial data reported by public companies, some requirements of SOX apply to private and nonprofit entities as well. Moreover, various non-SOX-related factors are motivating privately owned corporations to upgrade their IT controls — not the least of which is that they are no less vulnerable to criminal acts. The dependence of nonprofit organizations on grants and donations, coupled with an image problem caused by some well-publicized funds misappropriation incidents, has motivated many to tighten their internal controls. In the public sector, the Federal Information Security Management Act (FISMA) requires most federal agencies to implement information security controls specified by the National Institute of Standards and Technology (NIST), with each agency's ability to obtain future funding contingent on their compliance.

With the spotlight on IT auditing at all kinds of organizations, the field merits serious consideration by computer professionals. However, it is attracting so many new practitioners that there may be an oversupply now that most public companies have had to implement controls in accordance with SOX (the deadline for compliance by larger companies was the end of 2005). So, while the need to continually monitor controls and add new ones to reflect changes in operational processes and computer infrastructure will always exist, the level of IT auditing activities probably will diminish significantly. And, while new public companies are always being created, most will be small, such that their compliance initiatives will not entail the same massive effort exerted by large multinationals since 2002.

Two other trends may contribute to a glut of IT auditors: First, an increasing number of public companies are converting to private ownership; second, some foreign companies are delisting their securities from U.S. securities exchanges. The reason? The high cost of SOX compliance. In fact, in response to a spate of complaints from corporate executives about the financial burden SOX places on public companies, the SEC considered exempting smaller companies from complying with Section 404, the part of SOX that mandates the comprehensive internal controls that are causing companies to incur substantial costs. But the SEC seems disinclined to allow such exemptions, although it has extended the date by which companies with a market value of under $75 million, and newly public companies, must be in compliance.

Moreover, there are calls in some circles to repeal SOX. Yet even if that happened, any company that might consider abandoning its SOX compliance initiatives would have to deal with a fate worse than a regulatory investigation: the distrust of its investors, who, without the assurance of the SOX "stick" would question the company's reported results. Even worse, should investor suspicions prove out, the company would be facing their wrath. Thus, from a public relations standpoint, it would behoove any company that had promoted its compliance with SOX to investors to maintain the same level of attention to controls over the long term.

Understandably, SOX drove a substantial increase in the demand for IT auditors beginning in 2002, the result being that many employers at the time found it difficult to find candidates with industry certifications — as evidenced in their recruiting advertisements, which frequently prefaced such certifications with "preferred." One of my clients with a programming background became an IT auditor in 2003 after completing an introductory IT auditing course, but without obtaining a certification. More often now, however, advertisements for IT auditors almost always specify a Certified Information Systems Auditor (CISA) or Certified Information Security Manager (CISM) as a requirement, clear evidence of a much broader pool of certified applicants.

Notwithstanding the increased competition and probable future softening in the demand for IT auditors, you should view an IT auditing certification as one of several desirable arrows in your career quiver. Especially when coupled with certifications in computer forensics and forensic accounting, arming yourself in this way should provide you with a preeminent level of job security or a strong foundation for building a successful consulting practice.

POSITION TITLES

Information technology auditor, information systems auditor

JOB DESCRIPTION HIGHLIGHTS

Among your duties as an IT auditor, you will be expected to:

- Interact with corporate governance staff and internal/external financial auditors in defining audit objectives.
- Plan general controls audits of IT operations, systems development processes, and disaster recovery plans to identify weaknesses in the segregation of employees' duties, to determine the level of employee access to data necessary to do their jobs effectively, and to ensure the security of data.
- Plan audits of computer applications, for example, general ledger, HRIS.
- Interview non-IT managers and staff to understand the operational processes underlying their computer applications and to define the scope and level of access to hardware, software, and media they need to fulfill their responsibilities.

- Compare documentation pertaining to IT production, back-up, and archiving methods with information gleaned from interviews of operations personnel, with the goal of identifying discrepancies.
- Interact with legal counsel in defining controls to ensure compliance with laws and regulations governing the organization's business, e.g., Sarbanes-Oxley, HIPAA, Gramm-Leach-Bliley.
- Liaison to IT security staff in reviewing and addressing exposures to internal and external threats.
- Develop/update IT audit procedural manuals.
- Write reports and deliver presentations on audit findings and recommendations for remedial actions.
- Follow up to verify implementation of recommended remedial actions.

TYPICAL WORKDAY

To gauge your level of interest in the IT auditing profession, assume the following is a typical workday for you, an information technology auditor at Williams Reinler, a fictitious manufacturer. As you read, enter your reaction to each activity in the adjacent cell in the Rating column: an "L" (for like), "D" (for dislike), or "N" (for neutral, or no reaction). If you must conduct research before deciding, leave that cell blank for now.

Time	Activity	Rating
8:30– 9:40	Meet with Steve T., Manager of Contract Administration. Need to establish unique passwords for sales and customer service staff to limit their access to only their assigned customer files. Also, temporarily expand access for employees who cover for absent staff. Discuss design of an Audit Trail Log Analysis Report for Client Contract Database to flag incidents of employees retrieving excessive numbers of client contract files — could signal misappropriation of proprietary data.	
9:40– 10:00	Download an e-mail from Ray D., Chief Risk Officer, listing all personnel approved for remote access to the network, the telephone numbers each will use, each person's allowable day/time access periods, and the operating system on each person's computer. Forward Ray's e-mail to Pete E., NOC Director, with a request: Immediately *(cont...)*	

Time	Activity	Rating
(cont...) 9:40– 10:00	initiate modem callback capability, along with permissions reflecting each user's day/time parameters. E-mail request to Ray to ask Karl F., Director of HR, to establish a procedure for informing NOC management prior to the termination, or immediately upon resignation, of any remote user's employment, so that remote access can be revoked.	
10:00– 10:45	Prepare a report on last week's interviews of Penny H., Data Center Supervisor, and Kyle M., Data Center Operator, regarding physical and logical security procedures. Highlight concerns about five discrepancies between their responses to questions about employee access to servers and archived media, as well as the segregation of duties among data center staff. Itemize other discrepancies between several responses they gave and documented procedures.	
10:45– 12:10	Prepare report on findings of interviews of eight software engineers. Note that six can still access applications they participated in developing even though these apps have been in production for at least three months and none of the six has been assigned maintenance responsibility. Follow up with e-mail to Carleen M., IT Security Manager, instructing her to immediately revoke their access.	
1:00– 1:40	Write report on last week's test of the Accounts Payable System controls: Describe the vulnerability of spreadsheet templates to inadvertent changes that can cause calculation errors. Recommend implementation of version numbers for spreadsheets and related controls.	
1:40– 2:00	Conference call with Nina R., CIO, and Teresa P., Corporate Attorney. Discuss proposed background checking process for consultants and their employees/subcontractors granted access to corporate data centers, the network, systems, and applications. E-mail details of the process we defined to Sid R., Manager of IT Procurement — and give him a heads-up on an e-mail coming from Teresa that contains a clause covering the background checks for incorporation into all consulting contracts.	

Time	Activity	Rating
2:00–2:40	Meet with Ray (Chief Risk Officer) to plan a presentation to the VPs of Information Technology and Finance on 16 categories of data exchanged with divisions, partners, and vendors that are currently not encrypted. Adjacent to each category, describe the nature of the risk of transmitting unencrypted data, e.g., theft of intellectual property; theft of trade secrets; impaired ability to win bids.	
2:40–3:20	Meet with Derrick C., Manager of IT Audit, to get his approval for design of plan for upcoming general controls audit of client/server HR application. Key plan elements will be assessments of: physical security, on- and off-site locations of data, encryption method, back-up processes/frequency, personnel information, segregation of duties, and access.	
3:20–4:00	Visit websites of three vendors of anti-Trojan software. Send an e-mail to each seeking answers to several technical questions. Begin developing a matrix comparing their ability to prevent, detect, and remove Trojans.	
4:00–4:30	Review the NOC's plan for customizing the change management module of a software package it recently acquired. E-mail a number of questions to Pete, the NOC Director.	
4:30–5:30	Write a report on deficiencies in personnel access and segregation of duties identified during an audit of the Purchase Order System; raise flag on significant exposure to potential for an employee to establish a sham company or conspire with an actual vendor to create fictitious purchase orders.	
5:30–6:00	Prepare outline for tomorrow's meeting of the Software Development Controls Task Force. Important to focus on strengthening User Acceptance Test methods.	

JOB-HUNTING STRATEGIES

For a Position with an End User

Because Sarbanes-Oxley has been a strong driver of IT auditing efforts — and because so much of a company's business is computer-dependent — it's safe to assume that the vast majority of public companies have been focusing on meeting its requirements. At the same time, it's important to point out that the level of effort needed for compliance has ranged considerably, because some companies' preexisting controls anticipated those required by SOX, while at others, controls were woefully inadequate. One reason for this disparity is that companies in regulated industries have historically paid more attention to controls because of external pressure to do so. An article in the *Wall Street Journal* reported that, according to Institutional Shareholder Services, Inc. (ISS), a corporate-governance monitoring and rating service, "Companies with some of the highest corporate-governance ratings are in the utility, real-estate and banking industries, while household and personal products, food, beverage and tobacco, and media companies were among the lowest-scoring ones...."[2]

While the quality of a company's IT controls is only one of many factors comprising corporate governance effectiveness, SOX did motivate many public companies in unregulated industries to upgrade their IT auditing functions. And although the deadline for large companies to implement controls was the end of 2005, some have found — as others no doubt will — areas of noncompliance, whether independently or through a third-party audit. Thus, a job-hunting campaign focusing on companies in unregulated industries may prove especially fruitful.

Another useful strategy for finding companies with a welcome mat out for IT auditing candidates is to target those with weak corporate-governance ratings, regardless of whether they operate in unregulated industries. The *Wall Street Journal* article cited earlier also noted that Institutional Shareholder Services, Inc. provides corporate governance ratings at no charge through Yahoo Inc.'s personal-finance website. To find these ratings:

1. Go to http://finance.yahoo.com.
2. Enter the ticker symbol for a company that interests you.
3. When the company information is displayed, click on "Company Profile" on the lower right-hand side of the page. The resultant page will contain the ISS corporate governance quality (CGQ) score, as well as a link to an explanation of the factors comprising the score.

---

2 "Free Web Link Offers Corporate-Governance Scores," *The Wall Street Journal,* May 10, 2005, p. D2. Reprinted by permission of *The Wall Street Journal,* © 2005, Dow Jones & Co., Inc. All Rights Reserved Worldwide.

An earnings restatement by a company may signal a need for upgraded IT controls and, depending on the cause, may also result in an SEC enforcement or administrative action. Earnings restatements, as well as enforcement and administrative actions, can be found at www.sec.gov.

Once you have identified a prospective employer, try to learn the name of the IT auditing executive or, alternatively, the CIO. If a search doesn't yield the name, the *Directory of Top Computer Executives* may (see Information Sources).

For a Position with a Consulting Firm

Contact the executives at midsize to large consulting firms who oversee their IT auditing practices. If you can't find their names on the corporate websites, a search using the firm's name and practice area could lead to panel discussions, white papers, or other material revealing it. When approaching dedicated SOX-compliance firms, the CEO would be the optimal person to contact.

In light of the increasing numbers of IT professionals interested in the field, you should absolutely acquire an appropriate certification before embarking on a job hunt. But you should also use your resume, cover letter, and other communications with employers to describe any experience directly or tangentially related to the activities of an IT auditor — such as IT security, ISO certification, and technology due diligence. Obviously, any experience working with IT auditors in defining the scope of general or application controls and audit trails should be highlighted.

RECESSION RESISTANCE

Given the consequences of noncompliance with SOX (including a possible prison term for CEOs found to be culpable), a sales decline, whether due to a recession or other factors, should not lead to the diversion of resources from IT auditing. Moreover, even if noncompliance does not result in something as serious as the conviction of the chief executive, the prospect of a public accounting firm rendering a qualified auditing opinion — or inexplicably resigning from an account — should be a sufficient deterrent. While privately owned companies are not regulated under Section 404 of SOX, their computer infrastructures and e-business operations are just as vulnerable to criminal acts, which should constitute a strong motivator to ensure the adequacy of their IT controls, regardless of the economic environment.

OFFSHORE OUTSOURCING SITUATION AND OUTLOOK

U.S. public companies have found the cost of complying with Sarbanes-Oxley extraordinarily high and, not surprisingly, are increasingly turning to offshore companies to reduce their financial burden. These vendors are getting involved in various SOX compliance initiatives, including the design of financial transaction databases and tracking mechanisms, as well as the creation and administration of internal audit reporting processes. As the quality of the SOX compliance services provided by offshore vendors is validated through third-party audits, attesting to the strength of the controls they implement, their clients will gain the confidence to offshore increasingly higher-level IT audit responsibilities.

In addition, if it has not yet been implemented, it's only a matter of time before at least the preliminary interviews that IT auditors administer to management and staff are replaced by an online, interactive interview process involving computer analyses of responses. Furthermore, since the explosion in the demand for IT auditors has been driven by SOX, as U.S. companies undergo one or two successful audits after investing substantial resources in implementing controls, the IT auditing function will evolve into a maintenance activity that will be managed in a fashion no different from payroll and order-processing functions — in other words, it will become a prime candidate for offshoring.

But none of these factors should deter you from obtaining a certification in IT auditing. You should also consider acquiring certifications in other investigative disciplines — such as computer forensics, forensic accounting, and fraud examination — as valuable adjuncts to an IT auditing certification. With all four credentials, you should have a very high level of protection from a decline in the demand — or greater competition — in any one of them.

INFORMATION SOURCES

Information Systems Audit and Control Association (www.isaca.org). This organization offers educational and certification programs for IT audit professionals, including the Certified Information Systems Auditor (CISA) and the Certified Information Security Manager (CISM). The Career Centre lists employment opportunities.

Compliance Week (www.complianceweek.com). Articles in this publication's weekly newsletter and monthly magazine will educate the newcomer to the IT auditing profession on issues and opportunities. Announcements of public companies' restatements, delays, and other actions could prove to be valuable leads to employers that are expanding their IT audit staffs.

Directory of Top Computer Executives. The print version of this directory, which is widely available in libraries, includes the names of IT executives (primarily in companies with 500-plus employees), along with information about each company's technology department. The directory is published in East, West, and Canada editions, with each including a geographic index. Job-hunters can purchase the directory data in electronic form through a variety of list-rental and license options, which can be found at the website of the publisher, Applied Computer Research, www.acrhq.com.

INFORMATION TECHNOLOGY AUDITOR
YOUR RATINGS AND NEXT STEPS

How compatible is this field with my skills?

Assign a score of 0–10 (10 is highest): _____

Skills/Knowledge I Need to Acquire Before Contacting Employers

1._____

2._____

3._____

4._____

Typical Workday Task Ratings

After conducting research to fill in any ratings you initially left blank, calculate the total for each type of reaction (like, dislike, neutral). A field may be a good choice if you have at least six Ls and three or fewer Ds.

Total **Ls:**_____ Total **Ds:**_____ Total **Ns:**_____

Research Notes

_____

_____

_____

_____

_____

_____

_____

_____

_____

_____

Contact Log

Date:_____ Name/Title:_____

Phone/E-mail:_____

Comments:_____

_____

_____

_____

Date:_____ Name/Title:_____

Phone/E-mail:_____

Comments:_____

_____

_____

_____

Date:_____ Name/Title:_____

Phone/E-mail:_____

Comments:_____

_____

_____

_____

Date:_____ Name/Title:_____

Phone/E-mail:_____

Comments:_____

_____

_____

_____

CAREER OPTION:
BUSINESS CONTINUITY PLANNER

SECTORS OF THE ECONOMY
Private, public, nonprofit

PRIVATE SECTOR INDUSTRIES
All

END-USER ORGANIZATIONAL DEPARTMENTS
Risk Management, Information Technology, Finance

OVERVIEW OF THE BUSINESS CONTINUITY PLANNING FUNCTION
It has long been common practice for businesses, nonprofits, and government agencies to take measures to protect themselves against events with the potential to impede their operations, such as power outages, computer system crashes, and natural disasters affecting both them and their suppliers. To address these contingencies, they purchase back-up generators, devise disaster recovery plans, and establish relationships with multiple suppliers. Add to these the more recent and sinister threats of terrorism, computer hackers, and malicious employees, it's no wonder that responsibility for ensuring the continuous operation of an organization has evolved into a profession: business continuity planning. BCP, as the field is widely known, is aimed at anticipating potential threats and implementing actions to prevent or minimize the likelihood of their occurring. And the role of a business continuity planner's job is ongoing. Once a plan has been developed, it's not filed away, to be taken out only for periodic review. Rather, business continuity professionals are expected to monitor changes in operational processes and internal/external relationships, implementing appropriate modifications on a timely basis.

According to Cheyene Haase, the founder and president of BC Management, Inc., a recruiting agency in Irvine, California, "One indication of the growing importance of the business continuity planning function is that companies are increasingly implementing enterprise BCP processes to ensure that all divisions and branch operations adopt a standardized, high-quality method of assessing and addressing their vulnerabilities."

As an occupational class, computer professionals can claim the greatest exposure to an activity widely regarded as the forerunner to business continuity planning: disaster recovery planning. This, coupled with the fact that the majority of business processes rely on computer technology, means that IT professionals are well positioned to make a transition to the field. That said, much more than knowledge of computer technology is needed to perform well as a business continuity planner. As Haase pointed out, "Because such a large part of a business continuity planner's job involves gathering accurate information about the client organization's activities and vulnerabilities, it demands the highest level of relationship management and communication skills."

In fact, the work of a business continuity professional is in some ways similar to a business analyst's: Both must acquire an in-depth understanding of the processes underlying the operations they are assigned to support. From this point on, though, their responsibilities diverge. The business analyst uses the knowledge he or she has gained to define the requirements for a computer application. In contrast, the business continuity planner uses it to identify and prioritize the potential impact of vulnerabilities to disruptions in the activities of the client organization, as well as to define and implement steps to eliminate or mitigate the most significant exposures.

Although some threats will, of course, be unrelated to the computer infrastructure, the universal dependency on computer technology today means that many will be directly or indirectly associated with it. Furthermore, because so much of a computer professional's training and experience is focused on understanding and dissecting complex processes, a transition to the business continuity planning profession is quite feasible, regardless of whether one has experience as a business analyst. Nevertheless, you should consider acquiring a BCP certification before attempting to make such a transition, as doing so will only enhance your candidacy. (See Information Sources for organizations offering professional certifications.)

POSITION TITLES

Business continuity planner, business continuity manager, business continuity director, business continuity analyst, business continuity associate, business continuity consultant

JOB DESCRIPTION HIGHLIGHTS

As a business continuity professional, expect to:

- Conduct interviews of personnel involved in business processes (e.g., supply chain, payroll) and develop flowcharts detailing those activities.
- Define and prioritize the severity of events with the potential to interrupt the organization's activities (e.g., bomb threats, fire, computer denial of service, political upheavals in foreign countries where the company has operations).
- Prioritize the degree to which the occurrence of each identified threat can undermine the company's ability to conduct business, as well as the time period within which it is critical for recovery to occur.
- Develop policies and procedures to prevent operational disruptions and respond to those that occur.
- Prepare RFPs for products and services to both prevent and immediately respond to business interruptions; for example, back-up generators, colocation data centers, PCs to replace equipment damaged in a catastrophe, real estate brokers to assist in locating temporary facilities.
- Devise procedures to monitor changes in the internal and external environments — for example, new laws in each jurisdiction in which the organization operates — and implement new or revised BCP policies and procedures accordingly.

TYPICAL WORKDAY

Imagine you are a business continuity planner for Moselle Wand, a (fictitious) chemical manufacturer, by going through this typical workday, to see if the field interests you. As you read, enter your reaction to each activity in the adjacent cell in the Rating column: an "L" (for like), "D" (for dislike), or "N" (for neutral, or no reaction). If you must conduct research before deciding, leave that cell blank for now.

Time	Activity	Rating
8:30–9:40	Lead a meeting of the Global Financial Records Task Force. Objectives: (1) itemize the documents that must be retained to comply with state, federal, and foreign tax regulations; (2) establish the length of the retention periods; (3) determine current back-up method and off-site storage arrangement; and (4) assign the department/individual who will control back-up processes and access to off-site records.	

Time	Activity	Rating
9:40–9:50	E-mail Allison B. a request to administer the Vendor Business Continuity questionnaire to an executive at Moselle Wand's payroll-management vendor. What measures have been taken to prevent disruptions to its services, including the timely filing of customers' state and federal 941 tax returns?	
9:50–11:00	Write a progress report on the Physical Facility Vulnerability Task Force for last month; include: (1) recommendations for new security measures for both employees and visitors; (2) a plan for implementing remote network access for employees who can work from home.	
11:00–11:50	Meet with the SAN BCP Task Force regarding the technical capabilities of three vendors' clustered storage devices. These will enable the replication of data across multiple company locations and the virtual real-time recovery of computer operations affected by a disaster.	
11:50–12:20	Download the e-mail from Ram G., Director of U.S. Risk Management, with the inventory of the company's regulatory certifications and license documents, and the name of the computer file containing copies of all such documents. Forward the e-mail to Maureen Q., Manager of Enterprise Content Management, along with the names of three employees authorized to have access to that information. E-mail Violet C., HRIS Administrator, to ask her to flag the personnel files of those employees to note their access, and to notify Risk Management of any changes in their personnel status, such as a new position or termination.	
1:00–1:35	Meet with Laurette V., Manager of International Risk Management, to plan the agenda for next week's BCP webinar for executives overseeing European, Asian, and Middle Eastern operations. E-mail the agenda to Rene M., Associate General Counsel, and Howard B., of Cremer Geopolitical Risk Advisors, inviting them to add any agenda items.	

Time	Activity	Rating
1:35– 2:40	Draft a Vendor Integrity Program RFP for submittal to investigative firms. Under the program, the physical addresses of all current and prospective vendors will be verified, background checks of their executives conducted, and a financial stability assessment prepared from a review of their responses to a questionnaire, as well as interviews with creditors.	
2:40– 3:30	Review the report prepared by the Network Vulnerability Assessment Task Force recommending the acquisition of software capable of performing deep inspection of packets — this will replace the current method of using application proxies. E-mail Vince F., Task Force Lead, a request to invite three vendors of such software to deliver a virtual sales presentation to the task force.	
3:30– 4:00	Meet with Christine P., Manager of Training, to review the content of the BCP module that will be incorporated into the company's management training program.	
4:00– 4:30	Outline tomorrow's presentation on the Logistics Interruption Analysis Task Force. Detail: (1) vulnerability assessments of owned and leased warehouses, (2) exposures inherent in shipping methods and containers used by the company, and (3) the impact of strikes by union truckers and port authority workers.	
4:30– 5:30	Attend a presentation by Bernington Partners on its colocation facilities in conjunction with the establishment of a redundant e-commerce operation.	
5:30– 6:15	Meet with Sunny R., IT Auditor, to develop a Software Testing Business Continuity Plan. Include a form that project leads can use to update the status of application testing within two business days of any such activity; specify a method for auditing employee compliance with software testing procedures.	

JOB-HUNTING STRATEGIES

Because disaster recovery planning has elements in common with business continuity planning, be sure to highlight any experience you have in that function in your resume, cover letter, and other communications with employers. Other experience to emphasize: systems conversions, ISO certification, vendor/acquisition due diligence, and Y2K initiatives.

For an End-User Position

Employers who engage recruiters to find business continuity planners only want to be presented with candidates with experience in BCP. That should not discourage you, for if you undertake a proactive job-hunting campaign that directly targets employers, you may be considered a viable candidate for BCP positions. And I can recommend some strategies for researching employers that will maximize your chances for a successful outcome.

- **Target companies whose BCP processes are more likely to involve computer technology.** This means companies in the information technology industry. But do not limit yourself to these. Any midsize or large company is likely to have a business continuity plan in place or be on the verge of implementing one.
- **Pay particular attention to companies in industries where you have experience.** Emphasize your knowledge of their unique business processes and exposures when communicating with them. (See page 15 for guidance in capitalizing on your industry, functional, and/or product usage experience to find employers that fall in this category.)
- **Identify companies in regulated industries.** These are more likely to have business continuity plans. For example, utilities must comply with state and federal regulations aimed at ensuring their ability to deliver services in the face of a disaster.

It also may be useful in targeting employers to review surveys conducted by Cheyene Haase's company, BC Management. They yield information about the allocation of company resources to BCP by industry category. You can access these surveys at www.bcmanagement.com.

When seeking a position with any organization, try to identify the executive in charge of the business continuity planning function. Although his or her name may not be on the corporate website, an online search may produce it. Or you may come up with the name of the chief risk officer, another suitable person to approach.

And if you're planning to job-hunt in the public sector, be aware that some states have enacted legislation mandating that its agencies develop business continuity planning processes. Also note that all federal agencies are required to comply with rigorous business continuity planning regulations specified in the Federal Information Security Management Act (FISMA), passed in 2002. And though many federal agencies have not yet met FISMA's requirements, they are under pressure to do so by Congress and the Office of Management and the Budget, suggesting that they may have more position openings than they can fill with experienced BCP professionals — especially since private sector compensation is typically higher. Thus, they might be more receptive to computer professionals, who can seize the opportunity to establish themselves in the field. To identify federal government BCP employment opportunities, visit www.jobs@opm/gov. You should also directly contact the personnel executives of all federal agencies, regardless of whether such positions are posted.

For a Position at a Consulting Firm

If you are targeting a midsize or large consulting firm, begin with a visit to its website to find the name of the head of the practice providing business continuity consulting services. (Note: It will probably include "risk" in the name.) If that person is not identified there, a search using the company and practice name may lead you to articles, panel discussions, or white papers containing the executive's name. A search will also lead you to the websites of a number of small consulting firms that exclusively provide business continuity planning services. The CEOs of those companies are the appropriate people to contact.

RECESSION RESISTANCE

According to Haase, "While business continuity planning would seem to be so vital to a company's continued operation that it would be immune to recession-related cutbacks, in reality it is highly susceptible." She has, however, observed (both in her own practice and through discussions with other BCP recruiting executives) one factor that may motivate a business to sustain its focus on BCP in the face of a sales decline; that is, companies that have BCP functions are increasingly requiring their vendors to also have such processes as a condition of doing business with them.

Another trend that will undoubtedly increase the resistance of BCP to an economic downturn: More and more businesses are interested in purchasing business interruption insurance. This reflects the same heightened sensitivity to their exposures that is causing them to require their vendors to have business continuity plans. As part of the underwriting process for business interruption coverage, insurers require evidence of an applicant's business continuity plan, the quality of which will be instrumental in both the decision to offer such a policy and the price of the coverage. A company that seeks business interruption insurance would, therefore, be compelled to invest in both the establishment and ongoing management of a business continuity plan, even if its sales are affected by a recession.

OFFSHORE OUTSOURCING SITUATION AND OUTLOOK

Planning for the continuation of a business is a vital activity that demands an understanding of the interrelationships that exist among its various departments and personnel, as well as the organization's relationships with suppliers, customers, and other entities. As Haase noted, "While many companies will use consultants to assist them in establishing BCP processes, the ongoing management of the plan calls for a depth of knowledge that requires involvement in the day-to-day activities of the organization. Prior to the devastating hurricanes of 2005, I was aware of a few situations where companies had outsourced the management of an entire department that included the BCP function — for example, information technology — to large U.S. outsourcing vendors. In those cases, the business continuity professional became an employee of the vendor but continued to report to the same physical location and serve internal clients in the same manner as before the function was outsourced. However, the natural disasters of 2005 underscored the critical importance of BCP to the performance of the entire organization, leading many corporations to conclude that it should be completely under their control. In fact, some large companies that had previously outsourced their BCP functions are now considering whether they should transfer them back to in-house management."

INFORMATION SOURCES

DRI International (www.drii.org). This global organization awards the Certified Business Continuity Professional (CBCP) designation to qualified individuals. It offers educational programs and lists employment opportunities. A lower-level certification, Associate Business Continuity Professional (ABCP), is offered to those with experience in related disciplines who pass a DRI International examination and fulfill other application requirements.

Business Continuity Institute (www.thebci.org). This UK-based organization provides educational and career resources, including business continuity certifications at the Associate, Member, Specialist, and Fellow levels, to professionals in numerous countries. Those who lack BCP experience can apply for nonprofessional membership status.

Continuity Insights (www.continuityinsights.com). A bimonthly business continuity magazine is available by subscription. The publisher also offers an e-newsletter and sponsors conferences, which can help aspiring business continuity planners learn about and stay abreast of developments in the field.

BUSINESS CONTINUITY PLANNER
YOUR RATINGS AND NEXT STEPS

How compatible is this field with my skills?

Assign a score of 0–10 (10 is highest): _____

Skills/Knowledge I Need to Acquire Before Contacting Employers

1._____

2._____

3._____

4._____

Typical Workday Task Ratings

After conducting research to fill in any ratings you initially left blank, calculate the total for each type of reaction (like, dislike, neutral). A field may be a good choice if you have at least six Ls and three or fewer Ds.

Total **L**s:_____ Total **D**s:_____ Total **N**s:_____

Research Notes

_____

_____

_____

_____

_____

_____

_____

_____

Contact Log

Date:_____Name/Title:_____

Phone/E-mail:_____

Comments:_____

_____

_____

_____

Date:_____Name/Title:_____

Phone/E-mail:_____

Comments:_____

_____

_____

_____

Date:_____Name/Title:_____

Phone/E-mail:_____

Comments:_____

_____

_____

_____

Date:_____Name/Title:_____

Phone/E-mail:_____

Comments:_____

_____

_____

_____

CAREER OPTION: TECHNOLOGY RISK MANAGER

SECTORS OF THE ECONOMY
Private, public, nonprofit

PRIVATE SECTOR INDUSTRIES
All

END-USER ORGANIZATIONAL DEPARTMENTS
Information Technology, Risk Management, Security

OVERVIEW OF THE TECHNOLOGY RISK MANAGEMENT FUNCTION
Evidence of today's universal dependence on information technology can be seen in an emerging trend: the establishment of board-level technology committees to serve along with the traditional audit, finance, and compensation committees. In a *Wall Street Journal* article reporting this trend, a CIO explained his company's decision to join the growing list of businesses adopting this practice by describing technology as the "central nervous system" of his company — without which it could not function.[3] Another impetus for the formation of board-level technology committees has been the Sarbanes-Oxley Act of 2002 (see the Index for pointers to information about this legislation). Not surprisingly, this greatly heightened awareness of the critical importance of technology to organizations across all sectors has spawned a new profession: technology risk manager.

As with any profession in an embryonic stage of development, the roots of technology risk management lie in the consulting sphere, where specialists have been serving the client community on a project basis. But this is changing as technology exposures continue to grow. Many clients are acknowledging that such risks are beyond relegation to project-oriented activities that can be addressed through the occasional involvement of consultants. These risks, they realize, demand an ongoing dedicated focus — and on an enterprise-wide basis. This change in attitude first took hold at the largest multinationals, where the complexity and scale of their global operations created myriad exposures. Now, however, awareness is gradually cascading down

---

3 "Technology Committees Catch On in Boardrooms," *The Wall Street Journal*, June 30, 2005; p. B3.

the organizational scale. Companies in all size segments, in particular those that are exclusively or heavily engaged in e-commerce, are fast gaining an appreciation for the downside risks inherent in their reliance on computers, prompting many to follow the lead of the large multinationals.

A good way to look at technology risk management is as a form of technology due diligence, with this difference: Rather than being focused on a counterparty to a transaction, it is self-directed at the initiating enterprise. In fact, the same consulting staff members who conduct technology due diligence of client acquisitions are often assigned to technology risk engagements as well. Certainly, technology due diligence will encompass an examination of weaknesses in IT security and other facets of an organization's computer infrastructure, but its emphasis will be on determining the cost of addressing identified exposures, so they can be factored into the price of the transaction — assuming they are not deal breakers. In contrast, the primary focus of a technology risk manager is to identify and prioritize exposures to reflect their impact on the business, thus enabling the most judicious allocation of resources.

Because of the newness of the profession, many of those chosen to head startup in-house technology risk management functions have been recruited from the staffs of the consulting firms used by the client companies. Others are being tapped from the IT security and IT auditing professions.

Businesses and other organizations that have not addressed their technology exposures, as well as those that have done so exclusively by drawing upon consultants, will increasingly join the ranks of those establishing proprietary organizations. Some of these initiatives will be internally motivated, but many will stem from external pressures — investors, regulatory agencies, legislation, and a growing body of case law that is gradually shaping best practices standards for enterprises entrusted with custody of third-party data. Two other trends will loom large as impetuses to action:

- First, just as it is becoming routine for businesses to require their vendors to demonstrate both the existence and adequacy of business continuity plans, expect to see more and more enterprises using their RFPs to elicit information about vendors' attention to managing their technology risks.
- Second, the awareness of technology exposures is driving robust growth in the demand for insurance products for cost-effectively transferring such risks, which insurers are eagerly meeting by designing a potpourri

of offerings. And a key factor in a policy applicant's ability to obtain such coverage — not to mention the cost — will be an insurer's assessment of the actions it has taken to mitigate its technology exposures.

Understandably, as the demand for insurance products is rapidly growing, the insurance industry itself is emerging as a third segment of technology risk employment opportunities, along with the end-user and consulting environments.

NOTE: To learn about other insurance industry opportunities for computer professionals, read the Technology Insurance Broker/Agent (page 161) and the Technology Insurance Underwriter (page 175) career options, which follow this one.

Because insurers only recently began offering cyberliability and technology risk insurance products, many have exclusively turned to technology consultants to evaluate the risks inherent in their applicants' operations. But the past few years have seen the formation of alliances between insurers and companies that specialize in assessing and mitigating computer-related exposures. This trend reflects the dramatically expanded technology loss control needs of insurers as they compete to establish a foothold in what promises to be a very lucrative market over the long term. I predict that some of these casual relationships will become formalized through insurers' acquisitions of their technology partners. Indeed, some insurers have already established in-house technology loss control functions employing personnel recruited from traditional IT environments; and some large insurance brokerages have formed in-house technology risk solution teams staffed by IT professionals.

In the not-too-distant future, it will be as common for insurers and brokerages that market cyberliability and computer industry professional liability policies to staff their loss control and risk management functions with IT professionals as it has long been for life, health, and disability insurers to employ physicians and nurses, and for structural and civil engineers to be on staff at property and casualty insurers.

Whether you would prefer to practice technology risk management at an end user, a consulting firm, or an insurance carrier or broker, obtaining an IT auditing or IT security certification would be an important first step. And because the development and administration of budgets is a key component of a technology risk manager's job, add an MBA to your list of important credentials if you want to attract the attention of the most discriminating employers, or build a thriving consultancy.

POSITION TITLES

Technology risk manager, technology risk consultant, technology risk associate, information technology asset manager

JOB DESCRIPTION HIGHLIGHTS

As a technology risk manager, you can expect your responsibilities to include some or all of the following:

- Oversee the development of standardized processes for identifying, prioritizing, reporting, and remediating technology risks.
- Interact with corporate governance, risk management, and finance management in analyzing technology risks across the enterprise; establish priorities for remediating these risks to reflect their potential impact on the organization.
- Perform technology risk assessments of auditing, compliance, e-business, network administration, and software development processes.
- Work with managers in all departments, both individually and on a cross-functional basis, to define and prioritize their technology risks; define and communicate policies and procedures to mitigate those exposures.
- Develop and administer budgets for technology risk management initiatives; prepare reports on the status of expenditures versus budgets.
- Manage RFP preparation, contract negotiation, and vendor relationships associated with the acquisition of software, services, and products to address technology risks.
- Prepare reports and deliver presentations on identified exposures and mitigating actions.
- Develop and administer policies for granting third parties access to company data centers and other facilities, networks, systems, and proprietary/customer data.
- Lead the development of standardized processes for conducting technology due diligence of companies, business units, product lines, and

technologies considered for purchase; evaluate and report due diligence findings as they pertain to particular transactions.

TYPICAL WORKDAY

To get a better idea of whether the preceding responsibilities might appeal to you on a daily basis, read about them "in action" in this workday of a technology risk manager at Kingsler Industries, a fictitious manufacturer of medical diagnostic instruments. As you read, enter your reaction to each activity in the adjacent cell in the Rating column: an "L" (for like), "D" (for dislike), or "N" (for neutral, or no reaction). If you must conduct research before deciding, leave that cell blank for now.

Time	Activity	Rating
8:30– 9:10	Conference call with Harriet N., IT Security Manager, and Howard S., Director of Network Operations, to discuss updating Kingsler's network topology diagram — which, alarmingly, dates back to before the integration of the networks of the last two acquisitions. Institute a plan of action to ensure currency of topology diagrams at all times. Document the elements of the plan and assignment of responsibility for each; e-mail the doc to Harriet and Howard for their approval.	
9:10– 9:55	Review the Social Engineering Vulnerability Assessment prepared by Neshultz Group, an ethical hacking firm. It reported 16 instances where their staff improperly gained access to Kingsler data centers and branch offices by pretending to be utility repair technicians, pizza and furniture deliverers, and Kingsler personnel. In three situations, employee passwords — in plain view on notes taped to their computers — were used to access Kingsler's A/P, HRIS, and CRM applications.	
9:55– 10:15	Download an e-mail from Sid T., Kingsler's Chief Risk Officer, including the attached letter from Belsinger Risk Management, the company's insurance broker. The letter details the results of the network pen testing of Glarina Publications, a planned acquisition. Sid wants to know whether the deficiencies that permitted numerous network *(cont...)*	

Time	Activity	Rating
(cont...) 9:55– 10:15	intrusions can be eliminated before the deal is consummated. If not, Kingsler will have to pay $80,000 in premiums above the increase just for adding Glarina to its policy. Sid also wants to know the cost of fixing these problems, as it must be factored into the purchase price. Forward Sid's e-mail to Arlene C., CIO, along with a note asking for a low-to-high dollar range for eliminating these problems — can enough NOC and IT security staff be assigned to guarantee remediation within two weeks, or will we need outside help?	
10:15– 11:00	Review the proposal from Holliman Seminars for licensing its interactive cybersecurity training program to Kingsler. E-mail the proposal with a cover memo to Sid (copy Liam F., Director of Training). Note that the program seems comprehensive enough to meet our needs; suggest he make participation mandatory for all employees and new hires. E-mail Kate L., Associate General Counsel, asking her to draft a clause requiring third-party personnel to complete this program as a condition of accessing Kingsler's network. (Memo to Self: Tell the Holliman account executive that we expect the unlimited seat license we're buying to include our vendor and consultant personnel.)	
11:00– 11:40	Download the e-mail from Mary S., IT Audit Manager, listing discrepancies her staff found in the back-up and archiving procedures of Kingsler's two data centers. According to her description, both centers' procedures are noncompliant with the Electronic Media Task Force's retention policy issued last year to the data center managers. I should inform Sid about this during our meeting this afternoon — the problem is bigger than Mary thinks.	
11:40– 12:20	Draft two policies for presentation at tomorrow's Network Security Task Force meeting: (1) Define the criteria for designating a system as critical, so that inner firewalls would be installed to protect it. (2) Identify all servers that should be prohibited from making outbound connections, and establish a process for managing and modifying the inventory of those restricted servers.	

Time	Activity	Rating
1:00–2:20	Meet with Sid to go over the outline for the Technology Risk module of his presentation to the board's Technology Committee next week. Prepare him for questions from the board about Neshultz's Social Engineering Vulnerability Assessment. Make sure he's armed with information to defend the cost of the Neshultz license and other expenditures for high-priority risk-mitigating programs. Show him Mary's e-mail about the back-up and archiving deficiencies at the data centers, and discuss a "get-well" plan to bring them both into compliance and ensure that they remain so in the future.	
2:20–3:10	Prepare the tech risk management section of a greatly expanded checklist and questionnaire to use with all potential acquisitions. Can we get accurate and complete answers to all of these questions? This is a major concern, based on problems with three of our last five acquisitions, especially given that verifying them could add more time than Corporate Development could tolerate if we are to meet its "yesterday" deadlines for deal closings. (Memo to Self: Ask Legal about getting the CEOs of potential acquisitions to certify their questionnaire responses à la SOX Section 302, with financial penalties imposed for any predefined discrepancies discovered during integration. Can part of the deal money be set aside in an escrow account pending completion of the integration?)	
3:10–3:30	Review Procurement's proposed upgraded RFP boilerplate model for use with all software vendors. Draft preliminary questions for inclusion in the new Technology Risk Assessment section: Can the vendor provide a customer satisfaction survey conducted by a third party? What were the voluntary and involuntary turnover rates of its IT personnel during the past five years? Has the vendor ever undergone a third-party audit of its software; if so, by whom and at whose initiation? Provide all documentation and correspondence between the vendor and all third-party auditing entities for the past five years. (Memo to Self: Ask Legal if we can do a routine check of any breach of contract or software malpractice lawsuits against any companies bidding on our contracts.)	

Time	Activity	Rating
3:30–4:00	Meet with Karen M., Kingsler's CFO, and Phyllis L. of Belsinger Risk Management, Kingsler's insurance broker, to finalize the RFP to be submitted to Kingsler's cyberliability and business interruption insurance carriers, and to four of their competitors. Phyllis is optimistic that if the current insurers will not significantly reduce renewal policy premiums, at least two of the other companies will beat their prices because they are known to be low-balling policy premiums in aggressive campaigns to win market share.	
4:00–5:05	Meet with Dave E., DRP Coordinator, to review each department head's list of applications that support their operations, along with projected losses (including both immediate financial costs and longer-term costs caused by customer defections) associated with recovery periods ranging from one to seven days.	
5:05–5:45	Review a report detailing the findings of a vulnerability assessment of four parts vendors under consideration for kanban agreements for six medical instrument models. E-mail Kristen F., Vendor Compliance Specialist, informing her that all four vendors fail to comply with the SLA in our contract, so none can be approved.	

JOB-HUNTING STRATEGIES

The demand for technology risk management professionals is increasing geometrically, and if you have a CISA, CISM, or CISSP certification and at least five years' related experience, your candidacy should elicit serious consideration for a management opening. And whether you seek a management or subordinate role, to the extent that you proactively search for opportunities — rather than just respond to ads — you will generate the most favorable results. To make the most productive use of your time, choose from the job-hunting strategies described in this section, based on the environment you prefer.

For a Position with an End User

If your preference is to work with an end user, you'll want to focus on these categories of employers:

- **Public Companies.** One factor makes these companies prime targets for employment: the Sarbanes-Oxley Act. Although public corporations have always had to comply with SEC regulations, SOX imposed much more stringent requirements for internal controls and financial reporting. And technology is the bedrock of the integrity of these processes, meaning public companies have an even greater incentive than previously to mitigate their technology exposures.
- **Midsize and Large Businesses in Regulated Industries.** Regulated businesses (e.g., financial services companies, utilities, chemical manufacturers, pharmaceutical companies, and medical-device manufacturers) are generally more attentive to technology risks than unregulated companies because their ability to meet compliance reporting, controls, and records retention requirements is strongly dependent on the quality of their computer infrastructures. And, needless to say, any company in a regulated industry that is also a public corporation would have the most compelling reasons to focus on technology risk management.
- **Technology Sector Companies.** Businesses that market computer-based products and services will have broader technology risks than those of any organization dependent on a computer infrastructure for its ongoing operation, regardless of the industry. Moreover, notwithstanding the limitations to liability that are ubiquitous in contracts and license agreements, the impact of product or service deficiencies on a company's reputation — which, inevitably, will be publicized on the Internet — can fuel mass customer defections, in addition to impairing the ability to win new customers. Considering the potential consequences of these contingencies, the management of technology companies should be highly motivated to focus on ensuring the quality of their commercial offerings — damage control always exacts a higher cost than preemptive measures.
- **Higher-Education Institutions.** These entities must comply with a broad array of regulations, including Gramm-Leach-Bliley, HIPAA, the USA PATRIOT Act, and FERPA. In this category, make large universities your prime targets because the complexity and scope of their operations create myriad technology exposures on a level similar to those faced by large businesses.
- **Large Urban Medical Centers.** All of the compliance regulations that apply to colleges and universities are equally relevant to this segment.
- **Federal Government Agencies.** The Federal Information Security

Management Act (FISMA), passed in 2002, established rigorous technology risk standards to protect federal agencies from both deliberate and accidental disruptions to their operations. Yet years after its enactment, many of these entities are still not in compliance. But pressure from Congress and the Office of Management and the Budget, coupled with some well-publicized computer security breaches at federal agencies, should accelerate the process.

After conducting an online search for employers headquartered in your preferred region, your next step will depend on whether you seek a technology risk manager position (for which you'll need a preeminent portfolio of qualifications) or a supporting role.

If you seek a technology risk manager position at a public corporation, try to identify the director on its board who chairs its technology committee. You may find this information in the Investor Relations section of the corporate website, possibly in the annual report. Alternatively, an online search using the company name, "board," "director," and the exact phrase "technology committee" may be effective. If neither step yields results, present your qualifications to any person designated as an independent director on the company's board.

In the event that a public company lacks a board-level technology committee, present your qualifications to the highest-ranking executive overseeing its risk management, compliance, security, or information security function. If you have a choice of two or more executives, opt for someone at the vice-presidential level, rather than a director.

Don't overlook private companies as prospective employers. Although not bound by the same compliance obligations that public entities face, the largest privately owned companies are likely to have a board-level technology committee — after all, they are no less vulnerable to technology risks. But their websites won't include an Investor Relations section, so if an online search using the keywords just specified is not productive, contact the chief risk officer or chief information security officer. Or, if the company operates in a regulated industry, it may have a corporate governance or compliance department, in which case the executive overseeing either area could be a good person to contact.

I want to emphasize that these steps are appropriate whether or not the company already has a technology risk manager in place. Why? Because if that person is recruited by another employer — highly probable, given today's risk-sensitive business climate — by following my suggestions, you will maximize the likelihood that your credentials will be reviewed *before* management feels the need to place an ad. And if your credentials are impressive enough, they may obviate the need for an ad — the most desirable outcome. Another possible scenario: The employer may be displeased with the current technology risk manager's performance, which could mean you may not have to wait long for an invitation for an interview.

If you seek a position reporting to a technology risk manager, make your initial target the chief information officer. But be prepared to learn that the function falls under the jurisdiction of risk management, compliance, corporate governance, or security because some companies are taking the stance that — as a form of internal auditing — technology risk management will be more objectively managed *outside* the department charged with responsibility for its technology. Due to the fledgling status of the field, organizations are undergoing a trial-and-error process as they strive to situate it within the optimal department. More clarity on this question should be forthcoming in the next few years, but even then there will probably be differences in the function's organizational "address" across industries and among the three sectors of the economy, reflecting the nature of the technology exposures unique to each.

For a Position with a Consulting Firm

An online search will unearth numerous companies providing technology risk management services, including all of the large multipractice global firms and small specialty consultancies. Contact the head of the technology risk practice of a large firm; and when approaching a dedicated technology risk firm, start with the CEO. Regardless of whether you find the name of the executive you seek on the corporate website, conduct an online search for that person, as comments attributed to him or her may guide you in preparing a compelling presentation of your qualifications.

For a Position with an Insurance Company or Brokerage

An online search for insurers that market cyberliability and computer industry professional liability products should reveal the names of the executives overseeing related product development, marketing, or loss-control functions. Any of these could be a suitable person to whom you should present your qualifications. If the search parameters you use to find insurance company executives do not also produce the names of the appropriate executives at large insurance brokerages, add "technology," "risk," and "solutions" to your keyword list.

No matter which technology risk management workplace appeals to you, highlight the same elements of your experience in your resume, cover letter, and interactions with executives. Keeping in mind the parallel I drew between technology risk management and technology due diligence, be sure to describe any experience in the latter endeavor, regardless of whether it relates to an acquisition, software/hardware vendor, or a technology service business.

Other types of door-opening experience you should convey to prospective employers include:

- Developing/upgrading software or hardware architectures and defining associated quality and risk management standards.
- Contributing to network architecture design and risk management initiatives.
- Participating in the development of enterprise risk management, compliance, or corporate governance applications.
- Designing system or application controls.
- Participating in data center design or renovation projects.
- Formulating security policies governing access by employees, vendors, and consultants to data centers, networks, operating systems, applications, and databases.
- Preparing RFPs for the purchase of IT security products and services, as well as evaluating vendors' bids.

Beyond these activities, which directly relate to technology risk initiatives, your background may include experience in a particular industry (such as banking) or function (such as field engineering), where you gained an understanding of their technology risks. If so, highlight that knowledge, as well as any related achievements, as they may strike a resonant chord with certain employers.

RECESSION RESISTANCE

Without question, the existence of a technology risk management function reflects management's appreciation of its importance. That's not to say, however, that in the face of an economic downturn the organization will maintain the same level of attention it initially allocated to it. Ongoing commitment will depend on whether management believes the initial effort was effective in identifying and remediating deficiencies. If so, it might have enough confidence to reduce the resources applied; for example, some companies might consolidate responsibility for technology risk management and IT security with an eye toward reducing the total number of personnel supporting both areas.

In general, public corporations are less likely to divert resources from their technology risk management functions because of today's heightened emphasis on corporate governance in a post-Sarbanes-Oxley environment. And any company, public or private, that operates in a regulated industry should be chary about dimming its focus on technology risk management because so much of its compliance strength is intertwined with its computer infrastructure. But a company need not be publicly held or regulated to be keenly aware of the potential financial cost associated with the loss, theft, or misuse of its or its customers' proprietary data. This alone should be sufficient motivation for maintaining a strong emphasis on technology risk management.

Even if you were to lose your tech risk management position because of the impact of a recession on your employer, you should have no difficulty finding a new position. Only a small fraction of organizations, business or otherwise, that should be addressing these exposures have done so. There is still a vast untapped universe of employers on the verge of taking action, or that will do so in the near future, and the ramping up of their technology risk management functions will demand substantial resources. Even among the large segment of "ostrich" organizations, more and more of those will have to pull their heads out of the sand to face the security breaches of computer systems, networks, laptops, and electronic media. These are now routine events at the largest companies in the world — which, presumably, have the most preeminent network and system security measures in place — so it stands to reason that smaller companies will finally get the message that they are even more vulnerable, thereby propelling them to action.

Another reason not to worry about the impact of a recession on your job security in technology risk management is that companies are increasingly buying cyberliability and business interruption insurance. An outcome of the underwriting process is that their insurers may require them to establish and maintain a predefined level of technology risk management resources consistent with their exposures. That means policyholders may not even have the option of adopting a more casual attitude toward it. And even if an insurer does not mandate such a requirement, a company that exerted a Herculean effort to qualify for coverage — only to later drain resources from it — could impair its ability to obtain renewal coverage. Or the company could risk having its premium increased to a level that — when compared with the cost avoided by diminishing the attention it pays to technology risk management — would at best be a "wash," causing it to rue the day it made such a penny-wise and pound-foolish decision.

Finally, remember that many businesses will remain unaffected by a recession, as will such nonbusiness organizations as educational institutions, healthcare institutions, and government agencies.

The clear message? More and more organizations will come to view cyberrisk and other technology-based insurance products as a fixed — rather than a discretionary — expense. Thus, increasingly, the impact of the economy on their financial performance will have an inconsequential impact on the decision to maintain a vigorous technology risk management function.

OFFSHORE OUTSOURCING SITUATION AND OUTLOOK
The fact that this career option is a risk-based activity will tend to motivate end users to exercise complete control over it, as discussed in Part 1. Naturally, an organization could establish a proprietary offshore technology risk management operation, but the depth and breadth of operational knowledge demanded of a technology risk manager argues against administering these responsibilities remotely, whether onshore or offshore. Consider just a few of the many kinds of changes in an organization's operations that should trigger an analysis of the resultant technology risk exposures:

- New software development initiative or a major software upgrade, conversion, or consolidation project
- Network upgrade, conversion, or integration
- Installation of vendor software
- Acquisition of a company, manufacturing plant, or technology-based product line
- Passage of a state or federal law mandating the implementation of new controls and reports within existing applications
- Construction or renovation of a data center

The diversity of this small sample of activities necessitating a technology risk assessment makes a strong case for assigning it to in-house personnel, as they are best positioned to have timely access to any change in the organization's "vital signs" that should precipitate a tech risk analysis. Add to this the need for regular communication with corporate governance, risk management, and auditing staffs, and you have the ingredients for a strong anti-offshoring argument.

Whether tech risk staff must be in the same physical space as those with whom they need to interact to perform competently is debatable. Many people might share my view that the most vital communications that occur within any organization are informal. They do not take place through e-mails, the distribution of reports, or meetings; rather, they occur as spontaneous interactions between people who accidentally run into each other at the elevator or in the company parking lot, or who learn about a project by sitting at a table in the cafeteria next to some coworkers from another department.

Still, it's inevitable that some companies, having completed their initial technology risk assessment and implemented remedial action to address exposures, will feel confident enough to offshore their ongoing management of the tech risk function as a cost-saving measure. Furthermore, a technology risk crisis at an organization that offshored its management would not necessarily mean that it could have been prevented if responsibility had remained onshore and under in-house control. But if a postmortem into the cause of the crisis pointed to a miscommunication between in-house and offshore personnel — especially if it stemmed from cultural differences — that should prompt management to revisit its decision.

As a matter of fact, it behooves any organization that establishes a technology risk management function — regardless of whether it is under full in-house control or outsourced to a vendor located anywhere — to test the integrity of the process. After all, it has long been a best practice for disaster recovery plans to be tested regularly through audits and rehearsals. Yes, disaster recovery planning is a reactive process, in contrast to technology risk management's preventive charter, but the latter function demands the same high level of attention to the integrity of the processes underpinning its structure.

To whatever extent the offshoring of technology risk management becomes prevalent in the end-user community, there is a much lower likelihood that insurers will offshore their technology-related loss control activities, or insurance brokers their technology risk solutions services. End users have intimate knowledge of their own technology exposures, which should give them a higher comfort level in delegating management of their technology risk function to a vendor, whether onshore or offshore. In contrast, each technology risk assessment undertaken by an insurance carrier or broker is conducted for the first time, unless performed in connection with a policy renewal. But even in the latter case, it must be managed with the same high degree of scrutiny that applied during the initial underwriting process because — in contrast to the full knowledge an end user has of changes in its proprietary operations — insurance carriers and brokers are not likely to be privy to the nature and scope of all operational changes made by each policyholder.

Both insurer and broker staff must orient themselves to the applicant's unique technology infrastructure, and understand the exposures unique to each policyholder's operations — which will vary widely among applicants. In conclusion, regardless of the degree to which end users gain the confidence to outsource their technology risk functions, I do not foresee insurers and brokers following suit for the long term.

INFORMATION SOURCES

Risk and Insurance (www.riskandinsurance.com). Reading this publication's articles on technology risk topics may help you assess your suitability for the field. It will also equip you with the knowledge to impress employers with the effort you have applied in preparing to enter the profession.

(ISC)² (www.isc2.org). The International Systems Security Certification Consortium offers a number of certifications that would be appropriate for aspiring technology risk management professionals to consider acquiring, including the Certified Information Systems Security Professional (CISSP) and related concentrations: Information Systems Security Architecture Professional (ISSAP); Information Systems Security Management Professional (ISSMP).

Information Systems Audit and Control Association (www.isaca.org). This organization offers educational and certification programs for the IT auditing profession, including the Certified Information Systems Auditor (CISA) and the Certified Information Security Manager (CISM).

Directory of Top Computer Executives. The print version of this publication, widely found in libraries, includes the names of IT executives at businesses with 500-plus employees, among whom are many who oversee their companies' technology risk management functions. The directory is published in East, West, and Canada editions, with each including a geographic index. Job-hunters can purchase the directory data in electronic form through a variety of list-rental and license options, which can be found at the website of the publisher, Applied Computer Research, www.acrhq.com.

ASIS International (www.asisonline.org). Many organizations have merged responsibility for physical and computer security under a chief security officer, and some entities have subsumed their technology risk management functions under that executive's role as well. Attending ASIS International's national or local chapter programs should help educate you on the enterprise security methodology increasingly being adopted by organizations, including where technology risk management fits into that model. You will also gain exposure to people who can provide leads to employment opportunities.

TECHNOLOGY RISK MANAGER
YOUR RATINGS AND NEXT STEPS

How compatible is this field with my skills?

Assign a score of 0–10 (10 is highest): _____

Skills/Knowledge I Need to Acquire Before Contacting Employers

1._____

2._____

3._____

4._____

Typical Workday Task Ratings

After conducting research to fill in any ratings you initially left blank, calculate the total for each type of reaction (like, dislike, neutral). A field may be a good choice if you have at least six Ls and three or fewer Ds.

Total **L**s:_____ Total **D**s:_____ Total **N**s:_____

Research Notes

_____

_____

_____

_____

_____

_____

_____

_____

Contact Log

Date:_____Name/Title:_____

Phone/E-mail:_____

Comments:_____

_____

_____

_____

Date:_____Name/Title:_____

Phone/E-mail:_____

Comments:_____

_____

_____

_____

Date:_____Name/Title:_____

Phone/E-mail:_____

Comments:_____

_____

_____

_____

Date:_____Name/Title:_____

Phone/E-mail:_____

Comments:_____

_____

_____

_____

CAREER OPTION:
TECHNOLOGY INSURANCE BROKER/AGENT

SECTOR OF THE ECONOMY
Private

INDUSTRY
Insurance

END-USER ORGANIZATIONAL DEPARTMENTS
Sales, Account Management, Business Development

OVERVIEW OF THE TECHNOLOGY INSURANCE BROKERAGE/ AGENCY FUNCTION
When organizations identify and prioritize the risks of their operations, they will take one of the following actions:

- Transfer part or all of selected risks to other parties, as with a shrink-wrap license for software, a click-wrap license on a website, and an indemnity clause in a contract.
- Purchase an insurance policy providing coverage for one or more identified risks, which is a form of risk transfer. In this case, the organization will still self-insure part of such risks in the form of the retention (deductible).
- Entirely self-insure one or more selected risks.

The decision to purchase an insurance policy is driven by an assessment of the probability that a potential risk will occur, coupled with the anticipated cost of dealing with it. To address risks associated with computer technology, insurers have developed a variety of products that fall into two categories:

- **Professional liability policies.** This segment includes errors and omissions (E&O) and directors' and officers' (D&O) coverage for companies that market computer products and services, such as software developers, systems integrators, consultants, website developers, ASPs, ISPs, and manufacturers.

- **Policies for companies in all industries.** Insurance products in this category address risks associated with *any* company's use of computer technology, with the most significant stemming from their operation of networks. Policies that address network exposures are referred to as "cyberliability" or "cyberrisk" products, and are designed to cover the theft of data belonging to the insureds and/or their customers, denial of service (DOS) attacks, viruses, and network extortion, and may also cover negligence by the policyholder. Some cyberliability policies include protection for Internet-related media risks, such as intellectual property infringement, libel, slander, and invasion of privacy. Traditional media companies faced these risks long before the advent of the Internet, but the damages potential of these problems constitutes a much greater threat today because of the ease and speed with which information can be transmitted through the medium. Moreover, because a website is considered an electronic publication, any organization — not just media companies — may need this kind of protection. Insurers have also created products addressing digital risks unrelated to the operation of a network, such as the accidental deletion or loss of electronic media, and deliberate damage by disgruntled employees.

These products are sold by brokers and agents, both of whom prospect for new clients and manage relationships with existing ones. Their performance is measured by the revenue they produce, which determines their compensation levels. Brokers draw upon their knowledge of the products and underwriting criteria of a variety of insurers to select the optimal one for each client; agents have formal agreements with insurers to represent their products. Each professional can operate as a sole practitioner, establish a company that employs agents or brokers, or — as you would begin your career — become an employee of an agent or broker.

As an IT professional, a number of aspects of your experience give you an edge as a technology insurance broker. Listen to what Scott Schleicher has to say. He's the Senior Vice President for ISG International's CCBsure Insurance Program for IT Companies, which offers professional liability coverage.

> I believe that insurance sales executives would consider an IT professional's training and experience an advantage in establishing credibility

with clients, performing preunderwriting, and assisting underwriters in evaluating issues that may inform their decisions. However, since computer professionals gravitate toward analytical work, they might want to begin their insurance careers as underwriters. [A section on the Technology Insurance Underwriter follows, on page 175.] This would allow them to apply their technical knowledge, while learning the challenges brokers face in meeting production goals. If they later decided to switch to sales, it would take about six months to become contributing members — somewhat less than if they made the transition directly from IT. And, while it usually takes three to five years to become a high-performing producer, the income potential far exceeds an underwriter's.

All states require the licensing of insurance sales personnel employed by brokerages and agencies. Obtaining such "producer" licenses, as they are called, is a relatively simple process, but an advanced credential is desirable to reach the pinnacle of the profession. Brokers and agents who specialize in E&O, D&O, cyberliability, and other technology risk products aspire to the Registered Professional Liability Underwriter (RPLU) certification.

Demand for the two categories of products should be strong over the long term. As Schleicher points out, "E&O and D&O policies are widely considered necessities by computer companies, and sales of these products have grown exponentially in the past decade. However, the potential size of the market is much greater, as it is estimated that approximately 50 percent of such businesses lack coverage. Usually it is because company management believes their general liability policies will provide protection for professional liability risks — but in most instances, they won't. As these companies become more established, their owners usually learn about this gap, often at trade shows and conferences." Cyberliability and Internet media risks that can apply to companies in all industries are also widely presumed by management to be covered under their general liability policies — and here, too, they are often excluded. The insurance industry is actively educating clients about these gaps, but an incessant stream of media reports of identity theft on the Internet may be more effective.

Here are some factors to consider when choosing which of the two types of products you might be interested in selling:

- The sales process for cyberliability, Internet media, and other technology risk products is more likely to entail discussions with clients about network technologies, security measures, NOC processes, colocation capability, and other matters related to computer infrastructure.
- Professional liability brokers and agents would probably discuss software development quality assurance, version control, and beta test processes; they would also review applicants' contracts with clients, subcontractors, vendors, partners, licensors, and licensees to understand the exposures inherent in those agreements. The sales process associated with cyberliability coverage may entail reviewing third-party agreements with network security, colocation, and telecommunications vendors.
- Professional liability brokers and agents often sell policies addressing risks unrelated to technology to their computer company clients, including general liability, automobile, and workers' compensation.

With these points in mind, if you would rather have your workday revolve more around analyses and discussions of computer infrastructure and related technologies than business processes and contracts, I suggest that you focus on cyberliability and other technology-risk products marketed to any type of organization.

POSITION TITLES
Broker, agent, account executive, sales representative

JOB DESCRIPTION HIGHLIGHTS
All of these responsibilities may apply to sales positions involving either professional liability or cyberliability products.

- Negotiate agreements with trade and professional associations to promote discounted insurance products as a membership benefit.
- Deliver presentations on risk management topics at trade shows and professional association meetings.
- Conduct cold-calling campaigns targeting executives at prospective client organizations.
- Design and deliver on-site and virtual sales presentations.
- Review client agreements with third parties to identify exposures that should be addressed by contractual risk transfer, the purchase of insurance, or self-insurance.

- Identify gaps in coverage resulting from clients' current and planned business initiatives.
- Guide clients in calculating their potential losses from uninsured risks, including damages and legal fees to defend claims.
- Interact with underwriters during the application review process. For example, provide information to supplement clients' application responses; discuss the loss control measures they require clients to implement to qualify for coverage; negotiate premiums.
- Inform clients of underwriters' requirements for supplemental information and loss control measures, as well as approval/denial decisions and premiums.
- Interact with internal brokerage/agency personnel in establishing new and renewal policies, adding endorsements, and processing claims.
- Monitor trends in underwriting practices, policy exclusions, competitive products and pricing strategies, and insurers entering/exiting the marketplace.
- Read legal rulings bearing on insurance specialty to anticipate trends that may signal a tightening/loosening of underwriting criteria or premium increases/decreases.

TYPICAL WORKDAY

Read this typical workday of a professional liability sales representative at Volksten Tech Insurance, a fictitious brokerage, to see if you would find the work appealing. As you read, enter your reaction to each activity in the adjacent cell in the Rating column: an "L" (for like), "D" (for dislike), or "N" (for neutral, or no reaction). If you must conduct research before deciding, leave that cell blank for now.

Time	Activity	Rating
8:30– 9:20	Review the Beta Test Manual of Washburn Corrigan, a developer of software for the engineering and architectural professions, in connection with its E&O application. E-mail Sue W., CEO, a request for the names of customers who participated in its most recent beta test — need to verify that the documented process was followed in the last release.	

Time	Activity	Rating
9:20–9:45	Telephone call from Craig V., attorney. He wants clarification of several terms in the D&O policy that his client, a software developer, is considering purchasing.	
9:45–11:10	Prepare for next week's presentation aimed at educating healthcare computer consultants on HIPAA regulations that may have implications for their client engagements. Address both third-party access to patient data and patient online access to their records; include exposures in states where minors can receive healthcare services without parental permission.	
11:10–11:30	E-mail Risa W., an underwriter at Collins IT Risk Solutions. Can she help find coverage for Cochran Pinellus Industries, a medical diagnostic test equipment manufacturer? Several insurers have declined the client because of the high damages potential of a faulty test result.	
11:30–11:45	Telephone call from Harry P., CEO of Gemano Solutions, a systems integrator. He's concerned about whether his current policy will cover a Canadian company he is considering purchasing. On the plus side, the Canadian company's sales are a low enough percentage of Gemano's to be covered under his policy. But the policy does not cover claims filed in foreign courts — will see if the insurer is willing to add an endorsement to expand the coverage, and get back to him.	
11:45–1:15	Cold-call the CEOs of two systems integrators and three consulting firms. Leave messages for three executives who were unavailable. Send an e-mail to a fourth who said he has E&O coverage — we can do better. Offer him a policy that covers claims by customers stemming from employee malfeasance — which his current policy lacks — and which will entail only a modest incremental cost. Enclose details of damages awards in such cases. The fifth executive says she neither has nor wants E&O or D&O coverage — and refused to give her e-mail address. Send her a letter itemizing judgments in cases against four similar companies that lacked such coverage. These eye-popping dollar amounts should change her mind — if she reads the letter.	

Time	Activity	Rating
2:00–2:15	E-mail Hank C., President of Burch Singular Solutions: A review of his business and website suggests that Castlewood offers the optimal policy, but it will not respond to an intellectual property infringement claim. Important that he consult his attorney regarding his intellectual property risks — including the exposure related to the Burch website's framing the websites of several companies whose products are used in the company's systems integration projects.	
2:15–3:00	E-mail Laura P., Underwriter at Colonial Plains Worldwide. Answer her questions about Highmount Tover's relationships with companies listed on its website's "Partners" page in conjunction with its E&O application.	
3:00–3:20	Call Dave W., CEO of Panorama Inter-Host, an ISP. Need to discuss several deficiencies in its procedures for complying with the Digital Millennium Copyright Act requirements for responding to proper notification of copyright infringement on a customer's website. These must be corrected before applying for a policy offering intellectual property infringement protection.	
3:20–4:10	Update an E&O competitive matrix comparing the policies of eight insurers for the computer industry SME marketplace to reflect recent announcements of new products, features, and exclusions by several of those insurers.	
4:10–5:00	Read the resumes of the officers and directors of Armington Chase Systems in conjunction with its D&O application. E-mail a list of questions to Carole M., Armington's COO — need more details about certain positions on four resumes, and the reasons for employment gaps of one to two years on three resumes.	
5:00–5:40	Conference call with Marion A. and Shep L. to discuss the services they plan to offer through the consulting firm they are in the process of establishing. Will think about an appropriate E&O coverage level and get back to them next week. In the meantime, alert them to legal fees and costs incurred by similar companies in recent software breach-of-contract and malpractice cases.	

JOB-HUNTING STRATEGIES

Regardless of which insurance product segment interests you, your resume and cover letter should describe any contributions you have made to business development proposals and presentations. To convey the impression that you are comfortable performing nontechnical responsibilities, detail any experience you have in preparing, reviewing, or negotiating contracts with clients, vendors, subcontractors, licensees, licensors, or partners. If the cyberliability segment appeals to you, describe your network security product knowledge and experience, including any participation in audits and the remediation of deficiencies identified through those processes. And highlight any background in ISO 17799 initiatives, regardless of which category you target.

Conduct an online search for insurance policy forms and applications for the product segment you target; the description of coverages and exclusions, as well as the questions asked of applicants, can guide you in presenting your qualifications to prospective employers. Also read media articles and white papers bearing on these risks. If you wish to enter the professional liability field, search for legal rulings in cases involving software breach-of-contract and malpractice claims. If you are drawn to the cyberrisk segment, research rulings involving network security breaches. When researching case law, always include "damages" and "plaintiff," along with other keywords specific to the product category.

It will be easy to find brokers and agencies that promote computer industry professional liability and cyberrisk insurance products, which will range from very small companies to large multinationals. In the case of large companies that have branch offices throughout the United States, ascertain whether one is in your area and, if so, contact the manager or regional sales executive. But do not limit your search to local companies because, as Schleicher pointed out, the larger brokerages and agencies sometimes employ personnel on a remote basis.

RECESSION RESISTANCE

Commercial insurance products are highly resistant to sales declines, regardless of when they occur — the fact that the purchase decision had already been made reflects management's belief that it is a necessity. That said, professional liability coverage is somewhat more likely to be viewed in this manner because computer professionals are keenly aware of the potential for software defects, missed deadlines, software incompatibility, and inadequate functionality — and their financial consequences. Aside from a company's internally driven decision to purchase E&O and D&O insurance, two external factors will motivate many companies to purchase — and maintain — professional liability coverage regardless of the economic climate and its impact on their business: First, companies are increasingly requiring their computer vendors to carry such insurance; second, venture capitalists and other investors routinely require the companies they fund to obtain D&O and E&O coverages.

As for the cyberliability and other technology risks that any type of company can face, once management is aware of its coverage gap, they should consider it a cost of conducting business. Just as it would be unthinkable for a brick-and-mortar retailer to drop its general liability policy and expose itself to damages resulting from a shopper's injury on its physical premises, so, too, should online retailers appreciate the damages potential from shoppers being injured on their cyber "premises" — albeit in different ways. But here, too, external forces may motivate companies to purchase and maintain cyberrisk coverage even if they are disinclined to do so because of weak sales results.

Appreciating these forces calls for a brief explanation of the distinction between first-party and third-party coverage. First-party coverage protects an insured's assets only. For a policy to respond to a claim resulting from the theft of customer data from the insured's extranet, it would have to provide third-party coverage — and might have to specifically affirm such coverage. How does this relate to the impact of a recession on the demand for cyberrisk coverage? Just as it is now routine for the customers of computer services companies to require those vendors to have professional liability coverage, expect to see more and more organizations requiring their vendors in all industries that provide extranet capability to carry third-party cyberrisk coverage as a condition of conducting business with them. Moreover, although individual consumers lack the clout of business customers, companies that operate e-commerce operations have a strong incentive to avoid seeing their names in media reports of network security breaches and the theft of confidential customer information. Beyond the harm to their brands and loss of customers, they may incur substantial financial losses from those events — and, in some cases, face regulatory action. These factors, coupled with the reality that the most exhaustive security initiatives are no guarantee against a breach, should motivate consumer-oriented companies to increasingly view third-party cyberrisk insurance as a nondiscretionary expense, making it highly resistant to the impact of a recession.

Finally, when a company's sales decline, regardless of the state of the overall economy, management becomes more aggressive in cutting costs, prompting them — almost universally — to put a "magnifying glass" to their insurance programs. Companies that automatically renewed their policies each year during boom times will, in down periods, typically try to negotiate more favorable premiums with their current insurers, while concurrently seeking bids from those companies' competitors. In either case, they will turn to their brokers and agents for assistance. In sum, brokers and agents may spend more time in a recession responding to the cost-cutting needs of their clients than selling new policies, but their services will be needed no less.

OFFSHORE OUTSOURCING SITUATION AND OUTLOOK

Brokers and agents in all industries have been affected by the Internet because of its capability to quickly and cost-effectively connect buyers directly with sellers. Initially, the impact was seen in low-technology transactions; but, now, more complex products and services — including the professional liability insurance offered through the CCBsure Program with which Schleicher is affiliated — are increasingly sold through the Internet. In only 15 minutes, a company can be approved for a CCBsure policy — but only if its application responses meet an insurer's predefined underwriting criteria. Other applicants must undergo a more in-depth, offline process with a salesperson. Says Schleicher, "Insurers have generally been resistant to online underwriting because they pride themselves on their ability to 'know' the risk, and they prefer to acquire that knowledge by having a broker or agent interact directly with the client."

As insurers become increasingly comfortable with online underwriting — which will probably happen to the extent that their projected claims liabilities are validated by experience — real-time underwriting will surely incorporate more sophisticated analyses. If insurers find that they can achieve favorable loss ratios with increasingly sophisticated online underwriting systems, should brokers and agents feel threatened? Probably not, for these reasons:

- In contrast to auto and homeowners insurance, the IT professional liability and cyberrisk underwriting processes — at least for midsize and large companies — require analyses of a multitude of variables, making them extremely difficult to automate above a certain level of complexity.

- Brokers and agents conduct periodic account reviews to learn about changes in their clients' product/service offerings, contractual arrangements, geographic span, and other aspects of their operations that may call for modifications in their insurance programs. But they may also initiate contact with clients at any time to inform them of risk management and other trends meriting their attention, as well as new products that can address their needs more cost-effectively.
- Insurers rely on brokers and agents to perform preunderwriting, which increases the productivity of their underwriters by limiting the applications they review to those with the greatest potential for approval.

Considered as a whole, these factors underscore the strong relationship management component of the broker and agent roles, which makes them highly resistant to offshoring.

Considering the matter from a regulatory perspective, U.S. residency is not universally required to obtain a state insurance producer (sales) license. Some states allow residents of another country to obtain a license valid for sales in their jurisdictions. For example, U.S. states that border Canada have reciprocal licensing arrangements with the adjacent provinces. And it is within the realm of possibility that a wider "door" would be opened by some states, such that residents of remote countries could qualify for producer licenses and, therefore, compete against those in the United States.

And a U.S. insurer could establish a proprietary offshore sales operation, whereby its employees would conduct telemarketing campaigns targeting U.S. customers. This approach might enable it to circumvent any state licensing restrictions against foreign brokers and agents. However, either of these approaches — using offshore brokers and agents, or hiring offshore employees — would be fraught with risk for the insurers; namely, that of undermining the quality of the underwriting process itself. As Schleicher explained, "Insurers rely on brokers and agents to present them with the most accurate and comprehensive information about the risks they underwrite, which demands a common understanding of vernacular by all persons participating in these discussions. Delegating the acquisition of this knowledge to people in any foreign country — even one where English is spoken — could impair this vital communication process."

INFORMATION SOURCES

Risk and Insurance (www.riskandinsurance.com). Reading this publication's articles on technology risk topics may help you determine your suitability for an insurance sales position. It will also equip you with the knowledge to impress employers with the effort you have applied in preparing to enter the profession.

Inside the Minds: The Insurance Business (Aspatore Books, 2004). The authors of this book include the chairs, CEOs, and presidents of insurance companies. They present their perspectives on how insurers manage risk, establish premiums, devise marketing strategies, and process claims. A newcomer to the industry should come away with a well-rounded orientation.

Professional Liability Underwriting Society (www.plusweb.org). This nonprofit organization awards the Registered Professional Liability Underwriter designation to brokers, agents, underwriters, and other insurance professionals. Its national and chapter programs and other events are open to anyone interested in the profession, and membership is available to people outside the industry.

National Association of Insurance Commissioners (www.naic.org). This website contains hyperlinks to the insurance commission websites in the 50 states. At the site of a state where you wish to obtain a license, look for "producer license" requirements.

TECHNOLOGY INSURANCE BROKER/AGENT
YOUR RATINGS AND NEXT STEPS

How compatible is this field with my skills?

Assign a score of 0–10 (10 is highest): _____

Skills/Knowledge I Need to Acquire Before Contacting Employers

1._____

2._____

3._____._____

4._____

Typical Workday Task Ratings

After conducting research to fill in any ratings you initially left blank, calculate the total for each type of reaction (like, dislike, neutral). A field may be a good choice if you have at least six Ls and three or fewer Ds.

Total **Ls**:_____ Total **Ds**:_____ Total **Ns**:_____

Research Notes

_____

_____

_____

_____

_____

_____

_____

_____

_____

Contact Log

Date:_____Name/Title:_____

Phone/E-mail:_____

Comments:_____

_____

_____

_____

Date:_____Name/Title:_____

Phone/E-mail:_____

Comments:_____

_____

_____

_____

Date:_____Name/Title:_____

Phone/E-mail:_____

Comments:_____

_____

_____

_____

Date:_____Name/Title:_____

Phone/E-mail:_____

Comments:_____

_____

_____

_____

CAREER OPTION:
TECHNOLOGY INSURANCE UNDERWRITER

SECTOR OF THE ECONOMY
Private

INDUSTRY
Insurance

END-USER ORGANIZATIONAL DEPARTMENT
Underwriting

OVERVIEW OF THE TECHNOLOGY INSURANCE UNDERWRITING FUNCTION

The role of an insurance underwriter presents an interesting dichotomy: On the one hand, these professionals are expected to play a key role in meeting their employers' goals for writing new and renewal policies; at the same time, they must avoid writing policies with the potential to adversely affect the companies' loss ratios. Thus, in one sense the underwriter is a business development specialist; in another, a risk manager. Inherent in the complexity of the underwriting process for the insurance products described in the Technology Insurance Broker/Agent section (page 161) — which is important for you to read before continuing — is a career opportunity for you, a computer professional.

My optimism about IT professionals making a transition to technology underwriting is shared by Scott Schleicher, Senior Vice President for ISG International's CCBsure Insurance Program for IT Companies. He began his career as an underwriter of professional liability coverage and is well positioned to know. As he explained, "I believe insurers that market E&O and D&O products to the computer industry, as well as policies covering technology risks, would be receptive to computer professionals as candidates for underwriter trainee positions. It would probably require one to two years of on-the-job training to become a seasoned underwriter, and this experience would be a very valuable foundation if one later wanted to switch to the sales side of the business."

Technology underwriters are employed by insurers, which market to brokers and agents, and by reinsurers, which market to insurers. They can also be found at large commercial brokerages that advise retail clients (end users) and wholesale clients (other brokers and agents) on selecting the optimal coverage, as well as represent them in discussions and negotiations with underwriters at insurance carriers. Sales representatives at these companies cultivate relationships with clients, coordinating the participation of underwriters in business development initiatives as the product experts. Underwriters routinely use models to quantify risks, but may override a model's rating to reflect information not factored into its algorithm. They will often specify loss control measures — essential actions — applicants must implement, along with other measures that, while not essential, are recommended. If the underwriter approves the applicant, he or she will determine the premium to reflect the risk.

Depending on an underwriter's product specialty, obtaining either the Registered Professional Liability Underwriter (RPLU) or Chartered Property and Casualty Underwriter (CPCU) credential would be an important professional objective. Regardless of whether you become an underwriter of professional liability coverage for computer companies or technology risk insurance products for all types of organizations, the RPLU would be the appropriate designation to seek.

POSITION TITLES
Underwriter, technology underwriter, technology account executive

JOB DESCRIPTION HIGHLIGHTS
Included among the following responsibilities are two that apply only to underwriters employed at reinsurers and brokerages, which I have noted with an "R" and "B," respectively.

- Confer with internal sales personnel to understand clients' needs, and provide product information to guide their selection of the most suitable type and amount of coverage.
- Confer with underwriters at insurance companies to assess whether and how much of their clients' risks can be reinsured, and at what price. (R)
- Confer with underwriters at insurance carriers to determine the suitability of their products for end-user clients, and to negotiate endorsements and premiums. (B)
- Review applicants' operational processes to understand their exposures to the risks covered by a policy.

- Review applicants' contracts with vendors, consultants, partners, licensees, and licensors to assess the degree to which they have transferred risk through indemnification and limitations on liability.
- Obtain information from brokers and agents to supplement their clients' responses to questions on policy applications.
- Convey underwriting decisions, loss control requirements, and premiums to brokers and agents.
- Review reports of third-party audits of applicants' operations — for example, ISO; privacy laws; network security.
- Interact with loss control specialists on their evaluations of applicants' operations and exposures as they relate to risks addressed by a policy.
- Design and conduct training programs in new products and underwriting criteria for agents and brokers.
- Monitor loss ratios to identify patterns in the nature, frequency, and industry sources of claims, formulating premium adjustments to reflect those data.
- Review media reports and case law relating to insurance specialty.

TYPICAL WORKDAY

See if the responsibilities in this typical workday of an underwriter of cyberliability and Internet media coverage at Northern Asset Sentry, a fictitious insurer, appeal to you. To assess your interest in and suitability for the field, as you read, enter your reactions to each activity in the adjacent cell in the Rating column: an "L" (for like), "D" (for dislike), or "N" (for neutral, or no reaction). If you must conduct research before deciding, leave that cell blank for now.

Time	Activity	Rating
8:30–9:10	Read a report on the findings of a network security audit of Hammond Forrester's e-business function, performed by a consultant selected by Northern Asset Sentry in connection with Hammond's application for cyberliability coverage. E-mail the report to Rich O., the broker, for presentation to the client. Need to have documentation detailing the status of his client's actions to remediate nine deficiencies cited in the report. After reviewing that documentation, a new audit may be required to verify the effectiveness of those initiatives.	

Time	Activity	Rating
9:10–9:40	Review the contracts Balmanich Gardening Galaxy, an applicant for cyberliability insurance, has with two vendors: its colocation services provider and MSSP.	
9:40–10:50	Download and read the contents of the website of Warrington Stylemasters, a furniture retailer that has applied for cyberliability and Internet media coverage. E-mail Robert P., Warrington's broker, the next steps: (1) the client must undergo a network security audit by one of two companies, at its own expense; (2) assuming the audit findings do not curtail the underwriting process, Warrington must discontinue framing the web pages of several manufacturers whose products it sells unless it can provide documentation of their permission, including whether it has been granted in perpetuity or with time limitations.	
10:50–11:05	Notify Rosalind L., an agent, that we will be sending a nonrenewal notice to her client, Richtermas Gourmet, on their cyberliability policy. The reasons: A loss-control review identified 16 discrepancies between the client's documented NOC change, problem, and request management policies and the actual handling of those matters. In addition, an employee of the consultant we hired gained entry into the client's data center by claiming that he worked for a local utility and needed to investigate an equipment trouble report.	
11:05–12:00	Begin the underwriting process regarding Internet media policy application of the publisher of *Merriman Geopolitical Quarterly*. Review its Editorial Fact-Checking Procedural Manual to assess its libel, slander, and defamation exposures, and its Freelance Writer's Agreement to evaluate its intellectual property infringement exposures.	
12:00–12:55	Download and read material sent by a subscription research service: recent court rulings in network security litigation, as well as a damages trend analysis in 30 such cases, categorized according to B2B and consumer litigation.	
1:30–2:10	Review the syllabus of Jamesworth Seckler's Employee Computer Security Awareness Program in conjunction with its cyberliability application. Seems comprehensive but need to ask Steve H., the broker: Does the client audit employees' compliance with the program and, if so, *(cont...)*	

Time	Activity	Rating
(cont...) 1:30– 2:10	by a third party or internal staff? (I'm not a fan of self-policing audits). Request all audit reports for the past three years.	
2:10– 2:20	Return telephone call from Marge Z., a broker. She's asking for a lower renewal premium for a client who has never filed a claim. Apparently she's uneasy about a new CFO who's initiating a competitive bidding process on all insurance programs. A lower premium may be feasible but will need updated information on the client's e-business operation first. Will e-mail her some questions by tomorrow. Afterward, visit the insured's website to see if its business has changed in any material way since the initial underwriting on the policy.	
2:20– 2:55	Prepare a list of security procedures that Freundmann Data Management, a credit card transaction processor, must implement to qualify for E&O coverage: videotaping of all workstations; a prohibition against removable media and writing instruments, criminal background checks for all employees; physical screening of personnel upon entering and exiting the facility. E-mail the list to Karin D., the broker — tell her it's important that her client understand the policy will not respond to any claim related to work performed by any subcontractor Freundmann may use, such as a service bureau.	
2:55– 3:45	Review the loss control report pertaining to a college's application for cyberliability coverage — a major red flag: no encryption of students' credit card account data, transcripts, or health clinic records, despite the client's stating on its application that it complies with FERPA, HIPAA, and Gramm-Leach-Bliley. The college has only a written policy instructing personnel who handle this information to "maintain the highest degree of confidentiality with respect to this information." E-mail the broker the decision: declined.	
3:45– 5:00	Read a report prepared by Detweiler Imhoff Group, an advertising conglomerate and current insured, on the technology due diligence it just completed of Ryerson Nagler, a British ad agency that it wants to buy.	

Time	Activity	Rating
5:00– 6:10	Prepare a presentation for next week's webinar for insurance brokers on the features and underwriting criteria for a new cyberliability policy targeting companies with annual sales of $10 million or less.	

JOB-HUNTING STRATEGIES

An important first step in your campaign will be a search for insurance policy forms and applications for the products you want to underwrite, which will be useful guides in developing your resume and letter, as well as preparing for interviews. Regardless of which category interests you, in your interaction with employers, highlight any participation in ISO 17799 certification activities, audits, technology due diligence, the development or enhancement of project planning or project management processes, business development presentations, and the design and delivery of training programs.

To find employers in either product category, conduct an online search for "underwriting," "insurance," "computer," and "technology," along with other relevant keywords. For example, for a cyberrisk underwriting position, add one or more of the following: cyberliability, cyberrisk, e-commerce; for professional liability, add these: professional, liability, E&O, D&O. When targeting an insurer, reinsurer, or brokerage, contact the highest-ranking underwriting executive responsible for your desired product category. If the company's website does not identify that person, an online search specifying the company name and product line may lead you to media articles, white papers, and panel discussions that contain it. And be sure to read these materials even if you find the executive's name on the corporate website, as their contents may prove useful in tailoring your presentation. If a search does not produce the name of the senior underwriting executive, try to identify the senior business development or sales executive overseeing the type of product that interests you.

RECESSION RESISTANCE

All of the recession resistance factors cited in the Technology Insurance Broker/Agent section apply equally to a technology underwriter's position since the need for a broker's services will almost always entail the involvement of an underwriter. However, be aware that those points relate to the recession's effect on the *demand* for the insurance products I described. An assessment of a recession's impact on an underwriter's job security should also consider the matter from the *supply* side of the business: the insurers themselves. According to Schleicher, "In a recession, insurers' investments in the stock market produce less favorable returns, motivating them to seek higher profits from their business operations. They typically tighten their underwriting criteria, which will improve their loss ratios and, therefore, their profitability — but I have not seen them react to a recession by eliminating underwriting positions." Schleicher's comment underscores the point I made in the Technology Insurance Broker/Agent section about clients' attempts to negotiate lower premiums on their current policies or seek bids from other companies. Just as these actions require the involvement of brokers and agents, so, too, will they entail the participation of underwriters, thereby bolstering the need for their services as well, during tenuous economic periods.

OFFSHORE OUTSOURCING SITUATION AND OUTLOOK

Insurers have been actively offshoring their business processes, such as policy billing and claims administration, for several years but, according to Schleicher, they have not done so with their underwriting functions. As he explained it, "Underwriting is effective to the extent that a risk is communicated accurately and completely to brokers and agents and, in turn, by those individuals to underwriters. The vernacular and nuances of the language used in the conversations among the parties — clients, brokers, and underwriters — will be instrumental in the quality of the communication process. And you can see evidence of the importance insurers place on the communication process in the fact that underwriting is most often performed at the regional level — not from a centralized headquarters location."

Of course, insurers might become receptive to expanding the scope of their offshoring to also encompass underwriting if they are satisfied with the results of their business process offshoring. If so, it will be interesting to see how far up the scale of complexity it will be feasible to offshore their underwriting functions, considering the critical importance played by the communication process in the assessment of their clients' risks.

But regardless of how broadly insurers embrace the practice of offshoring their underwriting activities, keep in mind that I have recommended technology underwriting because, as a computer professional, your understanding of industry best practices, processes, and jargon will provide you with an advantage that should be validated through favorable loss ratios associated with your decisions. And herein lies your greatest insurance policy for keeping an underwriting job over the long term. Indeed, given the complexity of the risks that must be understood when underwriting technology-related insurance products, any insurer, reinsurer, brokerage, or agency that wants to attain — or retain — a preeminent presence in the technology professional liability or cyberrisk segments should be aggressively recruiting computer science majors on campus.

INFORMATION SOURCES

Risk and Insurance (www.riskandinsurance.com). Reading this publication's articles on technology risk issues can help you determine your suitability for a career in insurance underwriting. It will also equip you with the knowledge to impress employers with the effort you have applied in preparing to enter the profession.

Inside the Minds: The Insurance Business (Aspatore Books, 2004). The authors of this book, who include the chairs, CEOs, and presidents of insurance companies, present their perspectives on how insurers manage risk, establish premiums, devise marketing strategies, and process claims. A newcomer to the industry should come away with a well-rounded orientation.

Professional Liability Underwriting Society (www.plusweb.org). This nonprofit organization awards the Registered Professional Liability Underwriter designation to brokers, agents, underwriters, and other insurance professionals. Its national and chapter programs are open to anyone interested in the profession, as is membership.

TECHNOLOGY INSURANCE UNDERWRITER
YOUR RATINGS AND NEXT STEPS

How compatible is this field with my skills?

Assign a score of 0–10 (10 is highest): _____

Skills/Knowledge I Need to Acquire Before Contacting Employers

1._____

2._____

3._____

4._____

Typical Workday Task Ratings

After conducting research to fill in any ratings you initially left blank, calculate the total for each type of reaction (like, dislike, neutral). A field may be a good choice if you have at least six Ls and three or fewer Ds.

Total **L**s:_____ Total **D**s:_____ Total **N**s:_____

Research Notes

_____

_____

_____

_____

_____

_____

_____

_____

Contact Log

Date:_____Name/Title:_____

Phone/E-mail:_____

Comments:_____

_____

_____

_____

Date:_____Name/Title:_____

Phone/E-mail:_____

Comments:_____

_____

_____

_____

Date:_____Name/Title:_____

Phone/E-mail:_____

Comments:_____

_____

_____

_____

Date:_____Name/Title:_____

Phone/E-mail:_____

Comments:_____

_____

_____

_____

CAREER OPTION:
TECHNOLOGY INDUSTRY RESEARCH ANALYST

SECTOR OF THE ECONOMY
Private

INDUSTRY
Research

END-USER ORGANIZATIONAL DEPARTMENT
End users that require computer industry research almost universally need it on a project — rather than a continuous — basis. Thus, it is more cost-effective for them to purchase it from companies that specialize in designing and conducting research studies.

OVERVIEW OF THE TECHNOLOGY INDUSTRY RESEARCH FUNCTION
Questions raised in the following scenarios typify those routinely posed by buyers and vendors of information technology products and services, lenders, venture capitalists, and other investors:

- A venture capitalist wants to know whether the three-year projections are realistic for IT support staffing levels stated in the business plan of a startup that intends to market project management and financial reporting software to the construction, engineering, and architectural segments.
- A manufacturer of a pocket PC wants to know which of four companies' operating wireless networks would be its optimal strategic partner based on their current technology, investment in R&D, company management, and brand image.
- A developer of a two-factor authentication product wants to devise a license structure to maximize its ability to capture at least 10 percent of the password security segment in two years, while achieving its investors' goals.
- An ASP wants to assess the potential for an online data warehousing application geared toward companies with annual sales under $50 million.

Whether the goal is to choose the optimal software or evaluate the potential market for a new product, the lightning speed of technological advances generates a continuous flow of new information that must be analyzed and interpreted to inform these decisions. An entire industry has sprung up in response to these needs, with companies offering a broad array of research products and services for sale. Depending on a research firm's business model, it might conduct and sell studies on: competing products in a market segment, trends in customer buying motivations, new technologies, the impact of legislation on the future performance of an industry, or other topics. Many firms sell customized proprietary studies tailored to individual client needs; some companies sell only off-the-shelf research; and some market both types of research products.

Depending on the goals of a research project, it may require access to data in the public domain or available only through subscription services. It may also require interviews or surveys of industry executives and other personnel. Although writing and presentation skills are key requirements of many technology research positions, the ability to answer the questions — indeed, to even *frame* the questions — at the heart of a research study demands an understanding of technology. And conducting an effective interview of a technology executive calls for much more than asking and recording responses to questions. It requires the ability to immediately pose follow-up questions, which presupposes a substantial mental data warehouse of computer terminology and concepts. Inherent in these requirements is an opportunity for computer professionals to position themselves as qualified candidates for research analyst roles.

Beyond a genuine interest by a potential buyer or investor to obtain information to support business decisions, there is another strong driver of the demand for research. Specifically, technology companies proactively cultivate relationships with industry research analysts to obtain favorable exposure for their offerings. Because the buyers of technologically complex products and services typically conduct extensive research about products and services to inform their purchase decisions, a favorable review by an analyst can be instrumental in supporting a vendor's marketing goals. As a matter of fact, many technology companies have established in-house Analyst Relations groups dedicated to this endeavor.

POSITION TITLES

Research associate, research analyst

JOB DESCRIPTION HIGHLIGHTS

As a research analyst in the computer industry, you will be expected to:

- Stay abreast of new trends and products, executive changes, acquisitions, and other developments in assigned segments by reading on a regular basis general business, trade, and, possibly, consumer print and online publications.
- Design the format and conduct studies of trends and issues in established and emerging markets.
- Meet with clients to discuss their needs for evaluating technologies, products, and companies under consideration for purchase, investment, merger, joint venture, or supplier relationships.
- Negotiate and conduct interviews of executives and professionals to learn their intentions to purchase particular products and services, as well as their assessments of the management, strategies, and competitors of industry participants.
- Write reports detailing research findings and recommendations.
- Design and deliver presentations to win new business and communicate the findings of studies to clients.
- Provide analyses and opinions of industry trends and developments during media interviews.
- Attend trade shows and conferences; deliver presentations at industry events.

TYPICAL WORKDAY

Assume that your typical workday as a research associate at Hartsglen Group, a fictitious research firm, is as detailed here. To assess your interest in and suitability for the field, as you read, enter your reaction to each activity in the adjacent cell in the Rating column: an "L" (for like), "D" (for dislike), or "N" (for neutral, or no reaction). If you must conduct research before deciding, leave that cell blank for now.

Time	Activity	Rating
8:30– 9:15	Meet with Mark W., Hartsglen's Director of Research. He wants to discuss the methodology for a planned study aimed at projecting public sector security software expenditures for the next three years, categorized by infrastructure, application, hardware, and physical security.	

Time	Activity	Rating
9:15–10:30	Develop the outline for a presentation to Argus HumanIT on the findings of a study it commissioned to evaluate the market potential for two- and three-factor authentication products in four healthcare industry segments. Prepare a matrix displaying the strengths, weaknesses, and prices of three such offerings that use biometrics technology. Design a spreadsheet categorizing the survey responses of 50 hospital risk managers to determine: satisfaction with current security methods, purchase intentions for new products, and the prices they would pay for security products offering advanced protection for physical and digital assets.	
10:30–11:40	In prep for contract bid for a market research study, write an RFP to send to three survey companies. Client wants to know the opinions of 100 CIOs of its planned new virtual data center product versus products currently on the market. Results will drive positioning, advertising, and pricing strategies.	
11:40–12:10	Search for online articles discussing CIOs' opinions of the pros and cons of using SOA in software development processes. E-mail Art C., Hartsglen's Contracts and Licenses Administrator: Can he get permission from the authors of two of the articles to include excerpts in our monthly client newsletter?	
1:00–1:35	Read e-mail from Jeanne R., Director of Marketing at e-BarEntry. She's agreed to an interview about its recently launched firewall. They're touting it as featuring stronger antihacking mechanisms than any product on the market. Prepare 12 questions for Ms. R., and e-mail them to her.	
1:35–2:00	Develop a list of proposed topics for studies on cutting-edge technologies for presentation at tomorrow's Product Development meeting, when research resources for the next three months will be allocated.	
2:00–2:35	Prepare two tables for inclusion in a report on the wireless security industry: In the first, list top 10 companies in declining order of annual sales; in the second, display those companies in declining order of ratings of functionality and quality by 85 CIOs interviewed by Hartsglen.	

Time	Activity	Rating
2:35–3:40	Review the RFP from Wishner Lyons, a venture capital firm seeking bids for a study of the smart container market to answer this question: Should it back a firm whose technology allows it to track the location of containers, use biometrics to permit access only to approved personnel, monitor changes in the weight of contents inconsistent with the manifest, and detect nuclear and radioactive materials? Outline the proposed research methodology and e-mail it to Rob A., Hartsglen's Marketing Coordinator.	
3:40–4:00	Write a report on the results of a study correlating 240 midsize companies' computer security expenditures as a percentage of their sales with their use of enterprise risk management, document control, and colocation services.	
4:00–5:15	Conference call with Rob (Hartsglen's Marketing Coordinator), and Kara S., Corporate Development Analyst for Seltzer Manchester. She wants a custom study of the proprietary technologies, products, revenues, and executive competencies of five digital rights management companies. Ultra confidential project — they're planning on acquiring one of the companies.	
5:15–5:45	Perform a trend analysis of managed security services companies' fee structures for the past two years. Price wars have left casualties on the competitive battlefield — four companies have packed it in.	
5:45–6:00	Visit the AvailaMax Solutions website. This marketer of application provisioning software is listing eight software engineer and two architect positions on its "Careers" page. For a company this small, this has to mean a major product development initiative is on the drawing board.	

JOB-HUNTING STRATEGIES

There are three ways you can provide services as a research analyst:

- As an employee of a research firm
- As a subcontractor to one or more research firms, whereby you would be engaged on a project basis
- As an independent consultant, whereby you would directly market your services to end users

If you would like to build a consulting practice, your contacts at technology companies may be able to introduce you to their marketing and corporate development colleagues, who are the primary buyers of research. Or you could contact those executives directly. And you could concurrently function as both a subcontractor and an independent consultant, as long as your client agreements would not disallow it and — importantly — there would be no ethical conflicts.

Understandably, you might be inclined to approach only those companies offering research in areas where you have expertise, but broaden your scope: Other firms might consider your experience advantageous in expanding or establishing client relationships. And, since research is not location-dependent, companies in any region should be on your list of potential employers. Use your resume, cover letter, and other communications with employers to highlight your functional, industry, and product knowledge and experience, referring to page 15 for guidance. Comparative analyses of alternative vendors and products are common research endeavors, whether in conjunction with custom projects to support client acquisition or product purchase decisions, or for off-the-shelf market studies. Thus, describe your experience evaluating software, hardware, and services, as well as participating in acquisition due diligence. And, because writing skill is an important requirement of research positions, don't forget to describe any contributions you made to proposals, presentation materials, case studies, sales brochures, and website content.

Most research firms are small enough that the CEO should be accessible. If a firm promotes expertise in multiple disciplines, its website may list the director of the industry or product segment that interests you, who would be a suitable person to contact. If you are unable to find the right contact person, a search using the company name may produce it in other venues, as these companies actively seek media coverage of their research products. Even if you can identify the optimal people to contact through visits to employers' websites, I recommend you still conduct a search that uses each name, as doing so may lead you to comments attributed to them, which may help you prepare for your initial contact.

RECESSION RESISTANCE

In an economic boom, a company whose stock price can finance an aggressive acquisition program might commission a study of the market of potential acquisition candidates. Conversely, if a recession caused its sales and stock price to decline, this same company might instead want a study to determine the price elasticity of its products, to understand whether, and to what extent, it could raise prices without losing sales or market share. However, since many businesses and assets have more attractive price tags during a recession, companies that have the cash or debt-financing ability to make acquisitions will often escalate their acquisition activity during a recession.

Moreover, even if a company is negatively affected by the economy, it would be a mistake to curtail all R&D initiatives since a recession is a predictable economic phase. If anything, a distressed cash flow situation would make it that much more critical to conduct research to ensure that the company allocates its limited R&D funds to projects with the greatest commercial promise. In sum, while the impetus for a research study may well shift in response to the economy, the demand should not diminish.

OFFSHORE OUTSOURCING SITUATION AND OUTLOOK

Depending on the nature of a research effort, the feasibility of offshoring it will range considerably. For example, consider the first question posed at the beginning of this career option section:

> A venture capitalist wants to know whether the three-year projections are realistic for IT support staffing levels stated in the business plan of a startup that intends to market project management and financial reporting software to the construction, engineering, and architectural segments.

Most, if not all, of the information needed to answer this question can be obtained through an online search using these keywords: customer, satisfaction, level, information, technology, helpdesk, staff, number. To supplement the search findings, one could contact a computer industry trade association to learn whether it had any survey data detailing the optimal ratio of technical support staff to the size of a user community. This type of research is highly susceptible to offshoring because the data acquisition and analyses can be performed by someone in any location. And the venture capitalist might well conclude that conducting the same search recommended here, augmented by information available from the trade association, would obviate the need to commission a research study.

Now consider the fourth scenario described at the start of this section:

An ASP wants to assess the potential for an online data warehousing application geared toward companies with annual sales under $50 million.

Of course, the ASP could hire someone located anywhere to research the number of businesses in the targeted size segment, but that information alone would not be sufficient to estimate the potential market. At the very least, answers to these additional questions would be needed:

- Would a sufficient number of businesses in the targeted segment view such an application as useful, since most small businesses do not use data warehousing — and may not even know what it is?
- What would be the optimal media for placing advertising to reach potential decision makers?
- How much would the ASP have to spend on advertising and promotion to achieve its customer acquisition goals?
- How should the application be priced to allow the ASP to establish a sufficient foothold in the market to fend off competitors, while achieving the investors' sales and margin objectives?

Current search engines are not capable of answering these questions. At the very least, a two-part study would be needed. Phase one could be a focus group of six to eight potential U.S. customers; phase two could be the administration of a questionnaire by a person — not a computer — to at least 50 potential customers. Furthermore, for the questions to produce the desired information, they would have to be open-ended, not yes or no or multiple-choice. In theory, both phases could be conducted on a remote basis, but in practice, the ability to communicate effectively with managers and executives, coupled with an understanding of U.S. business culture, management approaches, and technology would be vital elements in obtaining the highest-quality data.

NOTE: Most websites of prospective employers will provide sufficient information about their research methodologies to help you gauge the offshorability of their analyst positions.

Also, any company that markets custom research services would likely require communications between research staff and client personnel to: define the study objectives, negotiate agreement on the research methodology, and advise the client on how to interpret the study's findings to guide its decision making regarding the initiative that prompted the study. The point is, the strong relationship management component of this type of research makes it an unlikely candidate for offshoring — although the firm could certainly use offshore employees or vendors to perform data acquisition and analytical tasks.

Another argument against the offshoring of these types of positions may be evident from the display of analysts' biographies on a company's website, which would suggest that management regards both their technical expertise and past employment as key selling points.

INFORMATION SOURCES

Harvard Business Online (www.harvardbusinessonline.org). This website of Harvard Business School Publishing offers articles, case studies, and books on actual computer industry marketing, sales, corporate development, and turnaround programs, including both successes and failures. Reading these will provide insights into the drivers of industry research.

Consultants and Consulting Organizations Directory. This print directory, widely available in public libraries, lists consulting firms ranging from one-person businesses to the largest global firms. Use the subject index to find firms marketing IT-related services, the descriptions of which should help you identify those you should approach for a research position or a research subcontractor relationship.

TECHNOLOGY INDUSTRY RESEARCH ANALYST
YOUR RATINGS AND NEXT STEPS

How compatible is this field with my skills?

Assign a score of 0–10 (10 is highest): _____

Skills/Knowledge I Need to Acquire Before Contacting Employers

1._____

2._____

3._____

4._____

Typical Workday Task Ratings

After conducting research to fill in any ratings you initially left blank, calculate the total for each type of reaction (like, dislike, neutral). A field may be a good choice if you have at least six Ls and three or fewer Ds.

Total **L**s:_____ Total **D**s:_____ Total **N**s:_____

Research Notes

_____

_____

_____

_____

_____

_____

_____

_____

_____

Contact Log

Date:_____Name/Title:_____

Phone/E-mail:_____

Comments:_____

_____

_____

_____

Date:_____Name/Title:_____

Phone/E-mail:_____

Comments:_____

_____

_____

_____

Date:_____Name/Title:_____

Phone/E-mail:_____

Comments:_____

_____

_____

_____

Date:_____Name/Title:_____

Phone/E-mail:_____

Comments:_____

_____

_____

_____

CAREER OPTION:
TECHNOLOGY SECTOR EQUITY ANALYST

SECTORS OF THE ECONOMY
Private, public, nonprofit

PRIVATE SECTOR INDUSTRIES
Investment industry companies: Broker-dealers, investment advisors, independent research firms, private equity firms, hedge funds, mutual funds
Institutional investors: Businesses in all industries that invest their own and/or their employees' funds

END-USER ORGANIZATIONAL DEPARTMENTS
Investment industry firms: Research
Institutional investors: Pension Fund Management; Investment Office; Investment Management

OVERVIEW OF THE EQUITY ANALYSIS FUNCTION
Equity analysts try to predict the future performance of the stock of public companies to support trading decisions by investors. They can be found in a variety of workplaces:

- Those at broker-dealers are known as "sell-side" analysts because their research is sold or given to clients.
- Analysts at institutional investors are described as "buy-side" because their research guides their employers' investment decisions. Buy-side analysts are also employed at hedge funds, mutual funds, investment advisory firms, and bank trust departments, all of which routinely augment their proprietary research with sell-side research.
- Equity analysts are employed at independent research firms, which serve institutional and retail investors and, more recently, broker-dealers.

Equity research is typically described as *technical* or *fundamental* in nature. Technical research involves tracking financial market and industry sector performance using models and charts that incorporate a variety of statistical analysis methods. These tools help to discern relationships between trends in overall financial market performance and an individual stock's price. Fundamental research focuses on a company's historical financial performance, the influence of economic factors on its business, the strengths/weaknesses of its products or services relative to those of competitors, the soundness of its business plan, and management's ability to execute its strategies.

Some firms that engage in equity research use both technical and fundamental methods; others use one approach exclusively. A review of the biographies of fundamental equity analysts on the websites of broker-dealers, investment banks, and research firms shows that, while many have followed the traditional career path — prior employment exclusively at broker-dealers, investment banks, and/or research firms — others entered the profession after holding positions unrelated to the investment function at companies in the industries they now cover. That this path is most common among technology sector analysts should not surprise you since succeeding as a fundamental analyst in the technology sector — as opposed to, say, the food and toy industries — demands an understanding of highly complex products and services. Equity analysts who lack a technical background, regardless of how intelligent they are, may not be able to assess the novelty and commercial potential of a technological innovation, nor to understand the competitive and customer challenges a company faces in developing a commercially successful product, all of which can have an impact on its future stock price. My evaluation of the importance of a technology industry background to the performance of a fundamental equity analyst is backed up by a 2005 survey reported in the *Wall Street Journal* that named the top analysts in numerous industry sectors. An excerpt from the section on the software industry:

> The year's top stock pickers drew on their own experience in making and selling software to find winners in specialized corners of the industry, including health care, security and small-capitalization stocks.
>
> The No. 1 analyst in the sector, Paul Coster at J.P. Morgan Chase & Co. in New York, spent 16 years helping run the firm's information-technology operations before switching to J.P. Morgan's research team in 2000. Because he has developed computer systems himself, he says, he can tell whether a company's product-development plans are realistic. And as a former buyer, the 44-year-old London native says he can better evaluate a company's sales plans. .... The No. 2 analyst, Nitsan Hargil of Friedman, Billings, Ramsey Group Inc. in New York, says

his 10 years' experience in quality assurance, artificial intelligence and network design helps him avoid industry hype. ... The No. 3 analyst, Sean Wieland, 34 ... uses the insight gained from seven years as a health-care technology salesman and programmer."[4]

As for the 2006 *Wall Street Journal* survey, Sean Wieland again placed in the top three. And I have no doubt that the biographies of many other highly regarded computer industry analysts will similarly show that they began their careers in traditional IT roles.

Among the top analysts in any industry, some perform technical analysis exclusively, while others engage solely in fundamental analysis. Interestingly, an earlier article in the *Wall Street Journal* from the same year reported that the Smith Barney brokerage business of Citigroup decided to replace its technical analysis stock approach with a fundamental research function, despite the fact that the managing director of its technical analysis research function was "considered among the best stock-market technicians for years." The article quotes Smith Barney's director of global equity research as saying, "[W]e believe focusing our research investments toward fundamental company coverage best positions Citigroup to succeed in an increasingly competitive environment."[5]

Although technical research is used to great success by some analysts, I believe the Citigroup decision reflects a view that is gaining broad currency in the investment community: namely, that fundamental research may be more effective at ascertaining the actual and potential performance of a company — no doubt stemming from the recent rash of corporate accounting scandals that demonstrated the risks of relying exclusively on the financial data reported by companies. Indeed, one trend that underscores the investment community's heightened attention to due diligence is its increasing use of forensic accounting as a fundamental analysis tool. (See page 223 for a discussion of the Forensic Accountant career option.)

When it comes to the experience you'll need to enter the equity research

---

4   "Industry by Industry: Leading Analysts Look Back — and Ahead," *The Wall Street Journal*, May 16, 2005, p. R1. Reprinted by permission of *The Wall Street Journal*, © 2005. Dow Jones & Company, Inc. All Rights Reserved Worldwide.

5   "Not in the Charts: Entire Technical Team Is Out at Smith Barney," *The Wall Street Journal*, February 18, 2005, p. C3.

profession, computer industry background should be sufficient. But if you aspire to a preeminent level in the profession, you'll want to add an MBA and a Chartered Financial Analyst (CFA) designation to your list of credentials — not just for "window dressing," but to enhance your ability to critically analyze data on a company and its competitors.

POSITION TITLES

Equity analyst, stock analyst, equity research analyst, equity research associate, financial analyst

> **NOTE:** "Financial analyst" also widely refers to a professional who analyzes and reports the financial performance of a product line, program, or business unit in any industry. This is an entirely different position from the one described here.

JOB DESCRIPTION HIGHLIGHTS

Listed here are typical responsibilities of fundamental equity analysts, the type of position most feasible for computer industry professionals.

- Read trade publications to maintain current knowledge of new products, pricing initiatives, executive changes, and other developments in assigned industry segment.
- Attend industry trade shows and conferences.
- Conduct studies of the current/potential market for emerging and established technologies; review studies performed by research firms and consultants.
- Study the securities filings, balance sheets, and income statements of covered companies, as well as SEC actions against any of them.
- Review forensic accountants' analyses of companies' reported financial data to identify accounting improprieties and other issues that may signal material misrepresentations.
- Interview executives of covered companies, as well as those employed by their customers, vendors, and competitors.
- Participate in conference calls in which CEOs, CFOs, investor relations directors, and other executives discuss their strategies, planned

programs, and the obstacles they must address for those initiatives to be successful.

- Design models to forecast company revenues, earnings, and other key performance measurements.
- Communicate analyses and recommendations through reports, presentations, and conference calls with brokers and clients (if a sell-side analyst) or internal management (if a buy-side analyst).
- Present analyses and opinions of industry trends, technological developments, and company performance in reports and media interviews.
- Negotiate and participate in speaking appearances at industry conferences and other events.

TYPICAL WORKDAY

See if this typical workday of a computer industry fundamental analyst at Romanoff Analytics, a fictitious independent research firm, appeals to you. As you read, note your reaction to each activity in the adjacent cell in the Rating column: an "L" (for like), "D" (for dislike), or "N" (for neutral, or no reaction). If you must conduct research before deciding, leave that cell blank for now.

Time	Activity	Rating
8:00–9:10	Participate in a webinar for stock analysts held by Ferguson Rich Group, a manufacturer of handheld PCs. Peter L., CEO, will explain why last quarter's earnings per share were 2 cents below company estimate. Focus on his quality improvement plan, aimed at stanching the recent significant loss of customers — I'm skeptical.	
9:10–10:15	Finish working on a sales forecasting model for companies marketing information technology products to the OEM automotive industry, which incorporates regression and Durbin-Watson statistical analyses. Test the model's predictive capability using historical data for 2003–2005 to forecast sales performance for the 2006–2007 period.	
10:15–11:10	Analyze recent financial performance of 15 technology companies and prepare buy, sell, and hold recommendations for distribution to clients. E-mail recommendations and supporting data to Karen B., Managing Director of Technology Research.	

Time	Activity	Rating
11:10–11:25	Call Steve C., Investor Relations Manager of Carron Smythe, Inc., to arrange to visit its robotics plant next week. Review financial data on Carron and its two largest competitors for the last quarter, as well as media coverage of all three businesses. Prepare questions to pose during interviews of the company's Marketing, Sales, Engineering, Manufacturing, and Finance vice presidents.	
11:25–11:40	Search for media reports of Mernus Technology's response to a lawsuit filed by BoundarEase alleging infringement of a patent it holds on a three-factor authentication process. Read an article wherein Mernus states it can prove BoundarEase's patent was based on prior art. Draft commentary on the topic for next month's client newsletter.	
11:40–12:30	Download and read earnings announcements, restatements, and delays, as well as other corporate actions pertaining to eight software companies, sent by a subscription service. Need to revisit my buy recommendations for two companies based on a few items here. E-mail Karen (Tech Research) to hold off on distributing the recommendations on these companies that I sent her this morning.	
1:15–2:40	Search online for media coverage of Version 4.3 of Retrie-Valet's document control software. Update a matrix comparing RetrieValet with three competitive products to reflect V4.3's features. RetrieValet appears to have closed the feature gap with OmniDrawer, its leading competitor, but it will have to revamp its license structure to gain market share.

Another potential problem: RetrieValet's 10-K report stated that 65 percent of its sales were generated from three customers, making it the least diversified of the four companies by a wide margin — too much downside risk. | |
| 2:40–3:05 | Telephone interview with Arbor Lane Group's Investor Relations Manager, Chris M., and Doug T., its Director of Marketing. They're claiming 5–10 percent greater website availability for their new network load-balancing product versus competitive products. Ask for name and contact at the independent testing vendor — I may believe it when I see documentation of the methodology used. | |

Time	Activity	Rating
3:05– 3:40	Search online for comments by executives at FortreSense regarding media reports of vulnerabilities in its firewall software. Download and read three media items on the subject.	
3:40– 4:30	Download text of legislative bills pertaining to Internet security and privacy that will be voted on by ten states in the next few months. If passed, could mean significant growth for some companies — which? Review data on several possible beneficiaries.	
4:30– 5:10	Prepare for tomorrow's conference call with institutional clients. Based on last week's announcements of mergers, acquisitions, executive appointments and departures, product introductions, and pricing changes, what questions should I expect?	
5:10– 6:00	Download and read the report e-mailed by a research firm detailing projected federal government expenditures on FISMA compliance initiatives for the next three years, as well as the ratio of security expenditures to total IT budgets at 12 government agencies. Visit a website listing companies awarded FISMA-related contracts in the past three months. Draft commentary for client newsletter on the impact those contracts will probably have on the profitability of four contract awardees. Can also bet on four other public companies getting subcontracts from them.	

JOB-HUNTING STRATEGIES

The investment industry has received much media attention in the past few years because of allegations by the SEC and state regulators that some broker-dealers' stock recommendations were influenced by their desire to win investment banking business from companies covered by their analysts. Ten brokerages agreed to a settlement requiring them to purchase research from independent research firms and make it available, along with their in-house research, to clients for a period of five years. However, the anticipated strong demand for that research has not materialized, for various reasons. Some firms closed, and others laid off personnel. But this should not discourage you; there will always be a market for high-quality research and, as the previously mentioned *Wall Street Journal* article on the top-performing analysts demonstrates, your technical background can be a strong asset in reaching the pinnacle of the profession.

Conduct an online search for other research firms, as well as investment banks, investment advisory firms, and broker-dealers until you have compiled a comprehensive list. Next, contact the CEO of a dedicated technology research firm or a small firm that covers several industry sectors; when approaching a large independent research company, look for the executive overseeing the technology sector. If you're interested in a position at a broker-dealer, investment advisory firm, or investment bank, the highest-ranking research executive would be the optimal person.

> **NOTE:** If a targeted executive is not named on a company's website, conduct a search for mention of them in the media, where they are frequently quoted. Use their comments to prepare points to emphasize when presenting your qualifications.

Recruitment ads placed by investment banks and private equity firms for technology stock analysts typically state a preference for candidates with IT industry experience of one to four years, such as management consultants with experience in software services or business development. But don't be put off by that, as your expertise may be deemed relevant enough to elicit some interviews. Also, the briefer the experience sought by the employer, the greater your chances of getting an interview, since the firm may be willing to train you. One final word about ads: Although you may be able to obtain an initial position by responding to these postings, I recommend you devote most of your job-search time to contacting companies that have not placed ads.

I always advise my clients to demonstrate knowledge of a targeted employer's products or services during interactions with executives. Keep in mind that the "product" marketed by a firm that employs equity analysts is its assessment of *other* companies, so your telephone script and cover letter should include your assessment of the relative strengths (for example, high-quality technical support) and weaknesses (for example, limited scalability) of two to three companies in the segment where you are promoting your expertise, and on the significance and wisdom of price increases/decreases, acquisitions/divestitures, and other company initiatives. Your ability to use this technique effectively — essentially, a "demo" of what the employer can expect from hiring you — will be instrumental in the success of your job-hunting campaign.

RECESSION RESISTANCE

Although a company's performance and stock price may suffer in a recession, it may still be an attractive purchase to investors who believe that once the recession has ended the company will be poised to capitalize on a probable increase in demand. Moreover, interest in the future performance of a stock is not limited to the investment community. For example, as part of the underwriting process for directors' and officers' coverage, an insurer would want to understand the volatility of the stock of the company. Similarly, banks analyze the stock of public companies seeking financing in conjunction with their underwriting decisions. Information needs such as these occur during all economic cycles, making the equity analysis function highly resistant to a recession.

OFFSHORE OUTSOURCING SITUATION AND OUTLOOK

Large broker-dealers and investment banks have been offshoring equity research at a brisk pace, with some firms establishing proprietary offshore groups. As has been the case across all industries, the trend began with junior-level work and has been inching up the complexity scale. According to the website of the CFA Institute, which awards the highly regarded Chartered Financial Analyst designation, over 70,000 people worldwide — including many in countries that attract significant U.S. outsourcing business — have been certified. Do not let these factors deter you from setting your sights on an equity analysis career. Remember, my rationale for recommending this option lies in the advantage conferred by your industry experience, which will enable you to sift through the information provided by a company and separate the wheat from the chaff, an advantage validated by the stellar performance of the analysts featured in the *Wall Street Journal* survey cited earlier.

The comments of a client of mine who achieved the number-one ranking in a highly regarded survey of equity analysts in a nontechnology sector may also be useful in assessing the potential for offshore competition. He viewed his visits to company headquarters and manufacturing plants — including on-site interviews of management and staff — as vital components of his research method. First-hand observations of company operations, coupled with the face-to-face contact he had with executives, yielded insights he believed would not have been feasible otherwise. Yes, the questions he posed could have been administered by people located anywhere in the world, but he contended that the body language and facial expressions of the executives were very powerful indicators of the veracity of their statements. And, as I pointed out in Part 1, a key factor contraindicating the judiciousness of offshoring is the importance of a shared understanding of the language and vernacular by the parties to a communication. All this said, of course, the security of your employment as an analyst will ultimately rest on a single factor: the accuracy of your forecasts.

INFORMATION SOURCES

Chartered Financial Analysts Institute (www.cfainstitute.org). This organization awards the CFA credential to qualified professionals, including financial analysts, portfolio managers, and other investment professionals. Both the CFA Institute and many of its 130-plus member organizations sponsor educational programs and networking events, and provide job-hunting resources.

Institutional Investor (www.dailyii.com). Computer professionals interested in a career in equity analysis can learn much about the field by reading *Institutional Investor*, a print magazine. Its counterpart, www.dailyii.com, features articles and special supplements on sell-side and buy-side research trends, and on the top-performing analysts in each segment.

Investorside Research Association (www.investorsideresearch.com). This nonprofit trade association's membership includes more than 75 independent investment research firms. Clicking on the name of a member company will display a description of its research approach, enabling aspiring fundamental analysts to quickly identify potential employers.

TECHNOLOGY SECTOR EQUITY ANALYST
YOUR RATINGS AND NEXT STEPS

How compatible is this field with my skills?

Assign a score of 0–10 (10 is highest): _____

Skills/Knowledge I Need to Acquire Before Contacting Employers

1. _____

2. _____

3. _____

4. _____

Typical Workday Task Ratings

After conducting research to fill in any ratings you initially left blank, calculate the total for each type of reaction (like, dislike, neutral). A field may be a good choice if you have at least six Ls and three or fewer Ds.

Total **L**s:_____ Total **D**s:_____ Total **N**s:_____

Research Notes

_____

_____

_____

_____

_____

_____

_____

_____

_____

_____

Contact Log

Date:_____Name/Title:_____

Phone/E-mail:_____

Comments:_____

_____

_____

_____

Date:_____Name/Title:_____

Phone/E-mail:_____

Comments:_____

_____

_____

_____

Date:_____Name/Title:_____

Phone/E-mail:_____

Comments:_____

_____

_____

_____

Date:_____Name/Title:_____

Phone/E-mail:_____

Comments:_____

_____

_____

_____

CAREER OPTION:
COMPUTER FORENSICS SPECIALIST

SECTORS OF THE ECONOMY
Private, public, nonprofit

PRIVATE SECTOR INDUSTRIES
All

END-USER ORGANIZATIONAL DEPARTMENTS
Private and Nonprofit Sectors: Legal, Risk Management, Security, Compliance, Information Technology
Public Sector (e.g., municipal law enforcement agency; federal regulatory agency, such as the Bureau of Alcohol, Tobacco, Firearms and Explosives): Investigations

OVERVIEW OF THE COMPUTER FORENSICS FUNCTION
If a magnifying glass and fingerprints were visual symbols of the detective's tools in the twentieth century, then a computer and a stream of zeroes and ones would be the symbols in the second millennium. And the detective in the second millennium has a new name: computer forensics expert. Whether the purpose of an investigation is to collect evidence of identity theft, embezzlement, child pornography, or drug trafficking, or to support a civil lawsuit, one thing is certain: Some evidence sought will be resident on a computer hard drive or other digital media. Even large corporations now routinely staff a computer forensics function, where experts in the field use the methodologies to investigate computer security breaches, as well as matters unrelated to computer security.

Five types of work environments support this burgeoning profession:

- Federal, state, county, and municipal law enforcement; and investigative and regulatory agencies
- Companies that provide the full range of security and investigative services
- Large consulting firms with computer forensics and litigation support practice areas
- Dedicated computer forensics consulting firms

- Large companies with predictable, regular needs for computer forensics services (Details on these needs to come later.)

A critical goal of a computer forensics investigation is to extract data and information residing in files or fragments that, despite the user hitting the Delete key, have not been overwritten. When examining a computer in connection with a criminal investigation, a forensics specialist will first duplicate the entire hard drive of the computer and then search that copy for specified names of people, products, or other data relevant to the investigation. Because of the legal implications of forensic investigations, key elements of the process are the preservation of evidence and the establishment of a chain of custody.

Based on these requirements, what are the qualifications to become a computer forensics specialist? According to Thor Lundberg, a computer forensics expert, "Computer forensics investigators must have a thorough understanding of the data storage methods used by computers, down to the sector and bit levels. Because most software developers today write programs using languages that are compiled — rather than in machine language form — they may not have this knowledge, but they can acquire it by becoming certified in a computer forensics software package, which can search an entire hard drive relatively quickly."

NOTE: Lundberg is quick to point out another, less obvious aspect of computer forensics, which makes this a demanding profession. In a previous role as the director of Computer Crime Investigations for a law enforcement task force based in Massachusetts, Lundberg participated in a number of computer searches and seizures — including serving as the lead person during the execution of some search warrants. Remembering those days, he said, "These investigations can be very draining emotionally because the evidence you are seeking may be photographs of murder victims or children being sexually exploited. On the other hand, it is very rewarding to know you are assisting in bringing the perpetrators of these and other crimes to justice."

As noted, you need certification in computer forensics software. Currently, the most widely used such software in the world is EnCase, a product of Guidance Software. Obtaining certification in EnCase requires satisfactory completion of an appropriate EnCase course, as well as written and hands-on tests, a process that can be completed in several weeks. Beyond gaining proficiency in forensics software, Lundberg recommends that aspiring computer forensics specialists obtain complementary certifications, such as the Microsoft Certified Systems Engineer (MCSE) credential, as well as a mastery of intrusion detection software — the latter because forensic investigations often involve analyses of network traffic.

John Patzakis, the co-founder of Guidance Software, and its vice chairman and chief legal officer, is well aware of the numbers spurring the need for qualified candidates to fill positions in this rapidly growing field: "Over 90 percent of information today is in digital form, meaning that any investigation is virtually guaranteed to require computer forensics, which is why the industry is growing at an annual rate of at least 30 percent. Any government agency engaged in investigations, as well as all midsize to large municipal law enforcement agencies, have either hired computer forensics personnel or trained detectives in the methodology. Growth in the business sector has been equally dramatic, stemming from corporate use of computer forensics in both reactive and proactive ways."

Reactive Computer Forensics

One type of reactive computer forensics investigation — incident response — is triggered by intrusions or other threats to a computer infrastructure, such as customer-facing systems. However, a wide range of incidents that are not directly related to computer security, such as theft of trade secrets, falsification of payroll records, embezzlement, kickbacks, and inventory shrinkage (often due to employee theft), can also be impetuses for forensic investigations. It is even quite common for a party to a divorce proceeding to seek a court order to examine the family's computer for evidence to prove fault or identify hidden assets for the purpose of bolstering custody and financial demands. Another reactive application of computer forensics is *eDiscovery*, the process of identifying digital records required by subpoenas or requests for production in conjunction with civil litigation or regulatory investigations.

Proactive Computer Forensics

The proactive use of computer forensics in the business environment is aimed at ensuring compliance with laws, most notably the Sarbanes-Oxley

Act, passed in 2002. SOX, as it is widely known, primarily applies to public corporations, and imposes severe penalties on both companies and executives for noncompliance. It requires rigorous records management and retention processes to ensure the preservation of documents and facilitate the timely detection and reporting of fraud. Companies are increasingly using forensics software to analyze the contents of servers and PCs for weaknesses in accounting and nonaccounting controls. For example, they may monitor sales transactions and verify employees' adherence to company policies and controls.

Computer Forensics Knowledge Base

Not surprisingly, many colleges and universities have implemented curricula to prepare students for careers in computer forensics. Criminal justice undergraduate and graduate programs have added computer forensics courses, including instruction in Guidance Software's EnCase. Some institutions are offering associate's and bachelor's degree programs in computer forensics and digital investigations.

If you, an IT professional, acquire the knowledge base Lundberg recommends, you would bring a very valuable portfolio of skills to a computer forensics role. For example, if you have a corporate background, you might suggest to an attorney representing a plaintiff in a commercial litigation case that he or she discover whether the defendant had a disaster recovery plan, had undergone an ISO certification process, or used a software asset management process. Examining the documentation associated with these activities might be quite helpful in verifying the truthfulness of interrogatory responses relating to the defendant's software, hardware, back-up, and archiving procedures. In contrast, a computer forensics expert without a corporate background might lack the knowledge to provide this level of guidance to an attorney.

POSITION TITLES

Computer forensics specialist, computer forensics expert, computer forensics engineer, computer forensics investigator, digital forensics investigator, expert witness

JOB DESCRIPTION HIGHLIGHTS

Of the following responsibilities common to the computer forensics field, some are performed only in the public (government) sector, some exclusively in the private (business) or nonprofit sectors, and some in all three environments.

- Prepare proposals aimed at winning computer forensics consulting engagements.
- Prepare a project plan outlining the methodology that will be used to achieve the objectives of the investigation.
- Assist law enforcement personnel and attorneys in preparing search warrants and subpoenas seeking digital evidence.
- Assist attorneys in preparing interrogatories and requests for production aimed at understanding the opposing side's computer hardware, software, back-up, and archiving processes, as well as obtaining all responsive digital records.
- Review digital documents provided by the opposing side in a civil lawsuit in response to interrogatories and requests for production, as well as those responsive to subpoenas issued to third parties.
- Review digital evidence obtained by criminal prosecutors for attorneys who represent defendants.
- Participate in the physical impoundment of computers alleged to contain evidence vital to a criminal case; or, if a civil case, in conjunction with a court-issued *ex parte* order. (An *ex parte* order allows a party to a lawsuit to seize evidence, in the company of U.S. marshals, from the other party prior to filing the complaint, if a judge can be convinced there is a reasonable likelihood of evidence spoliation upon notice of the complaint.)
- Utilize computer forensics software to collect and analyze a company's sales transactions, e-mail communications, and other documents; and to analyze the contents of PCs and servers, with the goal of detecting fraud or other types of wrongdoing.
- Work with corporate auditors and security personnel to plan and conduct investigations into alleged criminal acts by employees, vendors, customers, and computer hackers.
- Assist attorneys in your employer's legal department in fulfilling eDiscovery obligations associated with civil litigation and regulatory requirements.
- Search permanent and removable media for evidence supporting criminal prosecutions and civil lawsuits.
- Serve as an expert witness in criminal and civil cases, which may involve

preparing reports, participating in depositions, and providing testimony in court proceedings, as well as reviewing the reports, deposition transcripts, and testimony of the opposing side, or the prosecution, if a criminal matter.

TYPICAL WORKDAY

The following responsibilities are tasks representative of a day in the life of a fictitious self-employed computer forensics consultant. As you read, enter your reaction to each activity in the adjacent cell in the Rating column: an "L" (for like),"D" (for dislike), or "N" (for neutral, or no reaction). If you must conduct research before deciding, leave that cell blank for now.

Time	Activity	Rating
8:30–9:00	Draft a motion for the preservation of digital evidence for Lou R., attorney for Sandra W., in her lawsuit against Floraliteas. She's alleging copyright infringement of eight botanical illustrations she had licensed in the print medium only, but which Floraliteas displayed on its website.	
9:00–9:30	Telephone conference with Hal E., forensic accountant, who has been engaged by Sagermann Lenz Novelties to investigate a suspected embezzlement by an employee. Discuss the investigative plan, including the need to inspect the hard drives of three computers during evening or weekend hours, as well as the chain of custody.	
9:30–9:45	Comment on draft of search warrant prepared by Harry F., Assistant District Attorney. He plans to present it to a judge tonight in a case alleging drug-trafficking and money-laundering, for execution over the weekend. Strengthen the scope of the search warrant by adding "data-enabled cell phones, digital audio players, and USB keychain drives" to the items specified for seizure. E-mail the revision to Harry.	
9:45–10:10	Telephone call from Dianne A., Associate General Counsel of RapiQuest International, regarding complaints from several employees that two coworkers have been using company computers to visit pornographic websites, in clear violation of a written policy on Internet usage. Advise *(cont...)*	

Time	Activity	Rating
(cont...) 9:45– 10:10	Diane to set up a conference call with RapiQuest's CIO to discuss the steps needed to preserve evidence of the two employees' use of the network and establish a chain of custody that can withstand legal challenges.	
10:10– 11:00	Download and read rulings in three cases involving discovery abuse claims, including two related to evidence spoliation and one entailing noncompliance with Federal Rule 26(a).	
11:00– 11:20	Telephone call from Doug A., Attorney for Hopmand Digital Group, which just sued Carlutteri Industries for violating a license allowing no more than 12 PCs to contain copies of Hopmand Digital's CAD software. Advise Doug to discover whether the defendant uses a software asset management system that scans each PC for installed applications, and a DRP that includes system redundancy at a vendor's location. If so, a subpoena should be issued to the vendor for any of Carlutteri's software and data in its possession.	
11:20– 11:40	Telephone call from Madeleine A., attorney, regarding her suspicion that the company her client is suing for breach of contract has not turned over all documents she sought through discovery. Ascertain that Ms. A. did not include any interrogatories aimed at determining how many servers the defendant operates, or all server IP addresses; nor did she attempt to discover the defendant's back-up and archiving processes. After verifying that she will have the opportunity to present a second set of interrogatories and requests for production, ask her to e-mail all technology-related items included in her first set, as well as information the defendant provided in response.	
11:40– 12:25	Review the damages report prepared by the computer forensics expert engaged by Dr. Arthur L. Dr. L. sued Rosekind Health Advisors for copyright infringement for displaying two chapters from his book, *Disease Management Strategies and the Measurement of Their Effectiveness,* on the subscription website it operates for physicians on staff at HMOs. *(cont...)*	

Time	Activity	Rating
(cont...) 11:40– 12:25	Send an e-mail to Cass D., Rosekind's attorney, confirming the accuracy of the expert's calculation of total page view counts for the four-month period. Rosekind admits the material was improperly displayed.	
1:05– 2:30	Read transcript of personal deposition given in regard to the forensic examination of the hard drive of a vice president of Coolidge Liberty Savings, who is accused of embezzling $5 million from private clients of the bank. Prepare an errata page of 12 items and e-mail it to Carla R., Coolidge's General Counsel.	
2:30– 3:20	Write a report documenting the results of a search of the hard drive of the computer used by the human resources manager of Merrimack Hillman, citing six queries she made of the HRIS system last year, seeking records on all employees over 50. E-mail the report to Randy B., attorney for Hannah R., a former employee, who is suing the company, claiming that its decision to fire her was based on age discrimination.	
3:20– 4:30	Review the auditing manual of Cyberpage Sentry, a company that certifies the accuracy of the page views claimed by Internet companies so that advertisers can accurately compare the costs/benefits of alternative sites for reaching potential customers. Note several areas where an audited company could potentially deceive Cyberpage's auditors with false website traffic figures. Prepare notes on actions to prevent and detect false data in preparation for tomorrow's conference call with three Cyberpage executives.	
4:30– 6:30	Conduct a forensic examination of the hard drive image of the computer used by a former engineer at Comstiel Environmental Engineering, now employed at Reedman Technology, Inc., in conjunction with Comstiel's lawsuit against the employee and Reedman for theft of trade secrets. Reedman introduced a portable soil analysis instrument that incorporates the identical advanced functionality as Comstiel's and was commercially available one month after Comstiel launched its product.	

JOB-HUNTING STRATEGIES

You'll want to take note of these employment trends John Patzakis has been tracking in the computer forensics field:

- The leading consulting firms have been actively recruiting computer forensics specialists, and are likely to continue doing so for the foreseeable future to meet their clients' growing needs for such services.
- Law firms, as well as end-user legal and IT departments, are adding computer forensics specialists to their permanent staffs.
- Large corporations are acquiring forensic expertise in two primary ways: (1) they are sending their security and auditing staff to obtain certification in EnCase software; (2) they are recruiting computer forensics specialists from law enforcement agencies who, in many instances, were formerly employed in traditional detective positions but who, after obtaining their certification, specialized in cybercrime.

Staff Employment Strategies

If you want to join a management consulting or investigative services firm, contact the CEO or president. But if the firm has a dedicated forensics or litigation support practice or division, you should contact the executive in charge of that organization.

If you would rather join a large end-user organization, use your investigative skills to find the Director of Electronic Discovery and Forensics, who should be in the Legal or IT department. If responsibility for those functions is divided between two executives, contact the person overseeing your preferred area. If he or she has no openings, ask for a referral to the executive in charge of the other area, since a second-choice position could pave the way to a more desirable opportunity in the future. And for public sector positions, check out the following agencies, which engage in investigative activities likely to involve computer forensics: FBI; Drug Enforcement Administration; Bureau of Alcohol, Tobacco, Firearms and Explosives; Department of Homeland Security; CIA; and Department of Defense (which has a very sophisticated Cybercrime Center). Regardless of whether these agencies list open positions on their websites, present your qualifications to the executives overseeing their investigative departments, either at the headquarters or a regional office. For other public sector positions, contact municipal police departments, as well as states attorneys' and district attorneys' offices. Even if no position is currently open, you may find work on a project basis if the agency either lacks in-house computer forensics capabilities or needs to augment its internal resources. As Lundberg noted, "While you may initially work in the computer lab, it could be a stepping-stone to more complex field investigative activities, such as participating in seizing a computer at the site of alleged criminal activity. It may also lead to a full-time position."

Self-Employment Strategies

The most fruitful path to self-employment will be to market your services to attorneys involved in civil litigation — especially commercial disputes and intellectual property matters, and criminal defense. You should not limit your search for consulting engagements only to attorneys in your locality since it is common practice for remote experts to be used in litigation. However, you might launch your practice by concentrating on local attorneys, who may view your accessibility as an advantage.

One more point: The success of a computer forensics initiative depends on the ability to identify and gain access to hardware and software likely to have been used in the act that triggered a lawsuit or criminal prosecution. And a prerequisite for achieving this critical goal is knowing what interrogatories and requests for production to present to an opposing litigant or, if a criminal matter, to specify in a search warrant. A computer professional with a working knowledge of the organizational practices and processes that involve the use of electronic media would have a significant advantage over individuals who lack that knowledge. Thus, regardless of whether you seek a job or wish to build a consulting practice, you should strive to distinguish yourself from others who, despite being proficient in computer forensics software, lack a traditional IT background. And the optimal way to accomplish this is to provide prospective employers or clients with details of any experience you have in disaster recovery planning, colocation service relationships, technology due diligence, document control software development, records management procedures, software asset management, IT controls and audit trails, and last — but certainly not least — back-up and archiving processes. An understanding of the workings of these functions and the extent to which they are used by organizations can be instrumental in unearthing hardware and media vital to a civil or criminal matter.

RECESSION RESISTANCE

Civil litigation (including divorce), the strongest driver of the demand for computer forensics, does not diminish in a recession; if anything, there is some evidence that it increases in a weak economy. With respect to a corporation or nonprofit organization, any cost-benefit analysis by their executives should lead to the conclusion that — regardless of declining sales or budget cutbacks — refraining from conducting reasonable risk management proactive and reactive forensic investigations can result in much greater financial liability than the expense of those initiatives. As for the public sector, criminal activity knows no season — if anything, it increases during hard times, creating a continuous need for computer forensics investigations by law enforcement professionals. While budget constraints have traditionally limited the resources available to law enforcement agencies, the events of 9/11 led to legislation that allocated significant funding to national and regional antiterrorism initiatives, some of which will entail computer forensics investigations, and this is likely to remain a high priority for the foreseeable future.

OFFSHORE OUTSOURCING SITUATION AND OUTLOOK

Thor Lundberg and John Patzakis share the opinion that computer forensics investigations related to both criminal prosecutions and civil litigation are not currently being outsourced overseas primarily because of the chain of custody requirement needed to refute any claim of contamination. In addition, Patzakis noted, "With respect to civil litigation, recent amendments to the Federal Rules of Civil Procedure impose requirements for an internal and systemized eDiscovery process, which cannot easily be outsourced overseas."

Since EnCase is an enterprise application, whenever a forensic investigation involves a computer network — as opposed to an examination of the contents of one or more offline computers — it can be used anywhere in the world where access to a network is provided. According to Patzakis, hundreds of people in other countries have been certified in EnCase, and the number of certification applicants is growing exponentially. The eDiscovery process is one area that is reaping the benefits of the enterprise capability of computer forensics software. Many corporate legal departments and law firms are outsourcing their eDiscovery to U.S. vendors, some of which use offshore personnel to produce responsive documents under the direction of onshore project managers. These companies also promote the ability to implement a chain of custody and provide expert testimony, which could involve the participation of personnel located anywhere. And some large law firms with a continuous, high-volume requirement for eDiscovery may establish proprietary offshore computer forensics operations as a means to maintaining greater control over the process.

A corporation's proactive use of computer forensics to ensure compliance with Sarbanes-Oxley or other legislation usually will not involve a deposition or testimony. However, depending on the findings, it could, thereby creating the need for a chain of custody in anticipation of that possibility. But establishing a nonrebuttable chain of custody should not be a problem. An employee or consultant with authorized access to a company's network from any location could collect and analyze data. In fact, a number of U.S. computer forensics consultants are promoting remote data collection services. One potential obstacle to dealing with a remote investigator, however — whether in the United States or abroad — could be the need for physical access to a computer.

Regardless of whether a forensics need stems from a reactive or proactive reason, it is inevitable that end-user organizations with a consistent, predictable requirement for this type of expertise will increasingly establish proprietary offshore operations. However, the need for computer forensics investigations to support civil litigation by smaller businesses and other organizations will only increase, offsetting any diminishment in the demand for U.S.-based practitioners that may result from offshoring initiatives by large companies.

INFORMATION SOURCES

High Tech Crime Consortium (www.hightechcrimecops.org). This organization was established to enable law enforcement agencies to draw upon experts in computer forensics and other investigative disciplines to leverage their internal, usually limited resources. It sponsors training programs and develops software tools useful to investigators in both the public and private sectors.

High Technology Crime Investigation Association (www.htcia.org). HTCIA offers training programs and conferences on the application of advanced technologies to support investigative and security activities. It also lists advertisements for technology-related investigative positions.

Forensic Expert Witness Association (www.forensic.org). With several chapters on the West Coast, FEWA provides resources useful to forensic experts in the computer industry, as well as many others. The organization also publishes a quarterly newsletter and operates a speaker's bureau.

Martindale-Hubbell (www.martindale.com). Computer forensics specialists can search for attorneys who specialize in those disciplines where their expertise is in particular demand, such as commercial and intellectual property litigation, family law, and criminal defense. Databases of attorneys, selected by legal discipline, geographic location, and other criteria, are available from the company for a fee.

COMPUTER FORENSICS SPECIALIST
YOUR RATINGS AND NEXT STEPS

How compatible is this field with my skills?

Assign a score of 0–10 (10 is highest): _____

Skills/Knowledge I Need to Acquire Before Contacting Employers

1._____

2._____

3._____

4._____

Typical Workday Task Ratings

After conducting research to fill in any ratings you initially left blank, calculate the total for each type of reaction (like, dislike, neutral). A field may be a good choice if you have at least six Ls and three or fewer Ds.

Total **L**s:_____ Total **D**s:_____ Total **N**s:_____

Research Notes

_____

_____

_____

_____

_____

_____

_____

_____

_____

Contact Log

Date:_____Name/Title:_____

Phone/E-mail:_____

Comments:_____

_____

_____

_____

_____

Date:_____Name/Title:_____

Phone/E-mail:_____

Comments:_____

_____

_____

_____

_____

Date:_____Name/Title:_____

Phone/E-mail:_____

Comments:_____

_____

_____

_____

_____

Date:_____Name/Title:_____

Phone/E-mail:_____

Comments:_____

_____

_____

_____

CAREER OPTION:
FORENSIC ACCOUNTANT

SECTORS OF THE ECONOMY
Private, nonprofit, public

PRIVATE SECTOR INDUSTRIES
All

END-USER ORGANIZATIONAL DEPARTMENTS
Accounting, Auditing, Security

OVERVIEW OF THE FORENSIC ACCOUNTING FUNCTION
Well before a spate of high-profile accounting frauds at public companies occurred several years ago, the forensic accounting profession was already on a high-growth trajectory. What those financial scandals did was to underscore the extent to which the use of intricate accounting techniques can hide a company's true financial picture. Because the boards of directors of public companies have a fiduciary responsibility to investors — not to mention liability exposure for being derelict in that duty — they are increasingly requiring the companies they oversee to exercise vigilance over their policies and controls. This vigilance has provided the impetus for companies to conduct investigations into their own financial activities. That's where forensic accountants come into the picture — but these professionals are called upon to provide services in many other types of situations.

First, it's important to understand the difference between forensic accountants and traditional accountants. The latter focus on evaluating the conformance of financial statements with generally accepted accounting principles, or GAAP, and limit their auditing to those procedures necessary to form such an opinion. In contrast, forensic accountants integrate their accounting training and experience with investigative abilities to prove financial statement fraud, employee embezzlement, money laundering, and tax fraud. Other common investigative objectives are to recover hidden assets and to establish the value of assets in conjunction with insurance claims, bankruptcy filings, and the dissolution of businesses and marriages. It is often said that — whereas traditional accountants look *at* the numbers — forensic accountants look *behind* the numbers.

Today, forensic accountants can be found in corporate audit and security departments, government agencies, insurance companies, public accounting firms, equity research firms, management consulting firms, and dedicated forensic accounting firms. Self-employment, too, is a feasible option for a forensic accountant, but becoming a successful solo practitioner presupposes the acquisition of experience under the auspices of an employer.

How can an IT professional make a move into forensic accounting? Explains Robert A. Garvey Jr., a certified public accountant, certified fraud examiner, and certified forensic accountant, who is a partner in McLean, Koehler, Sparks & Hammond, a public accounting and consulting firm in Hunt Valley, Maryland: "Forensic accounting is an excellent career choice for an information technology professional who is prepared to invest the time and effort to first become an accountant." Garvey, who heads his firm's forensic accounting practice and has served as an expert witness in civil and criminal legal proceedings throughout the United States, adds, "Gaining auditing experience within a general accounting environment is an important foundation for devising the investigative strategies needed to perform effectively as a forensic accountant."

Because, today, accounting and financial systems are almost universally in electronic form, forensic accountants work closely with computer forensics professionals (see page 208 for a discussion of the Computer Forensics Specialist career option). Clients requiring forensic accounting prefer to use firms that also have on-staff expertise in information technology to help them understand the nature and scope of vulnerabilities in financial and accounting systems that would allow controls to be circumvented. This dual demand for forensic accounting and computer expertise has provided the incentive for the establishment of firms promoting expertise in both disciplines. "Right now," Garvey noted, "firms marketing both types of expertise will assign a forensic accountant and computer specialist to work on any engagement. However, many clients would find it even more desirable to have one expert with proficiency in both disciplines."

You can choose one of a number of alternative paths to enter the forensic accounting profession, not all of which require first becoming an accountant. In descending order of the investment of time and effort required, Garvey described these approaches:

Maximum investment of time: Obtain a B.S. in Accounting. Assuming that you already have a bachelor's degree in a nonaccounting discipline, acquiring a B.S. in Accounting will entail completing a specified number of accounting courses in accordance with the requirements of the college or university where you are enrolled. After obtaining the degree, you could join a public accounting firm and gain the experience needed to qualify for the Certified Public Accountant designation, whose requirements vary from state to state. You could then participate in forensic accounting engagements at your firm, or, if it does not have a forensic accounting practice, join a firm that does.

Moderate investment of time: There are three options to this approach.

- **Option one:** Obtain a B.S. in Accounting and, upon graduation, join a public accounting firm. After gaining at least two years of auditing experience — but not the CPA designation — begin participating in forensic accounting engagements at your firm; or, if that's not feasible there, join another firm that offers that opportunity.
- **Option two:** Obtain a B.S. in Accounting and, upon graduation, apply for a position as a forensic accountant with a government agency, such as the FBI or IRS.
- **Option three:** Complete a two-year A.S. in Accounting program and, upon graduation, seek a position as a forensic accountant with a government agency.

Minimum investment of time: Complete at least two levels of accounting courses to acquire a basic understanding of the discipline. Augment this with courses offered by the Association of Certified Fraud Examiners (see Information Sources).

According to Garvey, certain types of forensic investigations can be successfully conducted by an expert in fraud investigations who is not also necessarily an accountant. "If bribery or a kickback scheme is suspected, it could be performed with equal competence by an accountant or nonaccountant. However, if financial statement fraud is involved, an expert in fraud investigation who is also an accountant would be required." He also noted that obtaining a certification in both fraud examination and forensic accounting would be highly desirable because clients are increasingly specifying the two credentials as requirements.

A number of colleges and universities offer forensic accounting certificate programs for accountants who are not CPAs, as well as for nonaccountants. At the same time, many CPAs are obtaining the Cr.FA credential (see Information Sources). As such, I believe that employers and clients presented with an increasingly larger pool of qualified professionals will become more discriminating in their requirements, leading them to favor those who not only possess certifications in fraud examination and forensic accounting, but who are also CPAs.

POSITION TITLES

Forensic accountant, fraud investigator, fraud examiner

JOB DESCRIPTION HIGHLIGHTS

A forensic accountant will typically perform the following responsibilities, but the first will apply only to a consultant.

- Develop proposals and deliver presentations aimed at obtaining consulting engagements, as well as negotiate the consulting contract.
- Develop an investigative plan for acquiring the data sought, and in a manner admissible in a court of law.
- Conduct interviews of employees, vendor personnel, and other individuals who may have information useful to investigations.
- Review records and dates of financial transactions to detect improper accounting procedures, embezzlement, money laundering, and bribery.
- Engage and interact with consultants contributing to investigations, such as computer forensics experts, economists, private investigators, and security specialists.
- Prepare reports and deliver presentations on investigative findings.
- Participate in depositions and provide testimony during court proceedings.
- Devise financial, accounting, and computer system controls to prevent and detect employee embezzlement and bribery, as well as fraud on the part of customers.

TYPICAL WORKDAY

To help you assess your suitability as a forensic accountant, imagine this is a typical workday at Kelmanjian & Associates, a fictitious public accounting firm. As you read, note your reaction to each activity in the adjacent cell in the Rating column: an "L" (for like), "D" (for dislike), or "N" (for neutral, or no reaction). If you must conduct research before deciding, leave that cell blank for now.

Time	Activity	Rating
8:30–9:30	Conference call with Harry F., General Counsel of Rushwell Mutual Savings Bank, and Lyle S., its Chief Risk Officer. Describe evidence gathered in the investigation into the fraudulent and material overstatement of the value of an asset used for collateral against a loan it provided to a customer.	
9:30–10:15	Conference call with Attorney Robert H., to discuss a plan for locating any hidden assets of the husband of one of his clients in the process of a divorce.	
10:15–11:40	Define and document financial controls to be implemented by a municipality to prevent employee embezzlement following the theft of $35,000 in cash receipts from its Recreation Department. E-mail it to Tony R., the municipality's legal counsel, along with five functional specifications that must be included in the RFP the town will be issuing to potential vendors for its planned new enterprise financial system.	
11:40–12:10	Meet with Ron E., Kelmanjian's partner in charge of the firm's audit practice. His client suspects employee embezzlement because eight purchase orders with eight contiguous numbers were issued for printing and design services. Discuss a proposed investigative plan, which Ron will present to the client.	
1:00–1:25	E-mail Kay S., Research Director for EquiTruth, a memo detailing preliminary results of an analysis of two years of balance sheets and income statements of a public electronics manufacturer. They indicate that its financial ratios and data are much more favorable than the performance of the industry during the same time period. Another anomaly found: Inventory turns declined while the company's sales increased. Tell Kay it looks suspicious; will e-mail a final report to her by Friday.	

Time	Activity	Rating
1:25–2:00	Prepare questions for next week's interview of Carolyn S., a new client and the co-owner of Day-Care Destination, which operates several day-care centers. She is suing her partner for allegedly diverting funds from the business to her husband's landscaping company.	
2:00–2:30	Conference call with Howard F., Chief Security Officer of Collins Woodruff Manufacturing, and Steve M., a computer forensics expert, to answer questions about the plan for conducting an investigation into suspected employee embezzlement.	
2:30–3:15	Review an exhibit prepared by Rich C., a freelance designer, for illustrating the trail of funds in the money-laundering investigation conducted for Lampinton County Savings and Loan. E-mail Rich several copy changes, a correction in the direction of an arrow, and two footnotes needed to translate financial jargon into simple language for the jury.	
3:15–4:00	Conference call with Liz N., Associate Counsel of Millenkamp Marts, a shopping center developer, and Marsha R., the company's CFO, to learn why they suspect that a tenant's financial statements understate its gross sales, thereby depriving Millenkamp of revenue due under the terms of the lease. Prepare the outline of an investigative plan and a retainer agreement for submittal to Millenkamp.	
4:00–4:20	Return phone call from Rochelle V., head of the Audit Committee of Brickman Lessing. Respond to her query about consulting to the Audit Committee on the design of policies and procedures to prevent, detect, and investigate accounting deficiencies and fraud following the identification of three years of improper accounting that required filings of earnings restatements.	
4:20–5:05	Review the transcript of the personal deposition taken in the Ofman Transportation breach-of-contract case. Prepare errata sheet to append to the transcript. Return transcript to Hamilton R., the defendant's counsel.	

Time	Activity	Rating
5:05– 6:15	Analyze Funsella Bakery's P&L, inventory, and production reports for the four months preceding the hurricane that shut the company down. Prepare a report for Perlinton Insurance, which issued a business interruption insurance policy to Funsella. Describe reasons leading to conclusion that Funsella overstated its income loss by approximately 15 percent. E-mail report to Les K., Perlinton's adjuster.	

JOB-HUNTING STRATEGIES

Though it will be a while before you obtain the credentials and/or experience to qualify for a forensic accountant or fraud examiner position, which will vary depending on the degree of investment you are prepared to make to enter the profession, there are steps you can take in the near term to enhance your future marketability. For example, since many forensic accounting firms employ both forensic accountants and computer professionals, you could seek a position that would allow you to participate in forensic investigations.

Begin by conducting a web search to find the names of forensic accounting firms. Their websites won't necessarily reveal whether such positions exist at their firms, but a call to the company should. When approaching an employer, contact the CEO, whose name will in most cases be displayed on the website. If it's not, do a search for the firm name (which you should conduct regardless, to obtain information to help you prepare your approach); this should lead you to white papers, panel discussions, or articles containing the name you're seeking.

Another preparatory step to take is to begin to make contacts in the profession. For example, the Association of Certified Fraud Examiners has many chapters throughout the United States. If one is in your locality, consider becoming an associate member, as the talks delivered by the program speakers will educate you on the profession, and the exposure to practitioners could be a fruitful source of leads. And when it comes to contacting potential employers, use your resume, cover letter, and other communications to highlight any experience they might consider relevant to their businesses, such as involvement in designing, enhancing, or maintaining general ledger, accounts payable/receivable, budgeting, and financial reporting applications. Discuss interactions you've had with finance, accounting, and IT auditing professionals in implementing or upgrading general or application controls, or designing audit trails. Don't forget to highlight any knowledge you gained of purchasing practices and controls through application development activities, because the establishment of sham companies and collusive relationships with vendors have frequently been mechanisms for fraudulent activities.

RECESSION RESISTANCE

The demand for forensic accounting is not linked to the performance of the economy. If anything, it is widely believed that embezzlement and fraud increase in an economic downturn, although such crimes may not be discovered until after the economy has turned the corner. Interestingly, some studies have linked higher rates of divorce to a deteriorating economy and it is increasingly common for a divorce litigant to engage a forensic accountant in an attempt to discover assets hidden by his or her spouse.

Neither is the volume of commercial litigation contingent on the economic environment. When it involves allegations of hidden assets and financial fraud, it will often trigger forensic accounting investigations.

OFFSHORE OUTSOURCING SITUATION AND OUTLOOK

Similar to the trend in other fields that encompass extensive data analysis, many accounting positions have already been relocated to offshore markets. To date, this has been limited to the large accounting firms, and, according to Bob Garvey, the practice is not likely to be adopted by small and middle-market accounting firms in the foreseeable future. As for the forensic accounting specialty, the Association of Certified Fraud Examiners has chapters in over 20 countries, including some that are popular offshoring destinations. The American College of Forensic Examiners Institute of Forensic Science has awarded the Cr.FA credential to professionals in other countries. And it is increasingly common for electronic depositions to be taken from witnesses in locations remote to trial venues.

While, in principle, these factors may suggest that U.S.-based forensic accounting positions are vulnerable to offshoring, there are countervailing factors operating as well. One such factor applies to anyone serving as an expert witness, which is described in detail in the Computer Expert section (see page 234). Garvey says, "At this time, I am not aware of any instances in which companies or individuals requiring forensic accounting services are using overseas experts. As a practical matter, it is not very feasible since one of the key responsibilities of a forensic accountant is to interview the suspect in a case of alleged fraud, as well as others who can provide information useful to the investigation. To be most effective, these interviews must be conducted in person."

INFORMATION SOURCES

American Institute of Certified Public Accountants (www.aicpa.org). The AICPA's website contains links to those of individual state affiliate organizations, where information about their licensing requirements is provided.

Association of Certified Fraud Examiners (www.acfe.com). ACFE awards the Certified Fraud Examiner (CFE) designation to professionals who meet particular educational requirements, are experienced in one of five specified functional disciplines, and pass an extensive written examination. The CFE would be an appropriate credential for IT professionals who wish to enter the investigative profession without becoming an accountant.

American College of Forensic Examiners Institute of Forensic Science (www. acfei.com). This organization awards the Certified Forensic Accountant (Cr.FA) credential. U.S. candidates for the Cr.FA must possess CPA licenses, the requirements for which vary from one state to another. The candidacy of applicants in foreign countries is evaluated on a case-by-case basis.

Forensic Accounting and Fraud Investigation for Non-Experts, by Howard Silverstone and Michael Sheetz (John Wiley & Sons, Inc., 2004). This book guides managers, crime investigators, and other nonaccountants in understanding those areas in an organization that are most vulnerable to financial fraud. It includes advice on conducting investigations to acquire evidence admissible in a court of law.

FORENSIC ACCOUNTANT
YOUR RATINGS AND NEXT STEPS

How compatible is this field with my skills?

Assign a score of 0–10 (10 is highest): _____

Skills/Knowledge I Need to Acquire Before Contacting Employers

1._____

2._____

3._____

4._____

Typical Workday Task Ratings

After conducting research to fill in any ratings you initially left blank, calculate the total for each type of reaction (like, dislike, neutral). A field may be a good choice if you have at least six Ls and three or fewer Ds.

Total **L**s:_____ Total **D**s:_____ Total **N**s:_____

Research Notes

_____

_____

_____

_____

_____

_____

_____

_____

_____

Contact Log

Date:_____Name/Title:_____

Phone/E-mail:_____

Comments:_____

_____

_____

_____

Date:_____Name/Title:_____

Phone/E-mail:_____

Comments:_____

_____

_____

_____

Date:_____Name/Title:_____

Phone/E-mail:_____

Comments:_____

_____

_____

_____

Date:_____Name/Title:_____

Phone/E-mail:_____

Comments:_____

_____

_____

_____

CAREER OPTION: COMPUTER EXPERT

SECTOR OF THE ECONOMY
Private

INDUSTRIES
Businesses in all industries can require the services of a computer expert.

END-USER ORGANIZATIONAL DEPARTMENT
Because, typically, the need for computer experts is of a temporary nature, they generally provide their services on a project basis, either as independent consultants or employees of consulting firms.

OVERVIEW OF THE COMPUTER EXPERT PROFESSION
If you can claim in-depth knowledge about a particular technology, you may be able to parlay it into a lucrative new occupation as a computer expert.

- Are you an ace C++ programmer? If so, you could provide expert testimony in a data warehouse developer's copyright infringement lawsuit against a competitor by rendering an opinion as to the similarity between the code in the two companies' applications.
- Are you proficient in managing large-scale, complex software development projects through all life-cycle phases? If so, you might be called as an expert witness for a software developer defending a malpractice claim.
- Are you an experienced IT security executive? If so, you might qualify as an expert in a class-action lawsuit brought by patients against a hospital, alleging that its negligence enabled hackers to steal their medical records and identities.

Computer experts have much in common with practitioners in several other fields covered in the book — computer forensics, forensic accounting, and IT auditing — all of whom routinely serve as experts in disputes, regardless of whether those conflicts have reached the litigation stage.

As noted previously, as a computer expert, you may work on a self-employed basis or as an employee of a consulting firm. The ease and speed with which you could build a successful consulting practice would depend on:

- The extent of your technical knowledge and how it compares to the qualifications of others in the field.
- Your ability to explain arcane technical concepts to juries, judges, and arbitrators.
- Your educational credentials, professional certifications, and reputation in your field.
- The reputations of your past employers and/or consulting clients.

Building a thriving practice does not necessarily take a long time. One of my clients drew upon 30 years' experience in a non-IT profession to establish an expert consulting practice and, within two years, had gained a national reputation among attorneys. To gauge your potential success as a computer expert, conduct an online search to compare your credentials and experience to those of experts against whom you would be competing.

POSITION TITLES
Computer expert, information technology expert, expert witness

JOB DESCRIPTION HIGHLIGHTS
As a computer expert, you would be routinely called on to:

- Assess the validity of complaints and defenses in computer-related disputes to help attorneys advise their clients on the optimal course of action — settlement negotiation, litigation, or no action.
- Assist attorneys in preparing interrogatories and requests for production pertaining to claims of breach of contract, breach of warranty, excessive charges, negligence, software malpractice, theft of trade secrets, and intellectual property infringement.
- Study the opposing side's interrogatory responses and documents to assess the strength of its claims or defenses.
- Compare the code in two software applications in conjunction with supporting or refuting copyright infringement claims.
- Compose technical questions for attorneys to pose to witnesses for the

opposing side, as well as examine witness responses for their impact on the strength of clients' claims/defenses.

- Calculate monetary damages for clients to claim from the opposing side, or refute damages claims against clients.
- Prepare reports describing evidence supporting or refuting liability claims and calculations of monetary damages.
- Participate in depositions and deliver testimony asserting/defending your findings and opinions.
- Serve as a court-appointed master, which may entail conducting technology tutorials for judges and attorneys, as well as advising judges on the technical issues underlying the cases over which they preside.
- Perform comparative analyses of the features, benefits, and price-value relationships of products/services that compete with the one at the heart of a dispute.
- Review and draft language for inclusion in software, hardware, and service agreements.
- Conduct technology due diligence in conjunction with mergers, acquisitions, joint ventures, investments, and loan workouts.

TYPICAL WORKDAY

Follow this typical workday of a fictitious self-employed computer expert whose background includes experience as a CIO, and as a manager of application development for proprietary and commercial software during employment at companies in both the IT and non-IT industries. As you read, enter your reaction to each activity in the adjacent cell in the Rating column: an "L" (for like), "D" (for dislike), or "N" (for neutral, or no reaction). If you must conduct research before deciding, leave that cell blank for now.

Time	Activity	Rating
8:30–9:10	Read the complaint alleging excessive charges, filed by Kelleher Continental against Shrobsen, Inc., which sells custom pattern-making software to apparel manufacturers. E-mail a list of questions to Harlan M., the attorney representing Shrobsen, regarding his client's project planning and project management processes, work performed, and manpower allocated to each phase of the project.	

Time	Activity	Rating
9:10–9:35	Do phone consult with Rita K., attorney for Couch Potato Caravans, a developer of video visits to tourist attractions worldwide that feature the capability to purchase mementos of those "trips" at venue gift shops. Couch Potato is suing a competitor for software copyright infringement. Explain the plan for applying the abstraction, filtration, and comparison method of analysis to determine similarities between the code in the two programs.	
9:35–12:20	Analyze the code in the metrics modules of the CRM data-warehousing packages of Sui GeneriSystems and SummiTarget Group. Look for similarities to support SummiTarget's lawsuit claiming copyright infringement. Report to Ted S., SummiTarget's attorney, on the degree of similarity between the two programs' code, lists of parameters, and macros, as well as the likelihood that any similarities were coincidences.	
12:20–1:00	Visit the websites of three vendors of document control software to help Nestino Worldwide select one for its use. Prepare a list of questions to ask the vendors' technical personnel to enable a comparison of their capabilities.	
1:30–2:20	Review the interrogatory responses and documents produced in discovery by Parmiczy Solutions, which was sued by Maylberg Essences for installing a logistics management software package that failed to perform in accordance with claims on its website and in written communications with the plaintiff. Write a report for Alicia N., attorney for Maylberg Essences, detailing beta test deficiencies evident in Parmiczy's internal e-mails and those between Parmiczy's staff and beta test participants. Highlight seven defects that were apparently never corrected.	
2:20–2:45	In prep for next week's depositions of the manager of product development and the account executive at ZiproMentor, a reverse auction software vendor, draft questions aimed at proving that its sales personnel knowingly misrepresented the software's capabilities to Demyan Industries. E-mail the questions to Charlie F., Demyan's attorney.	

Time	Activity	Rating
2:45–4:00	Test the medical laboratory management application implemented by Harrigan Myles, a systems integrator, to corroborate defects alleged by Smithson Analytics. Smithson is suing Harrigan for breach of contract. E-mail Peter R., Smithson's attorney, confirming all of his client's claims. Include a low-to-high range of costs Smithson will likely incur to correct the defects, which will be used to bolster its claim for consequential damages.	
4:00–4:20	Call Craig M., General Counsel of Coopman Manufacturing, to review the service deficiencies alleged by Coopman in its outsourced helpdesk services contract with Ridewell Digital. Discuss whether they support a breach of the contract's SLA clause.	
4:20–4:50	Prepare a proposal for Karen N., Corporate Development Director of Maricalle Universal, an HMO, for conducting due diligence of the disease management software package developed by a potential acquisition.	
4:50–5:10	Initial telephone conversation with Carlos D., attorney for Proskow, Inc., a real estate development and management company. Proskow claims numerous defects in the site selection software it recently began using. Ask Mr. D. for a list of the defects and the direct/indirect financial impact of each on his client's business.	
5:10–5:30	In a memo to Bill V., CFO of Dion Plastics, review the contract for a license for an HRIS package presented by the vendor. Note the inadequacy of the vendor's assertions that it will apply "best efforts" to inform Dion of all known defects and respond to its technical support needs in a "timely manner." Advise Bill to require the vendor to notify his company within three business days of learning of any defect. Include a table listing four increasingly critical categories of user problems that could require technical support, along with a minimal response time for each — which should be written into the contract.	
5:30–6:45	Read the transcript of the deposition of Marilyn M., a Senior Software Engineer at Thereault Systems, the developer of an enterprise risk management application, which has been sued for nonperformance by Carolman Engineering, a client of attorney Ron C. *(cont...)*	

Time	Activity	Rating
(cont...) 5:30– 6:45	Draw a three-column table, labeled: (1) "Software Functions" (list twelve capabilities the company's documentation claimed the package would have); (2) "White Box Testing"; (3) "Black Box Testing." Adjacent to each function in columns 2 and 3, rate — from 0 to 10 — Thereault's compliance with best practices for each type of test, to the extent that such information is revealed in Ms. M.'s responses.	

JOB-HUNTING STRATEGIES

Your technical knowledge can serve as a springboard to a career as a computer expert in three ways:

- **As an employee of a consulting firm.** When targeting firms that exclusively provide technology expertise consulting services, contact the CEO. Find out the name of the executive overseeing the relevant practice area of diversified midsize and large firms. Note: The names of these firms will probably include two or more of these keywords: technology, risk, advisory, litigation.
- **As a subcontractor to one or more consulting firms.** Some companies will engage experts on a project basis if their employees lack the type of knowledge required, if their expert staff members are too busy handling client matters, or if their business model is based on using subcontractors exclusively.
- **As a self-employed consultant.** In this realm, I recommend targeting law firms that engage in commercial litigation and that have 12 or fewer attorneys. These are most likely to lack in-house technology experts. Martindale-Hubbell, which publishes print and online directories of attorneys, offers a service that enables you to conduct a targeted mailing. (See Information Sources.)

You could concurrently be a subcontractor to consulting firms and an independent consultant to end users, as long as it is not prohibited by your agreement with any party. Even if no contractual limitations apply, be sensitive to the possibility of an ethical conflict that might be a reason to decline an engagement.

RECESSION RESISTANCE

Demand for computer experts primarily stems from civil litigation relating to claims of breach of contract, software malpractice, negligence, theft of trade secrets, and intellectual property infringement. Experts also prepare RFPs, evaluate vendor offerings, and review contracts. While sluggish sales may lessen the demand for assessing vendor offerings and reviewing technology-based contracts, in a troubled economy more companies are forced to sell businesses, product lines, and intellectual property — transactions that will all involve contracts. Thus, while the impetus for requiring the services of an expert may change, the level of demand should not be materially affected.

Experts often provide technology due diligence services. While merger and acquisition activity — a major driver of due diligence — usually declines in a recession, some companies view an economic downturn as an opportunity to buy businesses and technologies that are more attractively priced than in prosperous periods. And even if there is a net reduction in M&A-related demand for technology due diligence, it should be offset somewhat by an increase in the number of distressed companies, business units, and other assets on the market that their owners are forced to sell.

OFFSHORE OUTSOURCING SITUATION AND OUTLOOK

To understand why computer experts are well insulated from offshore outsourcing, consider one of the factors influencing the decision to offshore, cited earlier: the requirement for experience. Experts routinely render opinions as to whether the actions of one of the parties to a dispute conformed to an industry's best practices. To be a credible expert on what constitutes best practices presupposes two types of knowledge:

- Knowledge of what constitutes a best practice — as opposed to an acceptable practice. The fact that a company develops commercial software does not necessarily mean that it does so in accordance with an industry's best practices. Understandably, the more preeminent the reputation of companies of whose practices the consultant can claim knowledge, the greater the weight of his or her opinion.
- Knowledge of the practices of *multiple* enterprises. Notice the use of the plural "practices" here.

Thus, the most credible expert is one whose opinion reflects knowledge of the *practices* of the greatest number of companies that are acknowledged leaders in their industry segments. Certainly there are computer experts in the countries attracting U.S. offshoring contracts whose capabilities match those of U.S. experts, but on the whole the level of technological sophistication in those countries is less advanced than in the United States. However, computer professionals in those countries have already made — and will continue to make — significant strides in technical knowledge, and should be expected to compete for expert consulting engagements on an international level. In addition, as video depositions have become increasingly common, the relevance of the location of an expert has decreased in importance. Regardless, U.S. experts should not feel threatened by competition from offshore experts whose fees are substantially lower, for one simple reason: appearances.

When attorneys choose experts for jury trials (as opposed to bench trials, those decided by a judge), they pay as much attention to the impact of the expert's image and demeanor on the jury as his or her credentials. Attorneys know that, regardless of how objective people try to be, they bring biases into the courtroom. Thus, an attorney might choose an expert with a Midwestern background for a trial in a small Midwestern city on the basis that the jury members would identify with that person and, therefore, ascribe greater credibility to his or her opinion than, say, a Northeastern expert's. An attorney in *any* region of the United States who considers engaging an offshore expert would probably be sensitive to the possibility that some members of the jury might have been affected by offshoring, or know someone who has, and have a negative view of the practice. The attorney might conclude that this perception would accrue to their evaluations of the opinion rendered by an expert from any foreign country — whether a major western power or an offshoring market — regardless of whether his or her testimony is conveyed by video or in person. Consequently, in general, attorneys will resist using any foreign expert unless a qualified expert cannot be found in the United States.

INFORMATION SOURCES
Expert Testimony: A Guide for Expert Witnesses and the Lawyers Who Examine Them (National Institute for Trial Advocacy, 1998). This book by Steven Lubet provides guidance to experts in preparing for courtroom appearances, with an emphasis on effectively communicating their find-

ings, both on direct and cross-examination, as well as maximizing the credibility of their opinions.

National Institute for Trial Advocacy (www.nita.org). NITA is primarily engaged in developing educational programs for attorneys, which allow them to fulfill continuing legal education requirements. A new educational offering is aimed at training experts in delivering effective courtroom testimony.

Forensic Expert Witness Association (www.forensic.org). With several chapters on the West Coast, FEWA publishes a quarterly newsletter, operates a speaker's bureau, and provides other resources useful to forensic experts in many industries. The computer expert category encompasses over a dozen subcategories, including software design, computer evidence, and computer systems.

Martindale-Hubbell (www.martindale.com). This company publishes both print and online directories of attorneys throughout the United States. Databases of attorneys in selected specialties and geographic areas can be obtained for use in targeted mailings.

COMPUTER EXPERT
YOUR RATINGS AND NEXT STEPS

How compatible is this field with my skills?

Assign a score of 0–10 (10 is highest): _____

Skills/Knowledge I Need to Acquire Before Contacting Employers

1._____

2._____

3._____

4._____

Typical Workday Task Ratings

After conducting research to fill in any ratings you initially left blank, calculate the total for each type of reaction (like, dislike, neutral). A field may be a good choice if you have at least six Ls and three or fewer Ds.

Total **L**s:_____ Total **D**s:_____ Total **N**s:_____

Research Notes

_____

_____

_____

_____

_____

_____

_____

_____

_____

Contact Log

Date:_____ Name/Title:_____

Phone/E-mail:_____

Comments:_____

_____

_____

_____

Date:_____ Name/Title:_____

Phone/E-mail:_____

Comments:_____

_____

_____

_____

Date:_____ Name/Title:_____

Phone/E-mail:_____

Comments:_____

_____

_____

_____

Date:_____ Name/Title:_____

Phone/E-mail:_____

Comments:_____

_____

_____

_____

CAREER OPTION: INTELLECTUAL PROPERTY/ INFORMATION TECHNOLOGY ATTORNEY

SECTORS OF THE ECONOMY
Private, public, nonprofit

PRIVATE SECTOR INDUSTRIES
All

END-USER ORGANIZATIONAL DEPARTMENT
Legal

OVERVIEW OF INTELLECTUAL PROPERTY AND INFORMATION TECHNOLOGY LAW

As a computer professional, you know that project delays, inadequate functionality, and software incompatibility are routine occurrences. But to get an idea of the degree to which disputes about these and other software problems can escalate, go online and plug in these terms: software, breach, contract, plaintiff, lawsuit, damages. Next, use software, infringement, lawsuit, and damages, together with each of the following keywords in four sequential searches: Internet, copyright, trademark, patent. The number of hits produced by these searches will open your eyes to the demand for intellectual property (IP) and IT legal counsel.

Keep the results of those searches in mind as I explain why computer professionals who become attorneys will be well positioned to capitalize on that demand, which will only increase in lockstep with the growth in the use of technology. Legal matters involving computers are routinely presented to attorneys who lack knowledge of computer technology, often because those attorneys previously counseled the client on traditional contract matters. Clearly — and regardless of their level of legal competency — in such situations, these attorneys are operating under a handicap. Consider this scenario: An attorney untrained in computer technology is engaged by a software development company to defend a customer's claim that an application did not perform as specified. Certainly, personnel from the software company could tutor the attorney in such topics as project plan, SLA, beta test, white and black box tests, build, and user acceptance.

But would such tutoring sessions be sufficient, for even the most brilliant attorney, to provide the level of competent representation necessary in such a matter? I doubt it. You know first-hand that computer professionals master these concepts only through experience, over sometimes lengthy periods of time.

Now imagine that the attorney's client is not a software developer but a company that operates several restaurants, and does not employ in-house computer staff. The company entered into an agreement to license an enterprise financial package, only to find so many defects that it had to resort to managing the process manually. In this scenario, both the attorney *and* the client lack knowledge of software development processes and terminology. How could the attorney draft interrogatories and requests for production if he or she doesn't even know what terminology to use? For example, suppose the attorney prepared a request for production seeking "all documents and things relating to the design of the software." Since design is a phase distinct from testing, the defendant might not feel compelled to produce the results of a beta test that would reveal defects that were identified prior to commercial release but were not corrected. (Even if a request for production seeking the results of a beta test were presented, that would not guarantee that the defendant would provide them, as a search for "discovery abuse" would demonstrate.) The goal of discovery is to compose interrogatories and requests for production that make it impossible for the opposing side to avoid providing responsive information and documents.

Next, consider the discipline of intellectual property (IP), which encompasses copyright, trademark, and patent law. In the past, copyright law dealt mainly with licensing and distribution agreements, as well as infringements, pertaining to visual, literary, and aural works in traditional media; it also dealt with live and recorded musical and theatrical performances. Today, those products routinely involve distribution through the Internet, DVDs, and CD-ROMs. Moreover, software can be copyrighted and — if it embodies a novel process — it may be patentable. Trademark matters historically involved only print and broadcast media; but here, too, the Internet has given rise to new types of threats, making it more difficult than ever to protect such property. Providing IP counsel in the twenty-first century demands an understanding of RAM, framing, network and server technology, meta tags, encryption, copy protection, reverse engineering, browser cache, disk cache, digital rights management, source and object code, and a host of other technical terms and concepts.

Patent law has traditionally been practiced by chemical, mechanical, electronic, and electrical engineers who, because they are computer-savvy, should have no difficulty mastering the technology underlying these types of cases. In contrast, an attorney without an engineering or computer background, and whose IP practice has been limited to traditional copyright and trademark matters, could be at a serious disadvantage in providing representation. Even if he or she recognizes the need for a computer expert, the expert's fees added to the attorney's could impose a significant financial burden on the client. And I would not be sanguine about the attorney's ability to retain 100 percent of the information conveyed by a technology expert, such that there would be no errors or omissions that could contribute to an adverse outcome. On the other hand, having an attorney with a computer background could potentially preclude the need for a computer expert or, at least, result in significantly lower costs for the client.

My belief in the importance of understanding the technology underlying a legal matter is apparently shared by many leading law firms, as reflected in their websites, which promote the number of their attorneys with advanced degrees *and* business experience in computer science, biotechnology, chemistry, and other technical disciplines. These firms know that their clients want to be represented by attorneys who speak their language. Beyond saving considerable time and, therefore, money, dual-discipline knowledge is vital to providing competent representation in technology-based legal matters.

Computer professionals who become attorneys will find many opportunities in the public sector, including states attorneys' offices and federal agencies. The Department of Justice's Computer Crime and Intellectual Property Section employs attorneys who focus on computer crimes involving e-commerce, privacy violations, and hackers. It also deals with intellectual property matters since — although infringement claims are usually pursued through civil litigation — under certain circumstances they can be prosecuted under criminal statutes.

Obviously, computer knowledge is an advantage in the practice of IP and IT law, but it will be an asset in any type of litigation. The pervasiveness of computers today requires litigators to rely extensively on computer consultants, as a search for eDiscovery will bear out. While most midsize and large law firms employ attorneys or paralegals with computer expertise, attorneys in small firms or solo practices usually lack such support — unless the firm is an IP or technology boutique firm. True, a client of a firm that lacks in-house computer expertise could assign someone from its IT department to work with its attorney, but many clients do not have in-house IT staff and may even be unaware of the need for computer expertise.

And let's say an attorney recognizes the need for a computer consultant. That may constitute only superficial awareness, as he or she may mistakenly believe that *any* computer consultant will do, that is, be qualified in the technology involved in a case. As a computer professional, you know that, for example, an expert in software development and project management processes and best practices would be required for a case involving software malpractice, whereas an Internet trademark infringement matter would require a specialist in server technology and network traffic analysis. Yes, some consultants will be qualified in both areas, but this cannot be assumed. Nor can it be assumed that a consultant inexperienced in the computer discipline vital to the case will decline the engagement.

Some attorneys who specialize in IP and software matters confine their services to preparing trademark, patent, and copyright filings, and to drafting, negotiating, and reviewing license and distribution agreements; they do not engage in litigation. This is an important distinction. Among the biographies of attorneys on the website of Martindale-Hubbell (see Information Sources), which lists attorneys in all specialties, are many who describe their practice areas as "computer and intellectual property law." Unless "litigation" is mentioned, it might mean that the attorney does not provide litigation counsel. At some firms, IP litigation will be handled by two attorneys: one with expertise in IP law, the other a litigation specialist. I mention this because there is a widespread perception by the lay public that all attorneys engage in trial work, which may discourage those who prefer not to participate in adversarial legal matters to enter the profession. My point: You can build a very successful practice solely on the nonlitigation aspects of intellectual property or computer counsel.

In summary, if you are willing and able to obtain a license to practice law, you should be amply rewarded by the value you will be able to provide your clients through your dual-discipline expertise. And given the frequency of advertisements seeking corporate attorneys to provide IT and e-business counsel, your employer may be willing to fund your education in anticipation of your joining its legal department. Another option is to join the IT department of a university that operates a law school that you could attend on a part-time basis, since the tuition may cost you little or nothing.

POSITION TITLES

In a law firm: Associate, senior associate, junior partner, senior partner

In an end-user organization: Associate, senior associate, corporate counsel, assistant general counsel, associate general counsel, general counsel, staff attorney

JOB DESCRIPTION HIGHLIGHTS

Some of the responsibilities described here apply to attorneys engaged in either litigation or the nonlitigation aspects of IP or IT law; others will be performed solely by attorneys who provide litigation counsel. And still others will apply only to attorneys employed in federal and state government agencies who prosecute IP and computer crimes, which are noted with a (G).

- Structure and negotiate license, distribution, and other contracts for clients, as well as review such documents presented to clients by third parties.
- Evaluate client claims, and defenses against the claims of others, of breach of contract, breach of warranty, software malpractice, intellectual property infringement, and other offenses.
- Research case law to evaluate the strength of client claims/defenses and devise strategies to achieve the optimal outcome.
- Advise clients on the costs/benefits of resolving disputes through settlement negotiation versus litigation.
- Prepare and file complaints in the appropriate jurisdiction and court.
- Interact with opposing counsel in conveying client grievances and listening to those of their clients, establishing litigation schedules, and negotiating settlement agreements.
- Draft subpoenas for documents and witnesses.
- Plan and oversee investigations into intellectual property theft and computer crimes (G).
- Interact with representatives of domestic and foreign law enforcement agencies (G).
- Manage the prosecution of intellectual property theft and computer crimes (G).

- Draft interrogatories and requests for production for the opposing side, as well as review client responses to the opposing side's interrogatories and requests for production.
- Prepare motions for the court.
- Engage experts to evaluate the strength of client claims/defenses, as well as to quantify or refute damages claims.
- Depose the opposing side's witnesses, with the goal of obtaining information to support clients' cases.
- Oversee the deposition of clients, witnesses for clients, and experts supporting client claims of liability and damages, and review transcripts of these depositions for weaknesses the opposing side may exploit.
- Prepare presentations for and participate in hearings and trials.

TYPICAL WORKDAY

Read this workday of a fictitious attorney in a solo practice specializing in intellectual property and computer-related matters to gauge your interest in the profession. As you read, enter your reaction to each activity in the adjacent cell in the Rating column: an "L" (for like), "D" (for dislike), or "N" (for neutral, or no reaction). If you must conduct research before deciding, leave that cell blank for now.

Time	Activity	Rating
8:30–9:35	Review the contract presented to Croyston Theilman Industries by OmniScience Systems, a systems integrator, for implementation of an enterprise risk management application. Call Micki Z., Croyston's COO, advising her that a clause should be added to the contract to specify: (1) that the technical personnel who participated in the sales presentation that led to OmniScience's selection will be assigned to the project; and (2) that if any of those individuals cease working on the project for any reason prior to completion, Croyston will have the right to reject replacement personnel if it considers them less qualified and instead select their own contractors, who will be entitled to reasonable compensation for their services from OmniScience. Afterward, draft the two clauses and e-mail them to Ms. Z.	

Time	Activity	Rating
9:35–9:45	Telephone call from Les P., President of Linkmyer Supplies, a distributor, regarding a lawsuit served on him by a nautical books publisher. The publisher claims infringement of four photographs it owns that are displayed on Linkmyer's website. Mr. P. admits copying the photos. Inform him that if the plaintiff registered the copyrights in the photographs within three months of their first publication, he could be liable for as much as $150,000 in damages for each, in addition to the plaintiff's legal fees and costs. Ask Mr. P. to send a copy of the complaint.	
9:45–10:30	Read the complaint against Kaydent Riccardo, a systems integrator, by a customer alleging that the HRIS application Kaydent installed is incompatible with the client's payroll system, in violation of the contract. Review Kaydent's professional liability insurance policy before sending Pia R., CEO, an e-mail explaining that it does not cover any fees the plaintiff paid that she may be obligated to refund. Request a copy of the contract and all other communications with the client.	
10:30–11:15	Review the report prepared by Keith H., a software expert, on the results of the abstraction, filtration, and comparison test he performed to assess a copyright infringement claim by OptiChoice, a client that markets interactive software that helps students choose majors, against the Cochran Harnston Group, a competitor. Keith concluded that there was an unequivocal infringement.	
11:15–12:20	Review the colocation services contract presented by Ramjani Technologies to Whetmore Manufacturing. Re the clause stating that the vendor may relocate the server assigned to Whetmore from one data center to another at its discretion, advise Whetmore via e-mail to ask his insurance broker whether his company's cyberrisk policy requires the specification of the physical location of its servers. If so, a clause must be added to the colocation contract that requires the vendor to give Whetmore at least five business days' advance notice, by certified mail, of the server's relocation so that he can inform his insurance company.	

Time	Activity	Rating
1:00–1:30	Telephone conference with Douglas M., computer forensics expert, to discuss the court's approval of an *ex parte* order in the software infringement lawsuit that Larrimore Technologies, a client, will file against a competitor. Review the chain of custody that must be observed when Doug, two U.S. marshals, and I make a surprise visit to the competitor's offices next week to seize several computers.	
1:30–1:55	Respond to phone call from Jeff A., Vice President of Metri-Mart, a developer of portfolio management software regarding representing the company in a lawsuit against a licensee. Mr. A. says that, according to a letter received from a former employee of the licensee, it created unauthorized copies of MetriMart software and made it available to 24 personnel in two new European branches, exceeding the limit in the number of users granted under the license.	
1:55–2:45	Review a letter from the attorney for the operator of a website that displayed unauthorized images of eight botanical illustrations created by Doris S., a client, responding to a "cease and desist" letter that contained a demand for monetary compensation to avoid litigation. Draft a response indicating that the amount offered is inadequate, reflecting Ms. S.'s prior instructions re the minimal settlement she would accept; send the attorney's letter and response draft to Ms. S. for her approval.	
2:45–3:40	Read the copyright infringement complaint against Eloise B. by Craig D. alleging that portions of Ms. B.'s *The Influence of Asian Textile Arts on Fifteenth Century European Visual Arts*, were plagiarized from Mr. D.'s book, *Chinese Textile Design during the Ming Dynasty*. Call Ms. B.; explain that the degree of similarity and amount of text involved will make it very difficult to mount a successful defense. Advise her to be prepared to make a settlement offer, and that research into damages awarded in similar cases that went to trial must be conducted before recommending a figure.	
3:40–4:25	Read three recent rulings in cases involving contributory infringement on the Internet.	

Time	Activity	Rating
4:25– 4:45	Call Mel C. to discuss a letter just received from Sal W., attorney for DisCapers, a music publisher, offering $120,000 to settle his copyright infringement claim against the company for publishing the song he wrote 35 years ago in its Déjà vu Discorama album. Advise Mr. C. that all the evidence points to willful infringement by Dis-Capers, so he might be better off proceeding to trial and electing statutory damages under 17 U.S.C. 504 (b) since the judge has the option of awarding as much as $150,000, and his registration of the copyright within three months of publication will qualify him for reimbursement of attorney's fees and costs.	
4:45– 5:40	Prepare questions for next week's deposition of the operations manager of Ference Lockwood Industries. Focus on proving that the company falsely claimed its archiving process was much shorter than it actually was in an effort to minimize the period for which Harry E., the client, can claim damages for the infringement of his copyrighted landscape designs Ference displayed on its website.	

JOB-HUNTING STRATEGIES

Naturally, it will be a while before you can practice law, but there are actions you can take well before then to lay the groundwork for a successful start to your legal career:

To gain exposure to potential employers: Contact your local bar association to see if it has IP and technology bar association sections, and ask whether nonattorneys can attend their meetings. If yes, plan on doing so, as these events can be valuable venues for building contacts.

To gain exposure to potential clients: Whether you want to become an associate at a law firm or build a solo practice (as opposed to joining the in-house legal department of a corporation or other end user), you will need to generate business. As soon as possible, therefore, start attending the meetings of the local chapters of organizations whose members could be potential clients or sources of referrals. Contact the local chapter contacts of those groups to learn whether you qualify for membership; if not, ask if you can attend as a nonmember. A few suggested organizations are the National Association of Computer Consultant Businesses, Association for Women in Communications, National Writers Association, American Institute of Graphic Arts, and Organization of Black Designers. Consult the *Encyclopedia of Associations*, a reference book available in libraries, where you will find an abundance of other organizations whose members might need IT or IP legal counsel.

RECESSION RESISTANCE

The demand for some kinds of legal services is strongly linked to the economy (e.g., real estate closings decline and bankruptcy filings increase in a recession), but that is not the case for IP and IT counsel. Regardless of the economic environment, individuals and businesses continue to create works that can be copyrighted or patented; likewise, the misappropriation of intellectual property knows no season. If anything, a troubled economy drives an increase in all types of thievery. Also, some companies may more aggressively enforce their IP rights if their sales suffer in a recession. One software company executive said that her company viewed its efforts toward seeking damages for infringement of its IP as no different from its sales campaigns in a traditional distribution channel.

Companies with recession-related sales declines may be compelled to defer the acquisition of new technologies, which could affect the demand for legal counsel to draft, review, and negotiate software contracts. However, defects in software packages installed during an economic boom may not surface until after the boom has turned into a bust.

OFFSHORE OUTSOURCING SITUATION AND OUTLOOK

Junior attorneys in the United States are compensated at a rate roughly five times that of experienced attorneys in countries attracting U.S. outsourcing contracts, while the salary of a junior paralegal in this country is approximately three times that of an Indian attorney's. You do the math: Since an attorney possesses higher-level legal skills than a paralegal, it shouldn't be surprising that U.S. law firms and large corporations have been actively engaged in offshoring, with the greatest activity in the area of patent law.

India was initially the most popular offshoring destination of the U.S. legal community, for two reasons: First, its legal code is based on the same principles of jurisprudence that underlie the U.S. system; second, Indian lawyers speak English. However, the Philippines are another fast-growing source of offshore legal work. Law firms and large U.S. companies have trained offshore attorneys in research and writing approaches that conform to the particular requirements of the U.S. judicial system. And many U.S. law firms and corporations are bypassing the offshore vendor route and instead establishing proprietary offshore legal operations.

Junior attorneys in the United States — especially at large law firms — have historically been assigned the most mundane tasks. That is the type of work initially outsourced by U.S. firms, and so new associates at those firms now have the opportunity to handle more challenging matters at the outset of their careers. And even though the offshoring of legal work has gradually moved up the scale of complexity, as a practical matter there is a limit to how far up it is feasible, for several reasons:

- Much of the work of an attorney involves writing briefs and other communications, the effectiveness of which will depend on his or her understanding of U.S. jurisprudence, culture, and vernacular. And, when a trial is involved, the culture and vernacular of the region assume even greater importance. Thus, while law firms and corporations may find that offshoring allows them to reduce the number of U.S. law school graduates they hire, they will still need a sufficient pool of U.S. junior associates capable of advancing to a level that will qualify them to review the work of offshore attorneys to ensure that their communications are written in an appropriate manner.

- The requirement for confidentiality in providing legal counsel has deterred many law firms from engaging in offshoring. While the potential for a breach of confidentiality should be a concern regardless of the location of an outsourcing vendor, U.S. law firms would probably feel more confident about the protections accorded their client data under U.S. laws.

- Ethical issues may inhibit law firms from using the services of offshore attorneys. Proclamations issued by the American Bar Association impose obligations on attorneys to apprise clients on the progress of their cases, and to advise clients if temporary attorneys will contribute to their cases if the attorney has reason to believe that the client would want to know that. These and a number of other ethical issues that should be considered by law firms and corporations when deciding whether to use offshore attorneys are thoroughly examined in a paper presented at an ABA conference on lawyers' professional liability.[6]

Still, it is important to realize that some states will grant a license to practice law to attorneys who are neither citizens nor residents of the United States. And, certainly, those states that do not might do so in the future. Thus, we should expect to see increasing numbers of foreign attorneys obtaining U.S. law licenses, especially in light of the globalization of commerce. However, if any states that do not currently grant licenses to foreign lawyers who are neither residents nor citizens of the United States require changes in their attorney-licensing regulations to be approved by their legislatures, there is one factor that may act as a deterrent. According to the National Conference of State Legislatures,[7] approximately 15 percent of legislators nationwide are attorneys. While this percentage has declined from 25 percent during the past two decades, for a single profession to command a legislative representation of approximately one-seventh underscores attorney-lawmakers' ability to influence the outcome of bills proposed by other legislators (certainly not by them!) that would allow offshore attorneys to practice law in their jurisdictions. If you were an attorney, would you vote for a bill that would result in your income being decimated?

One more point: Establishing an offshore legal operation is most feasible in midsize and large law firms or corporations. But IP and technology legal counsel is widely in demand by writers, artists, and inventors, as well as small businesspeople, who are unlikely to become clients of such firms. Rather, these people usually rely on their networks of contacts to obtain referrals to local practitioners in solo, boutique, or small general practices.

INFORMATION SOURCES

Title 17 of the United States Code. Typically described as "17 USC," this is the federal copyright statute. Sections 501-513 cover copyright infringe-

---

6 "Offshoring of Legal Services: An Ethical Perspective on Outsourcing Abroad," by Mark Tufts. Fall 2004, National Legal Malpractice Conference, American Bar Association Standing Committee on Lawyers' Professional Liability.

7 Source: http://www.ncsl.org/programs/legismgt/aboutdemographic_overview.htm

ment and remedies, which any computer professional with an interest in a career as an IT/IP attorney should read.

Title 35 of the United States Code. Typically referred to as "35 USC," this is the federal statute that governs patent law. Computer professionals interested in a legal career should find Section 101 (Inventions Patentable) of particular interest.

International Technology Law Association (www.itechlaw.org). The membership of this nonprofit organization includes attorneys who specialize in providing technology counsel, as well as law students. ITechLaw sponsors educational conferences and other events, and publishes the quarterly *ITechLaw Bulletin*, which features news, scholarly articles, and case law of interest to attorneys who provide technology counsel.

Virginia Journal of Law and Technology (www.vjolt.net). Reading this publication's articles on intellectual property and emerging technologies should be helpful in assessing your suitability for a career as an attorney.

Computer Crime and Intellectual Property Section (www.cybercrime.gov). In addition to providing information about criminal intellectual property law, the CCIPS website lists criminal IP cases prosecuted by the Department of Justice. Employment opportunities for attorneys and technologists are posted.

Martindale-Hubbell (www.martindale.com). This company publishes print and online directories of attorneys throughout the United States. A review of the biographies of attorneys specializing in computer and intellectual property law and litigation will show that many have traditional IT backgrounds.

INTELLECTUAL PROPERTY/
INFORMATION TECHNOLOGY ATTORNEY
YOUR RATINGS AND NEXT STEPS

How compatible is this field with my skills?

Assign a score of 0–10 (10 is highest): _____

Skills/Knowledge I Need to Acquire Before Contacting Employers

1._____

2._____

3._____

4._____

Typical Workday Task Ratings

After conducting research to fill in any ratings you initially left blank, calculate the total for each type of reaction (like, dislike, neutral). A field may be a good choice if you have at least six Ls and three or fewer Ds.

Total **L**s:_____ Total **D**s:_____ Total **N**s:_____

Research Notes

_____

_____

_____

_____

_____

_____

_____

_____

Contact Log

Date:_____Name/Title:_____

Phone/E-mail:_____

Comments:_____

_____

_____

_____

Date:_____Name/Title:_____

Phone/E-mail:_____

Comments:_____

_____

_____

_____

Date:_____Name/Title:_____

Phone/E-mail:_____

Comments:_____

_____

_____

_____

Date:_____Name/Title:_____

Phone/E-mail:_____

Comments:_____

_____

_____

_____

CAREER OPTION: HEALTHCARE ADMINISTRATOR

SECTORS OF THE ECONOMY
Private, public, nonprofit

PRIVATE SECTOR INDUSTRIES
Healthcare, insurance

END-USER ORGANIZATIONAL DEPARTMENTS
Healthcare administrators can be employed in all departments and, potentially, can advance to CEO positions overseeing the entire organization.

OVERVIEW OF HEALTHCARE ADMINISTRATION
When the largest industry in the United States is on the precipice of a major phase of investment in new technologies, opportunity knocks for IT professionals. The driving force behind the adoption of technology is pressure from government agencies, HMOs, employers, and insurers — each of which has a compelling interest in controlling healthcare costs. They want hospitals, medical practices, and other healthcare providers to computerize medical charts and other functions to reduce errors and compress diagnostic, treatment, and administrative processes.

But the computerization of medical records is only one of a number of technology initiatives attracting the attention of healthcare executives. According to Lynda Nemeth, RN, MS, JD, In-house Counsel, Chief Compliance Officer, and Director of Risk Management for Norwalk Hospital in Norwalk, Connecticut, "Two technology projects that are high on hospital agendas are bar coding for patient/product/medication identification and computerized physician order entry (CPOE), both of which are aimed at improving quality and patient safety — the most important priorities in the industry today. Hospitals are also implementing interactive self-learning programs that enable clinical personnel to fulfill the continuing educational requirements of their licenses."

With so many large-scale technology initiatives in progress, IT professionals who are willing and able to acquire a graduate degree qualifying them for healthcare administrative positions will be poised to become beneficiaries of this trend. Nemeth agrees: "When a technology initiative affects more than one hospital department, it will be under the control of the CIO, who reports to the CEO or COO. The board of a nonprofit hospital would consider it advantageous to have a COO or CEO who is also conversant in the technology because that would strengthen their confidence in the decision to acquire the technology, as well as in their choice of the optimal vendor. If the technology will be used exclusively by one department, a hospital board would probably feel obliged to engage a consultant to assist them in the decision-making process. Having a computer-savvy CEO or COO should obviate the need for a consultant. In light of the financial pressures on hospitals today, avoiding the cost of consulting services would be highly desirable." Furthermore, even after the current wave of technology projects is completed, new technologies with the potential for additional cost savings and quality improvements will continue to be adopted by the healthcare industry.

Healthcare administrators can be found in a wide range of environments, including:

- Hospitals
- Long-term care facilities
- Assisted-living facilities
- Adult day-care centers
- Large medical practices
- Psychiatric facilities
- Clinics
- Health insurance companies[8]
- Managed care providers[9]
- Pharmaceutical companies[10]

Each of the preceding can be operated as a for-profit business, nonprofit corporation, or public sector entity. The highest-ranking administrator of a healthcare organization has P&L responsibility for the entire enterprise,

---

8 My rationale for recommending healthcare administration as a career opportunity stems from the large-scale emphasis on technology at organizations that dispense healthcare services. I have, therefore, limited my discussion to positions at these kinds of enterprises and at firms that provide consulting services to them.

9 Id.

10 Id.

including the clinical functions — those that directly provide care, as well as those engaged in the same activities that must be performed in any business, such as financial reporting, human resources management, and purchasing.

An initial position for a newly credentialed healthcare administrator might involve management of a hospital clinical department, such as ambulatory surgery or obstetrics, which would encompass budgeting, purchasing, staffing, and risk management responsibilities. A next step might be as chief operating officer or other administrative executive position reporting to the CEO; the ultimate objective would be an appointment to a CEO role.

People with healthcare graduate degrees are also in great demand by consulting firms, including those that serve the healthcare industry exclusively, as well as the largest international consulting firms, all of which have healthcare practices.

A number of graduate degrees can pave the way to healthcare administrative or management consulting roles. Traditionally, the MS in Healthcare Administration has been the most widely acquired degree, but in recent years many MBA programs have offered concentrations in healthcare. According to Nemeth, "An MBA in Finance — even without a healthcare concentration — would be very valuable in the current industry environment. However, an MS in Healthcare Administration would be equally valuable because the courses are usually conducted by healthcare executives, whose first-hand knowledge of the management issues would be especially useful. Having both an MBA and an MS in Healthcare Administration would be a very strong combination, and both degrees can be acquired through one of the dual-degree programs that are increasingly being offered."

Two other graduate degrees that may be appropriate for people with particular occupational interests are the MS in Public Health Administration and the MS in Long-Term Care Administration.

POSITION TITLES

Executive director, associate director, assistant director, chief executive officer, president, chief operating officer, department head

JOB DESCRIPTION HIGHLIGHTS

The responsibilities described here are typical of those performed by the highest-level administrator of a hospital or long-term care facility, although a COO or other administrative executive might participate in some or all of them.

- Oversee all clinical and nonclinical departments, including budgeting, financial reporting, capital appropriations, and the hiring of departmental executives.
- Lead organizational initiatives aimed at improving healthcare quality and patient safety.
- Manage merger and acquisition activities.
- Design organizational restructuring programs in conjunction with mergers, acquisitions, and streamlining programs.
- Review and approve the selection of HMOs whose members can receive services at the hospital, as well as the terms of contracts with those entities.
- Participate in qualifying physicians for attending privileges; review matters pertaining to their noncompliance with hospital policies and medical best practices in conjunction with medical/staff leadership.
- Oversee the implementation of policies and processes to ensure compliance with all applicable laws, regulatory authorities, accrediting agencies, and HMO contracts.
- Work with clinical executives to implement new and expanded health programs offered to the public.
- If a nonprofit hospital, manage the relationship with the board of directors in developing strategic and capital plans.
- If a nonprofit hospital, cultivate and manage relationships with area business leaders in coordinating their participation in capital campaigns.

TYPICAL WORKDAY

Study this typical workday of the CEO of a fictitious hospital called Curthwall Memorial to see if this type of position would be appropriate for you. As you follow this executive through the day, note your reaction to each activity in the adjacent cell in the Rating column: an "L" (for like), "D" (for dislike), or "N" (for neutral, or no reaction). If you must conduct research before deciding, leave that cell blank for now.

Time	Activity	Rating
8:30– 9:20	Meet with Irene P., Curthwall's Chief Financial Officer, Fred H., the CIO, and Darla M., Director of Risk Management, to compare three enterprise content management packages, with an emphasis on evaluating their ability to control and enable access to compliance and accreditation documents. Review each department head's plan for using the system, as well as his or her estimates of labor cost savings stemming from the elimination of redundancies in document production and distribution activities.	
9:20– 10:00	Meet with Darla (Director of Risk Management), to discuss strengthening the background-checking process for employment candidates. We must prevent another occurrence of an employee opening fraudulent credit card accounts in the name of a patient with the identical name. Review a list of all hospital databases containing the Social Security numbers of personnel, employees, and consultants. Call Ryan F., IT auditor, to request details on the audit trail processes of all computer applications that access those databases; discuss the feasibility of displaying only the last four digits of an SSN.	
10:00– 10:30	Review a report prepared by the Wireless and RFID Task Force on potential applications in the hospital, including the tracking of patients, pharmacy inventories, clinical instrumentation, and computers.	
10:30– 11:00	Review a report analyzing the strengths, weaknesses, and costs of alternative two-factor authentication processes, including token, smart card, and biometrics technologies.	
11:00– 11:30	Conference call with Lyle W. and Paulette G., members of the board of directors, to review a list of 40 area corporations targeted for donations in the upcoming capital campaign (focus on 35 with whom board members have a personal or professional relationship with their executives). Discuss the financial contribution to seek from each company — have handy the list of contributions from 18 in the last campaign.	

Time	Activity	Rating
11:30–1:00	Meet with Dr. Mack F., Director of the Bariatrics Program, Steve L., Registered Dietitian, and Kay M., RN, to discuss the structure and pricing for a planned counseling and support program for people who have undergone gastric bypass surgery for obesity, or who are considering the procedure. Develop a preliminary budget for marketing, staffing, and managing the program. E-mail the pricing and budgeting data to Rita D., Financial Analyst, asking her to incorporate them into a spreadsheet and prepare a three-year pro forma.	
1:45–2:30	Review a report prepared by Art D., a healthcare management consultant, on telemedicine programs at six hospitals, related HIPAA compliance issues, and a proposal for two to three telemedicine programs suitable for Curthwall. Evaluate revenue projections and cost estimates for hardware, software, telecommunications, and staffing. E-mail the report to Darla (Director of Risk Management), and Alex U., General Counsel, requesting their comments on the risk management and legal questions that must be answered before implementing a telemedicine program; in particular, determine whether the hospital can be reimbursed for services by state and federal agencies.	
2:30–2:50	Return phone call from Darla regarding a meeting she had with a nurse who claimed to have seen an attending physician modify an entry in a patient's chart a month after it was made. Ask Darla to corroborate and document the physician's acknowledgment of that improper action, then forward it along with the patient's chart, to Alex (General Counsel).	
2:50–3:35	Meet with Dan T., Facilities Manager, Regina G., Director of Nursing, and Sid R., Medical Director of the Pediatric Medical-Surgical Unit, to review the three best proposals sent in response to an RFP for a general contractor to oversee the renovation and expansion of the Pediatric Unit.	

Time	Activity	Rating
3:35–4:10	Review the Procurement Rx contract sent by Alex (General Counsel), whereby Curthwall will pool its purchases of hospital supplies and equipment with other nonprofit hospitals through an online reverse auction process.	
4:10–5:00	Meet with Darla, Fred (CIO), Alex (General Counsel), and Sonia T., Account Executive for Olship Group (Curthwall's insurance broker), to discuss the liability implications of offering patients online access to their account information.	
5:00–5:45	Review the proposed due diligence plan for the acquisition of Mossridge Rehabilitation Services, whereby Curthwall's due diligence team members would acquire data on incidents of patient injuries at the facility by questioning Mossridge staff. E-mail Ralph W., Due Diligence Team Lead, to inform him that this proposal will be inadequate for enabling Curthwall to assess its potential future liability. Advise him to contact Alex (General Counsel), to ascertain whether the confidentiality agreement Curthwall signed with Mossridge permits the Due Diligence Team to examine patients' charts without violating HIPAA; and, if not, to modify it accordingly.	

JOB-HUNTING STRATEGIES

It's a good idea to begin thinking about seeking a healthcare administrative position even before you have begun the requisite educational program — you want your campaign to encompass both near- and longer-term elements. In the near term, for example, you could obtain a position at a company that develops software for the healthcare industry, such as CPOE. Or you could leverage your technical background to join the staff of a consulting firm that serves the healthcare industry. Another strategy would be to join the IT department of a hospital or other healthcare institution. Any of these steps would serve to test your interest in the profession and, if validated, provide the resume-building experience to make you a highly desirable candidate for a healthcare administrative position when you complete your education.

Lynda Nemeth of Norwalk Hospital, who formerly served as president of the Connecticut Association for Healthcare Quality and of the

Connecticut Society for Healthcare Risk Management (state affiliates of national associations focusing on these disciplines), suggests, "People interested in the profession should learn whether their state affiliates of these national associations, as well as the state chapters of the American College of Healthcare Executives, allow nonhealthcare practitioners to attend their meetings. If so, they should take advantage of the opportunity to learn about the issues they would face as administrators from presentations at these events. In addition, these meetings may be useful in developing contacts to approach for a residency or permanent position."

RECESSION RESISTANCE

The demand for healthcare services usually does not diminish in a recession because federal and state programs continue to finance consumer utilization of healthcare services. That said, recession-related declines in state tax revenues can cause government agencies to tighten eligibility requirements or cut benefits. And businesses affected by a recession will typically shift even more of the healthcare cost burden to employees, who may, in turn, reduce their utilization of healthcare services — especially those of a preventive or elective nature.

Yet even when the demand for clinical services is affected by a recession, healthcare administrative positions are less likely to be eliminated. Of course, declining revenues might compel a hospital to undertake aggressive cost-cutting measures, such as eliminating higher-paying positions by consolidating multiple departments under a single administrator, or merging with another hospital. In either of these circumstances, the result could be elimination of healthcare administrative positions.

OFFSHORE OUTSOURCING SITUATION AND OUTLOOK

A number of healthcare business processes, such as medical claims processing, are already widely offshored. As for the clinical area, many hospitals have implemented telemedicine programs that provide remote diagnostic and treatment services to patients who live too far to visit a healthcare facility. Teleradiology is one type of telemedicine that entails the transmission of digital X-rays to radiologists in remote locations. This practice has been broadly adopted by U.S. healthcare providers to obtain initial assessments from radiologists in lower-cost countries, which are subsequently reviewed for a final interpretation by U.S. radiologists.

The offshoring of business and clinical processes will probably become more widespread as the feasibility and cost savings are demonstrated at increasingly higher levels of complexity. However, while today's technology makes it theoretically possible for healthcare organizations to outsource administrative management positions, it is very unlikely. One reason is that a key responsibility of senior executives of nonprofit hospitals is the cultivation of relationships with regional corporate executives and community leaders. Nonprofit hospital administrators often recruit them to serve on their boards, both because of their ability to generate community support for capital campaigns and the expertise they bring in the areas of finance, communication, legal, and other disciplines. The role of a nonprofit healthcare administrative executive has a strong public relations component, which demands frequent, face-to-face interaction with influential corporate and community leaders, and this makes the position an improbable candidate for outsourcing, whether onshore or offshore — that is, until the organizations headed by those influential leaders outsource their senior management positions.

INFORMATION SOURCES

American College of Healthcare Executives (www.ache.org). The largest association of healthcare executives offers educational and other professional development services.

National Association for Healthcare Quality (www.nahq.org). Membership in NAHQ, the largest organization for healthcare quality professionals, is open to people outside the field. Through educational and other activities, including publication of the *Journal for Healthcare Quality*, NAHQ promotes the continuous improvement of quality in all healthcare settings. On the "Affiliated Organizations" page of the website, you'll find links to state affiliates and their contact information.

American Society for Healthcare Risk Management (www.ashrm.org). Members of ASHRM primarily come from the healthcare, insurance, legal, and other professions, but the organization welcomes any person interested in the profession. Chapter information, including a schedule of ASHRM's programs, is listed on the site.

HEALTHCARE ADMINISTRATOR
YOUR RATINGS AND NEXT STEPS

How compatible is this field with my skills?

Assign a score of 0–10 (10 is highest): _____

Skills/Knowledge I Need to Acquire Before Contacting Employers

1._____

2._____

3._____

4._____

Typical Workday Task Ratings

After conducting research to fill in any ratings you initially left blank, calculate the total for each type of reaction (like, dislike, neutral). A field may be a good choice if you have at least six Ls and three or fewer Ds.

Total **L**s:_____ Total **D**s:_____ Total **N**s:_____

Research Notes

_____

_____

_____

_____

_____

_____

_____

_____

_____

Contact Log

Date:_____Name/Title:_____

Phone/E-mail:_____

Comments:_____

_____

_____

_____

Date:_____Name/Title:_____

Phone/E-mail:_____

Comments:_____

_____

_____

_____

Date:_____Name/Title:_____

Phone/E-mail:_____

Comments:_____

_____

_____

_____

Date:_____Name/Title:_____

Phone/E-mail:_____

Comments:_____

_____

_____

_____

Part 3

Charting Your Course of Action

SUMMING UP YOUR CAREER OPTIONS

No doubt you read this book because you are concerned about the effect widespread offshoring of IT jobs will have — or is already having — on your career, seeking guidance about how to protect yourself today and in the future. Now, as you reach the end of the book, I'm confident I've assuaged those concerns, that I've convinced you of the long-term viability of your skills and how you can translate and transfer those skills to a number of rewarding alternative career options. That sense of relief, I hope, will clear your thinking for the task in front of you now: to digest the details presented in the career option sections and focus on those with the greatest promise for fulfilling you, professionally and personally.

To help you do that, I've summarized some key aspects of these career options in the table titled "Career Options Overview"; then I've outlined the steps I recommend you take to sort through all this information.

Career Options Overview

Career Option	Overall Responsibilities	Applicability of Technical Knowledge[11]
Product Manager	Identify opportunities for new products and new features for existing products, and prepare the business case to justify funding for programs to capitalize on them. Oversee the product development process from concept through commercial launch; devise pricing and promotional strategies. Manage each product line to maximize sales, profits, and market share within its life-cycle phase.	Moderate
Account Executive	Conduct cold-calling campaigns targeting potential buyers of information technology products or services to the B2B segment; develop sales proposals and deliver presentations; negotiate contracts and manage relationships with customers to identify new opportunities and address competitive threats.	Moderate
Systems Engineer	Gather information about prospective customers' computer systems and applications to ascertain the potential benefit of their using a company's offerings. Oversee software/hardware installations; train users and provide support. Monitor and coordinate the resolution of software defects and documentation inadequacies.	High
Channel Sales Manager	Identify new distribution channels for selling IT products/services; negotiate and administer agreements with channel partners; train and provide direction to channel partner sales personnel.	Moderate

---

11 These assessments reflect my opinion of the degree to which you would use your computer knowledge in the course of a workday. But realize that a particular position in the specified field may entail responsibilities that would result in a different assessment.

Educational/ Regulatory Requirements for Entry[12]	Additional Requirements for Advancement	Self-employment Potential	Ratings Page Number
None	MBA	Moderate, as a consultant after period of employment	Page 35
None	None	Moderate, as an independent representative, if selling a product (e.g., off-the-shelf software)	Page 47
Certifications, as required by particular employers	Certifications, as required by particular employers	Low, but feasible if serving several small, noncompeting companies that cannot justify hiring a full-time employee	Page 56
None	None	Moderate, by serving several small noncompeting companies that cannot justify hiring a full-time employee	Page 65

12 The inclusion of an educational requirement in this column means that it is either required by a state regulatory agency or that the pool of applicants who meet the specified educational and/or certification requirement is large enough for employers to consider only candidates with those credentials.

Career Option	Overall Responsibilities	Applicability of Technical Knowledge	
Technology Partner Manager	Negotiate and manage alliances with companies that market technologies that complement or enable the use of your employer's products/services and/or that target the same customers.	Moderate	
Procurement Project Manager	Oversee the development of policies and processes to ensure the standardized, high-quality and cost-effective procurement of specified categories of products/services.	Low	
Corporate Development Analyst	Identify and initiate relationships with businesses for the purpose of entering into acquisition, merger, joint venture, investment, or asset purchase agreements. Oversee personnel during M&A due diligence and integration projects. Respond to overtures from other companies desirous of these transactions.	Low	
Technology Due Diligence Analyst	Assess the computer infrastructure of prospective acquisition and merger partner candidates. Assess the capabilities, compatibility issues, and competitive strengths of commercial software and hardware in connection with acquisitions, mergers, the purchase of technology, and selection of vendors.	High	
Information Technology Auditor	Design the framework for and conduct audits of information technology systems and applications, as well as define corrective actions to address identified weaknesses.	Moderate	

Educational/ Regulatory Requirements for Entry	Additional Requirements for Advancement	Self-employment Potential	Ratings Page Number
None	None	Low, but feasible if serving several small, noncompeting companies that cannot justify hiring a full-time employee	Page 76
None	None	High, after initial period of employment	Page 87
None	MBA	Moderate, after first gaining corporate end-user experience, followed by tenure at a venture capital or private equity firm	Page 100
None	None	High from outset	Page 117
Certified Information Systems Auditor (CISA)	Certified Internal Auditor (CIA), Certified Information Systems Security Professional (CISSP)	High, after initial period of employment	Page 129

Career Option	Overall Responsibilities	Applicability of Technical Knowledge	
Business Continuity Planner	Identify threats to the continuous operation of an organization, such as natural disasters, power outages, criminal acts, negligence, and other adverse events. Work with internal clients to implement threat-mitigating actions; purchase products and services to support those initiatives.	Moderate	
Technology Risk Manager	Define and prioritize risks inherent in using computer networks, systems, applications, and data. Develop and oversee initiatives to mitigate those exposures.	Moderate	
Technology Insurance Broker/Agent	Guide computer industry companies in defining their professional liability insurance needs, or direct companies in all industries, as well as other organizations, in defining their cyberrisk insurance requirements. Present client coverage requirements to appropriate insurers and negotiate premiums on their behalf. Assist insurance brokers/agents in securing technology-based coverage for their clients.	Moderate	
Technology Insurance Underwriter	Evaluate applicants for computer-related professional liability or cyberliability insurance coverage; coordinate and review the findings of related loss control assessments. Determine premiums to reflect the risk associated with each applicant approved for coverage.	Moderate	

Educational/ Regulatory Requirements for Entry	Additional Requirements for Advancement	Self-employment Potential	Ratings Page Number
Associate Business Continuity Professional (ABCP)	Certified Business Continuity Professional (CBCP), Master Business Continuity Professional (MBCP)	High, after initial period of employment	Page 140
Certified Information Systems Security Professional (CISSP) and/or Certified Information Systems Auditor (CISA)	Certified Information Security Manager (CISM), MBA	High, after initial period of employment	Page 159
State producer license required if not employed by an insurance carrier	Registered Professional Liability Underwriter (RPLU)	Moderate, after initial period of employment	Page 173
None	Registered Professional Liability Underwriter (RPLU)	Moderate, after initial period of employment	Page 183

Career Option	Overall Responsibilities	Applicability of Technical Knowledge
Technology Industry Research Analyst	Conduct studies of market segments, companies, technologies, customer buying motivations, and other factors to inform decisions regarding acquisitions, R&D initiatives, marketing strategies, and vendor selection.	Low
Technology Sector Equity Analyst	Predict the future performance of the stock of technology companies by analyzing their products/services, management, competition, and performance.	Low
Computer Forensics Specialist	Conduct investigations of computer hardware, software, electronic media, and network traffic to support criminal prosecutions and/or civil litigation; serve as an expert witness in related legal proceedings.	High
Forensic Accountant	Conduct investigations of suspected cases of embezzlement, hidden assets, fraud, and other financial improprieties through the examination of financial reports and other documents, as well as interviews. Advise organizations on measures to prevent and detect financial crimes.	Moderate

Educational/ Regulatory Requirements for Entry	Additional Requirements for Advancement	Self-employment Potential	Ratings Page Number
None	None	High from outset, depending on nature and marketability of expertise.	Page 194
None	MBA and Chartered Financial Analyst (CFA)	High, after initial period of employment	Page 206
Forensic software certification, Microsoft Certified Systems Engineer (MCSE), and self-study of network intrusion methods and detection software	Continued certifications to maintain knowledge of advanced software, operating systems, and networks	High	Page 221
BS Accounting	Certified Public Accountant (CPA) license, Certified Forensic Accountant (Cr.FA), Certified Fraud Examiner (CFE)[13]	High, after initial period of employment	Page 232

---

13 These credentials apply to the private sector. Advancing to the highest level in an investigative position at a government agency may be feasible with a BS in Accounting, employer-provided training, and on-the-job experience.

Career Option	Overall Responsibilities	Applicability of Technical Knowledge	
Computer Expert	Evaluate information technology products/services and contracts in connection with disputes related to contract performance, product/service quality, copyright/patent infringement, misappropriation of trade secrets, and other matters. Prepare/review contracts involving the purchase, lease, and licensing of computer products and services.	High	
Intellectual Property/ IT Attorney .	Provide counsel on computer transactions and disputes and on protecting computer-based proprietary rights. Draft contracts for computer-related transactions; review contracts presented to clients by third parties.	Moderate	
Healthcare Administrator	Manage the operational and administrative functions of a hospital, long-term care facility or other healthcare institution, or a department in such an organization.	Low	

Educational/ Regulatory Requirements for Entry	Additional Requirements for Advancement	Self-employment Potential	Ratings Page Number
None, assuming a preeminent level of experience and credentials in a marketable discipline.	Self-study and/or certifications, as appropriate, to compete against others marketing the same type of expertise	High; most experts are self-employed	Page 243
JD[14]; and must pass state bar exam to obtain license	None	High, immediately upon obtaining license	Page 258
MS in Healthcare Administration *or* MBA in Finance	MS in Healthcare Administration *and* MBA in Finance	High, after period of employment	Page 269

14 Seven states will grant a license to practice law to "law readers," i.e., individuals who are not law school graduates, but pass the state bar examination.

Narrowing Your Choices

As we both know, having too many choices can be just as daunting as having too few or none at all. And when it comes to a job search or career switch, it is imperative that you narrow your choices, so that you are better able to focus your efforts. The steps that follow will ensure you make optimal use of the information presented throughout the book.

1. For each career option that interests you, refer to the appropriate cell in the Ratings Page Number column of the Career Options Overview table. Turn to the page noted in that cell, where you will find the Your Ratings and Next Steps form you completed for that career.
2. Transfer the likes/dislikes ratings for all typical workdays where you rated five or more tasks as likes and no more than three as dislikes to the same cell in the Ratings Page Number column. Thus, if you rated five tasks as likes and two as dislikes, record "5/3" in that cell.

At this juncture, if you're like many of my clients, you will conclude that you need to eliminate a few options. To help with that winnowing process, continue with these steps:

3. Select the three options with the most likes and fewest dislikes, entering each as a column heading in the table on page 289, "My Comparative Analysis of Finalist Career Options." If more than three options qualify because two or more share identical scores, create your own table.
4. Develop a list of screening criteria important to you. If you need help identifying these criteria, refer to the sidebar, "Screening Criteria Checklist," which contains items that are almost universally considered key factors by people in your situation; then add three or four factors that reflect your personal preferences.
5. Enter each criterion from your list on a row in this table — do not be concerned with sequencing at this point.
6. Assign a number from 0 to 10 to each criterion to reflect its relative importance to you — 10 signifying the greatest importance and 5, average importance. If you consider two or more criteria equally important, assign them the identical value. Enter the importance rating for each criterion in the appropriate cell in the Weighting Factor column.

7. Use the information presented in the book, together with your research findings, to arrive at a score, from 0 to 10, to reflect the degree to which each criterion is met by each finalist option. Enter this number in the cell next to the relevant criterion in the Score column.

8. Multiply the weighting factor for each criterion by the score for that criterion to arrive at a weighted score for each criterion as applied to the particular field. Enter the product of those two numbers in the relevant cell in the Weighted Score column.

9. Add the weighted scores for all criteria for a single career to arrive at a total score. Compare the scores of all the options to see which one (or more) rises to the top of the list.

To clarify this process, the "Sample Comparative Analysis of Finalist Career Options" table on page 288 contains a hypothetical example that illustrates this scoring method.

Screening Criteria Checklist

When developing your list of evaluation criteria, omit items that do not apply to the selection of a career. For example, some clients seeking career changes have expressed the desire to work in an organization that promotes from within. This characteristic will vary widely among employers within the same profession, so it is not an appropriate screening criterion when choosing a field; rather, it belongs in the comparative analysis matrix that you should create when you begin to evaluate specific job offers.

Work Content
This criterion is justifiably high on most people's lists, as it is what motivates them to get out of bed on Monday morning. Presumably, because you are limiting the fields included in this exercise to only those with the most favorable likes-to-dislikes ratio, each will have an above-average score.

Compensation
Define your income goals for the next 1, 5, and 10 years; then compare

the compensation associated with these tenures for each finalist option. Next, conduct an online search for "compensation," "salary," and "surveys," which will lead you to websites providing data on hundreds of job titles, and within particular geographic regions. Also, look for online publications serving these fields that may have conducted surveys of their readership; and contact professional associations serving practitioners in your finalist options, as they routinely conduct member salary surveys (although you may have to become a member to access that information).

If you are willing and able to enter a field that offers modest compensation during the initial few years but has significantly higher long-term income potential, list "Near-term Compensation" and "Long-term Compensation" as separate criteria.

Overnight Travel Requirements

Some positions — especially in the consulting field — are known to involve moderate to high levels of out-of-town travel.

Ease of Entry

The bar to entry rises concomitantly with the level of educational requirements. Time and money are the primary considerations when deciding whether to undertake a substantial educational program. If you lack the financial resources, you may be able to find satisfactory funding sources. And to determine whether the investment will be worth it, subtract your age from 65 and ask yourself whether the length of your tenure in the profession would justify it.

If the answer is yes but you find the prospect of sitting in a classroom daunting, keep in mind that the curriculum will be relevant to the work you will perform. Thus, if it is a suitable choice, you should find the educational process enjoyable even if some material is uninteresting. If a career option that appeals to you requires completion of an educational program, compare the curricula of several schools. And do not choose a program based solely on discussions with faculty, as they have a built-in bias: Their continued employment depends on the program having a sufficient number of "customers." Instead, ask the department chair for references of at least three students: one who graduated a year ago, another three years ago, and a third at least five years previously. Ask each how well the program prepared him or her for the profession.

A more advanced level of due diligence would entail obtaining introductions to executives who hire practitioners in the profession you target, and eliciting their opinions of the preparedness of graduates from those educational programs.

Self-Employment Potential

Some of the fields will be more feasible springboards to independent employment than others. For example, it shouldn't be difficult for a computer professional to immediately build a computer forensics consulting practice upon acquiring the requisite product knowledge and certifications. In contrast, because the technology partner function calls for continuous management, it does not fit into the project mold that underlies most consulting work. That said, several small noncompeting technology companies that cannot justify hiring a full-time technology partner manager might welcome the opportunity to use a consultant's services at a fraction of the cost.

Long-Term Demand

No one can predict the long-term demand for any occupation. Even if data available today promise significant growth, it may attract so many practitioners as to make it highly competitive. But that alone should not justify eliminating it from consideration. As I have emphasized throughout the book, acquiring expertise in multiple disciplines will provide maximum protection from a decline in the demand for any single one. And the combined value of your computer industry experience and a graduate degree should constitute a very high level of protection as, for example, in the healthcare administrator and attorney careers, both of which demand a much higher investment and commitment than a certificate program.

Sample Comparative Analysis
of Finalist Career Options

Criterion	Weighting Factor	Technology Insurance Broker		Computer Industry Product Manager		IT/IP Attorney	
		Score	Weighted Score	Score	Weighted Score	Score	Weighted Score
Work Content	10	7	70	9	90	8	80
Ease of Entry (reflecting education and licensing requirements)	6	8	48	6	36	0	0
No further educational credentials to advance after entry	8	4	32	3	24	10	80
Compensation upon entry	6	5	30	4	24	7	42
Compensation potential after five years	9	9	81	7	63	10	90
Self-employment potential	7	10	70	0	0	10	70
Long-term job security	10	9	90	5	50	10	100
Overnight travel requirements	8	4	32	7	56	6	48
Ease of relocating and continuing in same profession	8	8	64	10	80	3	24
Total Weighted Score			**517**		**423**		**534**

My Comparative Analysis of Finalist Career Options

Criterion	Weighting Factor	Score	Weighted Score	Score	Weighted Score	Score	Weighted Score
Total Weighted Score							

Working Solo

If you still find yourself in a quandary as to how to choose — which I recommend you learn to think of as a delightful dilemma — consider this solution: Establish a consulting practice promoting your expertise in two or three fields instead of looking for a job in any one of those you find attractive. Given the unpredictability of the workplace, when you market your expertise in several disciplines, you dilute the negative effects of future trends on any one of them. For example, you could provide computer forensics services to attorneys, while promoting yourself as a contract research analyst to firms that will place a premium on your industry experience or product knowledge.

Many people view self-employment as embodying a much higher risk than having a job. I disagree. Think about it: How many people do you know who accepted a so-called permanent position, only to find it very temporary? Let's face it, all positions are temporary, some only less so than others. My point is, it may be easier to establish a consulting practice than to elicit an offer of employment. These days, it's a major commitment for a company to offer a competitive compensation package, especially when the total cost of an employee's compensation and benefits must be factored into the hiring decision. In contrast, a consulting engagement is a relatively modest commitment with a foreseeable end date, meaning that many companies will be more receptive to initiating a project-oriented relationship than to extending a job offer.

If the prospect of building a consulting practice seems intimidating, consider easing your way into it by first obtaining a job in one field that interests you. After gaining two to three years' experience, you should feel more confident about making the move. You could then either specialize in the discipline related to your job or diversify by adding one or two areas of expertise to your portfolio of offerings.

If flying solo appeals to you, be aware that before you "launch" you first must commit to following through on two tasks that will be critical to your success:

- **Aggressively and continuously market your services.** Some people gain the confidence to resign from a job if they first negotiate an initial consulting engagement projected to generate at least six months' income. However, all too often, they wait until the engagement has ended before undertaking a marketing campaign. This is a strategic error, as it can take 6 to 12 months before client relationships begin to bear financial fruit. Furthermore, some prospects will inevitably be lost to competitors. The result? The consultant feels pressured to again seek another in-house position.

- **Diversify.** With a full-time job, all of your compensation eggs are in one basket, exposing you to significant downside risk if your boss terminates your employment. As a consultant, you must cultivate a number of "bosses," so that if one of them fires you, it will have an inconsequential impact on your income. The lesson: Never become overly reliant on one or only a few clients, or you expose yourself to the same degree of risk as a staff employee. Strive to establish as many client relationships as possible — assuming, of course, that each generates a level of revenue that justifies your continued efforts. And if, eventually, your client list becomes too large to manage independently, you will have to decide whether to continue to accept more clients (in which case you'd need to hire employees or use subcontractors) or limit your clientele to a volume you can manage alone.

Making Decisions

By completing the preceding exercise, you're well positioned to make important decisions regarding your future career. One caveat is in order, however: Don't get caught up in the numbers. By that I mean, use them as a guide, not the only determining factors. For example, do not automatically eliminate a second-place option even if there is a significant difference between its score and that of the highest-ranked field. Instead, examine the criteria and weighting factors that led to its second-place finish and ask yourself whether you should reconsider the weight you gave any criteria. You might also want to conduct further research to verify the validity of the score you assigned to selected criteria to reflect the degree to which a particular field met them.

I also want to emphasize the importance of one decision-making factor that cannot be sorted mathematically: your intuition, your gut feelings — call it what you will — about these career options. Even as you "do the math" here, undoubtedly you will find yourself reacting instinctively to these career options. Pay attention to those reactions, as they, too, are vital input, and not to be ignored.

> **NOTE:** Remember, no decision you make today is cast in stone. You can always revisit this scoring process two weeks, two months, even two years hence. Regardless of whether you have already entered a new field when you perform your second evaluation, I predict that your reactions to at least some of them will have changed.

It's entirely possible that you found that none of the career options described in this book appealed to you as much as the IT positions you have held. If that is the case, probably the best strategy for you is to continue along the traditional career path of that profession. But stay open to the possibilities, for the second edition of this book (planned for publication in 2008) will include new career options, and one of them might appeal to you.

But if you find yourself reluctant, even resistant, to making a career change because your previous attempts ended in failure and frustration, perhaps the problem is due to a weakness in your job-hunting strategy or execution, which, once corrected, could open the door to markedly improved results.

> **NOTE:** My next book (anticipated publication date, 2008) is a job-hunting guide for IT professionals. It will offer more specific advice on improving your job-hunting strategy and execution, and whether you seek a position on the traditional career ladder or want more in-depth guidance on targeting one of the fields described in this book, it will be a valuable resource.

A Crucial Branch in the Flowchart of Your Life

You are now at a crossroads. You may think that choosing the most suitable field is the only decision you must make; it is not. Another decision will be at least as pivotal to your professional success: namely, whether you will assume the role of an applicant or a currency trader. The difference?

You are an applicant if:

- You participate in the daily Internet job lottery, a game in which "players" (job-hunters) choose their "numbers" (keywords) in the hope that their "entries" (resumes) will be "drawn" (downloaded) from the "bowl" (terabyte) of entries from which "winners" (candidates) are selected for "prizes" (jobs) awarded by the "lottery directors" (employers and recruiters).

- You exert extensive effort toward finding employment opportunities through your network of contacts, their networks of contacts, and so on. By doing so you allow the quality and financial rewards of the next 5, 10, 20, or more years of your professional life to be limited by the opportunities available only through the members of those networks.

You are a currency trader if:

- You realize that, as an *information* technologist in a world where information is a precious currency, your expertise in the processes and tools needed to capture, store, organize, analyze, compare, distribute, and secure information is critical to the performance of organizations across all sectors, industries, and geographic markets.
- You refuse to rely on intermediaries — job boards, recruiters, and networking contacts — to achieve your professional objectives. Knowing that the shortest distance between two points is a straight line, you cut out the "middle man" and seek out counterparties with whom to directly trade your intellectual capital, thereby reducing the risk of losing out on opportunities.
- You refuse to allow your career success to be limited by anything other than your imagination and the effort you are willing to apply.

The decision is yours and yours alone: applicant or currency trader? Which will *you* be?

INDEX